ROBERTA'S BOYS

Proceeds from this book will go,
in part, to support creativity in
the arts, humanities, and sciences
as they relate to cultural diversity
in its broadest sense.

ROBERTA'S BOYS

FOUR PITTS BROTHERS OF MACON, GA

- -

Ann B Carlson

for

The Pitts Family Trust

Ann Carlson
Publishing

ISBN 978-0-9962883-0-9

Library of Congress Control Number: 2015906670

Published in the United States of America

Ann Carlson Publishing
Malone, New York

www.threeoranges.net

ROBERTA'S BOYS

FOUR PITTS BROTHERS
OF MACON, GA

Ann B Carlson

for

The Pitts Family Trust

Ann Carlson
Publishing

ISBN 978-0-9962883-0-9

Library of Congress Control Number: 2015906670

Published in the United States of America

Ann Carlson Publishing
Malone, New York

www.threeoranges.net

for Ray

Acknowledgments

I wish to thank Nat Pitts for entrusting me with completing his father's final project, and for sharing his vast store of documents, photos, and tapes from the "Pitts Family Archive." Nat is the carrier of his father's vision for this history, and has given me extensive encouragement, support and guidance. Nat and his siblings—Frances, Ray Jr., and Kathy—all spent generously of their time with me, recounting family stories and memories, as did their cousin Mitra, nephew (Kathy's son) Kelvin, and Robert's wife Mattalyn. I thoroughly enjoyed getting to know this special family and feel privileged to count them as friends.

I am grateful to Ethleen Brooks and Barbara Dortch, Pitts relatives and avid genealogists, who shared with me their research on the family's more distant relations. I had many enjoyable discussions with other Pitts relatives and friends, as well as with several Macon, Georgia, residents who gave me valuable insights into the era during which the Pitts family made that city their home. The staff of Macon's 1842 Inn, where I stayed during my research trips, also deserve special mention for their warm welcome and helpfulness.

During the too-many-months I spent on this project my partner, Jan, has been patient, supportive, and my most enthusiastic cheerleader. Our cats, Amí and Sophia, were also enthusiastically helpful: habitually lying on the keyboard or sitting directly in front of the screen to enhance my writing experience. They made long hours in front of the keyboard probably less productive, but significantly more entertaining.

Finally and most of all, I feel deep gratitude to the men and women about whom I have written. Their lives are an inspiration to me. I hope what I have written will allow them to continue to inspire future generations.

A Note on Style and Sources

This book contains a considerable amount of material that is quoted directly from family documents, memoirs, letters, and taped interviews. To visually assist the reader in navigating the frequent switches between my writing and direct quotations, I have adopted the convention of indenting and italicizing all but the shortest bits of quoted texts. Where external sources are known and available, even if only in the institutional archives of the men's personal papers, the reference is given in a footnote. If there is no reference, the source is a private document, clipping, or audio file from Ray's extensive family collection.

In attempting to preserve the authentic voices of the Pitts family members and friends, the quotations have not been edited, even to conform with today's standards of terminology, usage or style—except, very occasionally, to correct spelling or add essential punctuation.

The rights to all quoted text and photographs used herein, unless otherwise noted in the caption or reference, are, to the best of my ability to ascertain, owned by the Pitts Irrevocable Living Trust or individual Pitts family members, and are used with permission. Poems quoted, except on the dedication page, are works of Raymond, Robert, or Willis Pitts, Jr. and have not, to my knowledge or unless indicated, been published elsewhere. The Dunkerley (Oxenham) poem, opposite the table of contents, was a favorite of Ray's and is in the public domain.

The Ways

by William Arthur Dunkerley

(John Oxenham)

To every man there openeth

A Way, and Ways, and a Way,

And the High Soul climbs the High Way,

And the Low Soul gropes the Low,

And in between, on the misty flats,

The rest drift to and fro.

But to every man there openeth

A High Way, and a Low.

And every man decideth

The Way his soul shall go.

Contents

Prologue

On a hot August day in 1988, nearly one hundred Pitts family members and friends met at Browns Grove Cemetery, Browns Crossing, Georgia. They were there to participate in a major family reunion: to enjoy the fellowship of close family, to reacquaint with family seldom seen, to meet new family members, and to jointly dedicate a new headstone to the memory of their common ancestor, David Peter Pitts.

Raymond Jackson (Ray) Pitts, President of the *Pitts Family Association of Central Georgia, Inc.*, addressed the crowd. He swept his arm to emphasize the vista of Baldwin County's bountiful woodlands, fields, lakes and streams. Then he indicated the humble, white-clapboard church their ancestor helped to build in the first years after the Civil War:

> *This is Hallowed Land. This is the land of our ancestors, and it is our land. It is Pitts land. This is where they were born. This is where they lived happy lives, and lives with some sorrows. This is where they worked, and where some of them slaved. This is where many of them lie.*

During the program, the youngest members of the clan were addressed by one of David's great-granddaughters—now a grandmother herself—and instructed to...

> *Look at me; and stand up straight and tall. Hold your chest out! Because you are part of me, and I am part of the past.*

It was Ray's dream to leave a tangible legacy of this shared past: in honor of his mother who instilled this family passion, and for the benefit of his own children and grandchildren. He wrote:

> *I have promised to [my children and grandchildren] that I will give to them, and to posterity, a history of the Family from which they came. This is a 'labor of love' for me. I travel everywhere to get the information that is needed for a complete and Authentic history of the People who were my ancestors.*

Most of all he wanted to leave them his own story, and the story of his three brothers—the lessons learned, the wisdom gained, and the successes they all achieved in those difficult and often forgotten years between the Great Depression and the Civil Rights Era.

They were David Peter Pitts' great-grandsons—through his first son Emanuel and Emanuel's fourth son, Willis Norman. Channeling the strength of their Pitts heritage, and the equal love, support and persistence of their indomitable mother—Roberta Jackson Pitts—these four brothers became prominent national leaders in education and government service: Dr. Willis Norman Pitts Jr. (1907-1988), Robert Bedford Pitts (1909-1982), Dr. Raymond Jackson Pitts (1911-2004), and Dr. Nathan Alvin Pitts (1913-1998).

Before he died, Ray managed to document most of the family's historical background and, in addition to his own, collected the memorabilia and professional papers of his three brothers. With his characteristic confidence, optimism and boundless energy, he expected and planned to live, at minimum, until he reached his one hundredth birthday. He had tasked himself with sufficient retirement projects to fill all of that time. Assuring himself that he would complete them all, he saved this most cherished family history for what he intended to be his last—his ultimate—contribution. Unfortunately for us, time caught up with him early: at age 93.

This book is not the book he would have written; yet, perhaps, the story he wanted to tell of this incredible family will survive in my retelling.

A Brief Pitts Family History

Peyton Taylor Pitts Sr. was a prominent and wealthy landowner in Jones County, Georgia. At various times he served as a member of the legislature, judge of the county's Inferior Court, delegate to the Secession Convention, and captain of the Civil War's Jones County Volunteers. He was fond of sports, guns and dogs, and was said to be a pillar of the Church. According to Carolyn White Williams' *History of Jones County Georgia:*[1]

He had a large two story white house with a long veranda across the front. In the rear he had a pigeon house and many pigeons, which he fed early in the mornings from a basket full of grain. His place was a village within itself as he had the slaves' quarters, wagonshops, cotton gin and grain houses and cribs for corn. Every house was painted white and situated in a large oak grove, a typical plantation of that time. ... Peyton Pitts built a nice Methodist church at the Crossroads and it was called "Pitts Chapel." He was the main supporter of this church and he also built the Negroes a church and helped support this.

After the civil war Pitts lost most of his wealth, sold the plantation, and lived in a small house nearby until his death in 1885. Many of his numerous descendants, both black and white, still live in Jones County, Georgia, or the vicinity. Others—"Roberta's boys" among them—left Georgia at the earliest opportunity, joining the general migration to points north and west.

But the events that concern this history began much earlier, when Jones and Baldwin Counties were in their ascendancy. This central Georgia land had been acquired from the Creek Indians in 1803, distributed to its new owners by land lottery, and immediately turned to the profitable cultivation of cotton. The Pitts family was involved almost from the beginning. The family's progenitor, Walter Pitts (1700–1770), had begun his career as a carpenter in North Carolina, but built his fortune in land and slaves, investing heavily in North Carolina and in Virginia. By the time of his death he was a noted gentleman-farmer with a large family, resident in Halifax County, North Carolina. Sometime before 1808, according to Pitts family records, one of Walter's youngest sons, John Pitts (1767–

---

1   Carolyn White Williams (1957). *History of Jones County, GA.* J. W. Burke Company, Macon, GA. p. 419.

1818), moved his family and many slaves to Baldwin County, Georgia. He, like his father, recognized the economic potential of the plantation and, taking advantage of the westward expansion of land availability, established himself there as a local planter. The war of 1812 had brought, at first, a large increase to the population of this area. Then the opening of other Indian lands further to the west caused the population to shrink by one third over the next decade, as the flood of would-be settlers continued west. But the John Pitts family remained, to become permanently ingrained in the fabric of central Georgia.

By 1820, thanks to the cotton boom, Baldwin County was prosperous and its city of Milledgeville, the state's capital, was becoming increasingly powerful and refined. Its neighbor, Jones County, was the most populous county in Georgia, with 43.5 people per square mile (9,821 whites; 6,886 slaves).[2] Two of John's sons became plantation owners in Jones County. The 1830 Federal Census shows that the younger son Peyton Pitts, at only eighteen years of age, was already the owner of his own plantation; it was not far from the larger plantation of his elder brother, Captain John (Jack) Pitts. These Pitts plantations were situated only five miles from the county seat of Clinton, and fifteen miles equidistant from the sedate capital of Milledgeville and the upstart village of Macon, in Bibb County.

Peyton was recently married to Ann Marie Moore, the younger sister of his brother Jack's wife, and she was expecting their first child. Head of his own household, he was already well on the way to a high standard of antebellum wealth and prominence. Although still a teenager, he owned fifteen slaves. His brother Jack owned twenty-two. Peyton's slaves, as listed in that 1830 Census, included only one female between the ages of ten and twenty-three. That slave girl was known to the Census as only a number—sex, age, and race—but she is remembered by her descendants as "Hess." She was also destined to soon have a child: Peyton's child.[3]

Peyton's wife Ann Marie gave birth in December 1830 to a little girl, naming her Mary. Perhaps Ann Marie was unable to resume her "wifely duties" quickly enough to please her husband, or perhaps he, along with so many of his compatriots, was already accustomed to taking mistresses from among the family's slaves. Whatever the case, the following November Hess gave birth to David Peter, who was in all likelihood Peyton's firstborn son. The descendants from this child, born "on the other side of the blanket," rival the recognized Pitts heirs both in number and in contributions to their community and their country.

Today the surname name of Pitts is ubiquitous across Georgia's Jones, Bald-

---

2   William H. Bragg (August 15, 2013) *Jones County*. New Georgia Encyclopedia. www.georgiaencyclopedia.org, (All references in this chapter to the web-based New Georgia Encyclopedia were verified April 24, 2015).

3   There is another tradition, supported by his death certificate, that David was born in 1823 and his father was John (Jack) Pitts. However, census details and most family records do not support this alternative history.

win, and Bibb Counties. The brothers each had several children by their legal wives, and each owned dozens of slaves and likely fathered several more. Nearly all the slaves of the family took the surname of Pitts after emancipation, including those to whom it belonged, whether acknowledged or not, as a genetic birthright. David Peter Pitts was one of these.

Pitts' descendants on both sides of the family tree had large, interconnected families that stayed on the land, or migrated to nearby Macon or Atlanta after the Civil War. David himself had 18–20 children with two successive wives, and through them, almost innumerable descendants. His descendants remain a close family group.[4]

David Peter Pitts

The early details of David Peter Pitts' life are illumined only by family legends or by his occasional mention in legal documents, church records and family archives. His grandson Willis Sr. recorded that he grew up with five brothers and one sister: children of Hess.[5] Some of their given names appear in wills; marriage, death, and tax records; and in census documents of that time period. However, multiple uses of the same name in extended families was common, which complicates the process of using these documents to understand family relationships or the circumstances of their lives. David, additionally, had at least two younger half-brothers—Alexander Pitts and John Wesley Pitts—said to be fathered by Peyton through Carrie, another of his slaves.

Born a slave in a land where cotton was king, David was only too familiar with the hard labor of the fields. To quote another descendant of cotton plantation slaves, "If you talk to elderly blacks today who have worked in the cotton fields, a negative response is always given, such as 'I don't ever want to see another cotton field as long as I live.'"[6] But as an acknowledged son of his master, he may have had a somewhat more privileged position than his fellows. Writing with the characteristic "rose colored" memories of a Southern white woman of her era, Ms. Williams wrote about life on just such a prosperous Macon plantation.[7] She states that it was customary for each son in the owner's family ...

> *to have given to him an older negro boy to go with him everywhere, to protect him from harm or wait upon him, when necessary. The negro boy taught him woodcraft, how to fish, to make and set traps for turkeys and quail, to find bird nests and identify the eggs. Although they were comrades the dif-*

---

4   And still hold biennial family reunions.

5   According to Willis Sr., they were Emanuel Pitts, Isaac Pitts, Peter Pitts, Balam Pitts, Asburn Pitts, and Rhonda Pitts Cook.

6   Jeanne C. Herring (2000). *Macon, Georgia* (Black America Series). Arcadia Publishing, Charleston, SC.

7   Carolyn White Williams (1957). *History of Jones County.* p. 67-68.

*ference in social status was not lost sight of by either. The negro boy enjoyed a
standing among his fellows by reason of his position, in which he took great
satisfaction. He came into the big house on rainy days and cold days and there
he learned many things of the white folks that helped him, their stories, songs
and lore.*

David might have played some version of this role for a younger son of one
of Peyton's legal wives.[8] Clever and ambitious, perhaps he learned far more from
this arrangement than "stories, songs, and lore."

David and his half brother John Wesley were, again according to family stories, fairly light-skinned "mulattoes" (half black – half white)[9] and were sent
away by Peyton as young men to be educated. They would have been unusually
accomplished for slaves of the day.[10] In fact, some of the family believe that David had already been granted his freedom before the Civil War (but no documents supporting his early manumission can be found). Peyton was, however,
known to have several skilled black carpenters and artisans working for him
who were also hired out in the village as artisans.[11] Such work would go to those
with privilege, training, or unusual capability. These skills and an education
would have greatly enhanced their social standing after the war. And indeed,
David and John Wesley did fare rather better than most freed blacks. They were
ultimately able to adopt and maintain the dress and manners of typical, middle-class southern gentlemen.

David married fellow slave Lucretia Woolfolk. Their first son Emanuel was
born in 1850.[12] David and Lucretia had at least six additional children[13] before she died, somewhere around 1862—possibly at the birth of her youngest
daughter Leah. He was married a second time to Martha Gray Allen, and had
an additional 11–13 children with her.[14] There is a family legend that some of
David's children by Lucretia had been sold away from the family before the end
of the war (John Nelson, in particular, to Alabama), and that after the war David scoured the countryside to bring them all home. Their belief is that he was

---

8   He was married three times, successively, to Anne Marie Moore, Rebecca Moore, and Mary Buford Hill.

9   Light skin generally conferred a higher status.

10   Although educating slaves was discouraged and often forbidden, literacy was highly desired and sought
out by slaves. By 1860, perhaps five percent of slaves had obtained some level of literacy. [Eugene Genovese
(1976). *Roll, Jordan, Roll.* Vintage Books, New York.]

11   Carolyn White Williams (1957). *History of Jones County.* p 419.

12   The existence of an elder sister, Mary, is possible. A "Mary" is noted (age 25) in the 1870 Census as a
member of the household, but may not have been David's biological child. She could possibly have been
Lucretia's or Martha's from an earlier relationship, or could even have been Martha herself, as the accuracy of
information in those old census records is notoriously poor.

13   Hester, John Nelson, David Jr., Carrie, Henrietta, Leah.

14   Asbury (Jace), Fannie, Marietta, Osborn (Andrew? Also possibly also called Abraham), Joseph B., Lu-
crecia (Lucy, Cressie), Samuel, William (may be the same person as Samuel), Florine (Corine), Oliver, Mattie,
and Ruben Thomas.

ultimately able to reunite the entire family during the Reconstruction period.

The Civil War devastated Jones County. A pistol factory in Griswoldville, only a few miles from the Pitts plantation, had been a major supplier of arms for the Confederacy. The only major confrontation of 1864's Savannah Campaign was fought at Griswoldville during Sherman's advance to the sea, and the pistol factory was burned to the ground. In the course of Sherman's campaign Milledgeville was ransacked, vandalized, and largely burned. The entire surrounding countryside was essentially laid waste; although the city of Macon, now the temporary state capitol, was spared.[15] The Pitts plantation was also spared. According to a story passed down by David Pitts' descendants, General Sherman came to the plantation house and sat down to negotiate with Peyton Pitts. One of the slaves, a housekeeper or cook, overheard the conversation. She said that Sherman requested livestock in exchange for not destroying the plantation. The livestock were delivered; the plantation survived intact.

When the war was over the central Georgia area suffered political turmoil, population decline, crop failures, and plummeting land prices.[16] The first Ku Klux Klan existed from roughly 1867 to 1870 and had its roots in the notorious antebellum slave patrols. It succeeded, through terror and intimidation, in driving many blacks from the land and into the cities. There they were cut off from their social networks, frequently could not find work, and were sometimes utterly destitute.

Property tax records from 1869 show that David and his eldest son Emanuel remained, at first, to work for Peyton Pitts as farm laborers. The 1870 Census indicates that David continued on in the area as a farm laborer, but by then was working at a different farm, assisted by his many children. Martha was a cook. The 1880 Census lists David as a tenant farmer, now renting a farm in Jones County not far from the site of Peyton Pitts' former plantation. Most of his large brood of children still worked with him as farm laborers. His third son David Jr. rented the next farm down the road. Only Emanuel,[17] also living nearby, was in a different occupation—working for the railroad. Tax records reveal that David, although just a tenant farmer, was relatively better off than most of his neighbors, probably because of the labor of his large family.[18] By 1890, Emanuel was apparently the wealthiest of the family, and had even managed to purchase some land.

---

15   A cannonball struck one house (now known as The Cannonball House) in Macon during a nearby battle on the Clinton Road, but Sherman was turned away from attacking Macon in his rush to reach Savannah.

16   William H. Bragg (2013) *Jones County*. Web-based New Georgia Encyclopedia.

17   Because David also had a brother named Emanuel, it is difficult in some cases to determine which one is referred to in public records. Best guesses, judging from likely age and proximity of immediate family, have been employed in this history to distinguish one from the other, but conclusions remain uncertain.

18   Also, 1873 Jones County records show that David was paid ten dollars by the county for "making coffin and furnishing articles for burial of Mrs. Catherine Spear, a pauper."

At first in the Reconstruction era there was optimism and some measure of opportunity for freed blacks. The Federal government kept a watchful eye on the former Confederate state and enforced the Union's abolitionist agenda. But the situation became much worse after the withdrawal of Federal troops in 1877. Tenant farming was seldom a good deal for former slaves, and it became less and less so over time. If they were fortunate, they might make a small profit. Most actually lost money in the process, going further and further into debt. Denied bargaining rights or access to the political process, tenant farming could feel very much like simply a new form of slavery.

The late 1880s and the 1890s were particularly tumultuous. In addition to worsening disenfranchisement at the polls and intimidation by white supremacists, numerous Jim Crow laws were passed to limit black, or "colored," access to public spaces and facilities. Race discrimination in employment, finance, housing, and property ownership was rife. Georgia's 1877 enactment of the cumulative poll tax had resulted in systematic disenfranchisement of the majority of black citizens, reducing the percentage of blacks that could vote from fifty-three percent in 1876 to just eight percent in 1900.[19] Blacks did organize, and tried vigorously, but vainly, to fight back against such policies. The Union Brotherhood was formed in 1888 to promote Negro rights, and that same year a Georgia Consultation Convention of the state's black leaders was held in Macon.[20] Ordinary black citizens banded together, formally and informally, to fight against Jim Crow laws and the tolerance of lynchings, and to petition for basic rights. Nevertheless, Georgia's rival political parties successfully used race-baiting strategies to unite both poor and wealthy whites of various political stripes in the common cause of ensuring perpetual white supremacy.[21]

According to the 1890 tax records, David and Emanuel were two of the very few freedmen[22] who had paid the poll tax, and thus were eligible to vote. Whether they were actually able to vote, however, is another question. Violence at the polls was common,[23] and those few blacks that were, against the odds, elected to various positions were frequently prevented from serving.

Although the specific reasons for their move are not known, in the early 1890s both David and the children remaining with him, as well as Emanuel and his young family, left Jones County for good.[24] David moved to the area of Browns Crossing in neighboring Baldwin County. He continued to tenant farm and still employed several of his children. Emanuel also initially moved

19   Andrew M. Manis (2004). *Macon: Black and White.* Mercer University Press, Macon, GA, p. 19.

20   Donald L. Grant (1993). *The Way is Was in the South.* Birch Lane Press, New York, NY, p. 134.

21   Edward A. Hatfield, (April 7, 2015) *Segregation.* Web-based New Georgia Encyclopedia.

22   A separate category on the tax rolls.

23   In 1872 and again in 1874 several blacks were killed attempting to vote in Macon.

24   One possibility is that "Whitecappers"—who used violence to oppose black ownership of property, and are known to have been active in the area at the time—may have driven them off their Jones County property.

his family to Brown's Crossing, and commuted to work as a laborer in Macon. Later, in the wake of the city's strong commercial and industrial growth, he and his family moved permanently to Macon.

David Peter Pitts was still living in Browns Crossing in 1920, the head of a farming household that included his wife Martha, a younger son, and two grandchildren. He died in Milledgeville in 1924. He was a strong man, a religious man, and a leader of the community. He was instrumental in the construction of the Friendship Colored Methodist Episcopal (CME) Church in Gray, Georgia (c1870) and the Browns Grove CME Church in Browns Crossing (1871), where he served as a trustee and where he is buried.

Emanuel Pitts

Emanuel would have been about twelve when the Civil War first came to Jones County, and fifteen when it ended. The War had left everything in the South in chaos, and education was not exempted. In the 1870 Census Emanuel, at the age of twenty, is reported to be the only one of his father's children who could read and, at least according to that Census, neither he nor any of his siblings could write. None had attended school within the year. Nevertheless for the Pitts family and generally for the black community, despite the devastation that the war had brought, there was optimism and an eagerness to better themselves. Former slaves flocked to schools opened by the Federal government's Freedmen's Bureau, by Northern freedmen's aid and missionary organizations, or by literate former slaves. Adults as well as children struggled for literacy: for just as the withholding of education was a hallmark of slavery, the gaining of an education was seen as the route to respect, prosperity and success.

Although many of the teachers were whites—often white women from the Northern missionary societies—many were local blacks, women and men, who had already managed to obtain some measure of education. The commitment of the newly freed to their community's success is evidenced by the dedication of their teachers. Technically operating under the auspices of the Freedmen's Bureau or one of the Northern aid societies, they often labored without pay almost to the starving point—going without food, clothing and housing; to say nothing of teaching supplies.[25]

By 1870 the Freedman's Bureau schools were closed, and the post-war flow of funding for black education had dwindled to a trickle.[26] But although the opportunities and the optimism were short lived, the Pitts determination was not. However they managed it, by the time of the 1880 Census Emanuel and most

25 Titus Brown (2002). *Faithful, Firm & True: African-American Education in the South.* Mercer University Press. Macon, GA, p. 4.

26 Ronald E. Butchart. (October 29, 2014) *Freedmen's Education during Reconstruction.* Web-based New Georgia Encyclopedia.

of his brothers were reported to be able to read and write. His wife and most of his sisters were, unfortunately, not similarly accomplished.[27]

Emanuel married Emily Morris on February 18, 1871, in Jones County. David and Martha were witnesses. Their firstborn son, Dorsey, was born the following year. By 1880, Emanuel was a landowner and a railroad worker with five sons: Dorsey C., John Nelson, Hope Hull (Hoppie), Willis Norman, and Rufus Franklin (Tick). He and Emily later had two daughters, Angie Dequilla (Quilen) and Amanda Bell (Mandy). Through his hard work, intelligence, and adaptability, the family was earning a place in the tiny, but growing, black middle-class.

Success was precarious, and required sacrifices. In about 1890, Emanuel (known by then as "Big Bud") went to Macon to obtain work as a laborer. He lived there as a boarder, leaving his family in with the extended Pitts clan. The population of Macon had almost doubled in the 1880's and it could provide jobs, while they were becoming increasingly scarce in the countryside. An economic depression, centered around 1893, accelerated the migration to the cities to find work. Macon was fast becoming a major transportation and distribution hub for the entire state.[28] Another motivation for Emanuel's move may have been better educational opportunities for his sons, if they were so inclined. Macon's Lewis High School (that later became Ballard Normal School) was the only school in central Georgia offering greater than a sixth grade education for black students.[29] It was run by the American Missionary Association and was a full, college-preparatory school. It also offered industrial education in carpentry for boys and homemaking/needlework for girls.

It must have been a difficult life for Emanuel, especially during the depression years of the middle 1890s, but he eventually prospered as a laborer and carpenter, to the degree that he was able to reunite with his family in the city. City directories show him as a laborer in the Fort Hill vicinity in 1890, and for a few years thereafter. They show that his son Willis Norman was working in Macon by 1892, and living nearby. At least by 1899, the directories show that two other sons, Dorsey and Rufus, were living and working in Macon, while the 1900 Census shows that Emily and Quilen (and, presumably their youngest, Mandy) had moved to be with Emanuel; they were all living in the black neighborhood of East Macon. By that time Hoppie and John Nelson had also likely lived and worked in Macon for some years: military records show that Hoppie enlisted in the Army from Macon in 1899.

---

27 The early census data are notoriously unreliable, however. Many blacks mistrusted how the data would be used and were, understandably, less than honest with the census takers. Many census takers also filled in what they assumed to be the case, without bothering to ask.

28 The New York Times in 1895 dubbed Macon "The Central City," in reference to its being the regional transportation hub.

29 Titus Brown (2002). *Faithful, Firm & True: African-American Education in the South*, p. 78.

Emanuel was a member of Holsey Temple, Macon's CME church. The CME Church had split from the southern half of the Methodist Episcopal Church after the Civil War. Less politically active than the Northern-based African Methodist Episcopal (AME) Church, the CME denomination maintained ties with the white Methodist Episcopal Church, South. It was both culturally more familiar to black Southerners and also more optimistic about the future of racial relations than its Northern counterpart. David had been one of the denomination's earliest members and elders. For Emanuel and his children, Holsey Temple would become their center of social and spiritual life. A fellow member—Mr. Frank Hubbard, the undertaker—was a family friend. When Willis Norman came to East Macon early in the 1890's, he lived with Mr. Hubbard and worked for him as a clerk. One of the early construction projects that Emanuel and Willis Norman worked on together was building Holsey Temple's new sanctuary. The congregation had been founded in 1867, but the old church building had been destroyed by fire. The new one was erected in 1895.

Emanuel's eldest son Dorsey returned at some point to the country and made a career of farming in nearby Browns Crossing, Baldwin County; marrying a local girl named Irene in 1891. John Nelson, who made his living as a carpenter in Macon, had married Eugenia Mitchell and the two already had several children by the early 1900s. They were living in East Macon with Eugenia's father, Henry Mitchell. Hoppie enlisted in the Army in 1899. He served in the ninth Cavalry unit at Fort Apache in the Arizona territory until 1900, and then was deployed to the Phillippines during the Spanish-American War. He made the Army a career, serving another twenty years as a farrier at West Point in Highland Falls, New York. Willis Norman briefly followed Hoppie into the Army, after completing a degree in industrial arts from Booker T. Washington's famed Tuskegee Institute. He returned to East Macon in 1904, married to his college sweetheart Roberta Jackson, and worked as a carpenter with his father.[30] Rufus was married to Ellen Griswold in 1907. She was from Browns Crossing, and already had small children from an earlier relationship. He returned there with her to farm, and to ply his carpentry skills on the side. They had an additional four or five children together. Mandy also married in 1907, and moved south to Dooley County with her farmer-husband, Probel McCormick. They eventually moved back to Browns Crossing, to be near her family and raise their own. Quilen lived with her parents until Emanuel died in 1908. Afterwards, she moved with her mother Emily back to Baldwin County to live with Dorsey and his family. She married a neighbor, Albert Bonner, but died childless when she was just thirty-eight. Emily died in 1915 at age sixty.

---

30   The 1904 city directory indicates that he was a boarder in Emanuel's home on Bernard Street. By 1907 he is listed as the owner of 108 Bernard Street, with his father and mother as his boarders.

Left: Peyton T. Pitts (1812–1885)

Below: Conceptual likeness of
David Peter Pitts (1831–1924)
(*from 1988 family reunion documents*)

He is buried in
Browns Grove Cemetery,
Browns Crossing, Georgia

Gravestone inscription:

PITTS

IN MEMORY OF DAVID PITTS

DAVID PITTS BORN JONES COUNTY GEORGIA
NOVEMBER 1831. MARRIAGES TO LUCRETIA
AND MARTHA GAVE RISE TO OUR FAMILIES
BEGINNINGS

EMANUEL	DAVE	HENRIETTA	FLORINE	JOSEPH	WILLIAM
HESTER	CARRIE	FANNIE	ASBURY	LUCRETIA	MATTIE
NELSON	LEAH	MARIETTA	OLIVER	SAMUEL	RUBEN

Above: Gravestone of David Peter Pitts listing (most of) his children

Below: Some of David's children:
Left: Carrie Pitts Mabry (front) and Mary Etta (Marietta) Pitts Benford
(who once boarded with Emanuel and Emily in Macon) Right: Leah Pitts
(a blind seamstress) Bottom Right: Reuben, David's youngest

Marriage Certificate of Miss Emily Morris to Mr. Emanuel Pitts
(David and Martha Pitts as witnesses, signed by David Lester)

Mrs. Dequilla Pitts Bonner oldest daughter of Emmanuel and Emily Pitts. Grand daughter of David (Dave) and Lucertie Pitts.

Above Left: Emanuel Pitts
Above Right: Emanuel's daughter, Dequilla (Quilen)

Below: Holsey Temple CME Church

Photo: Ann Carlson

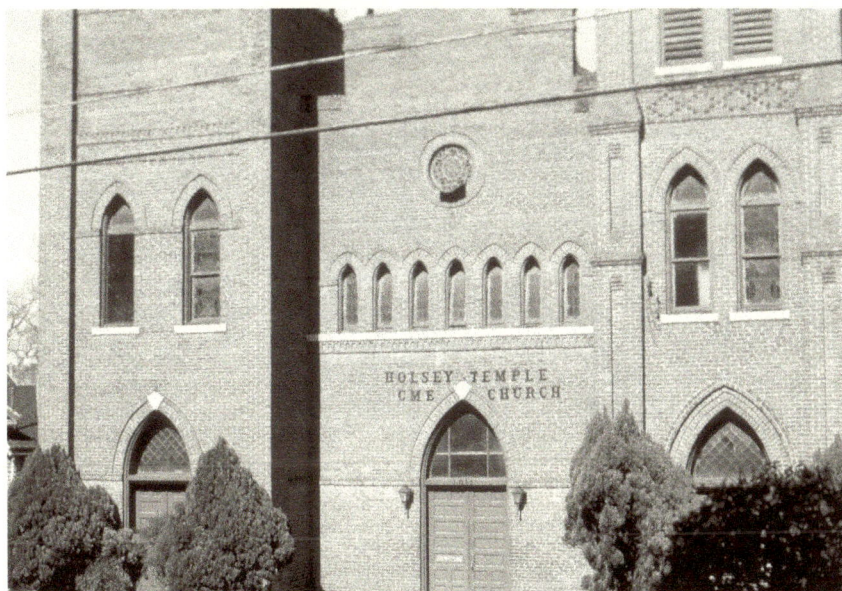

Sons of Emanuel Pitts
Seated (l to r): Dorsey, John Nelson
Standing: Hoppie, Rufus, Willis Norman

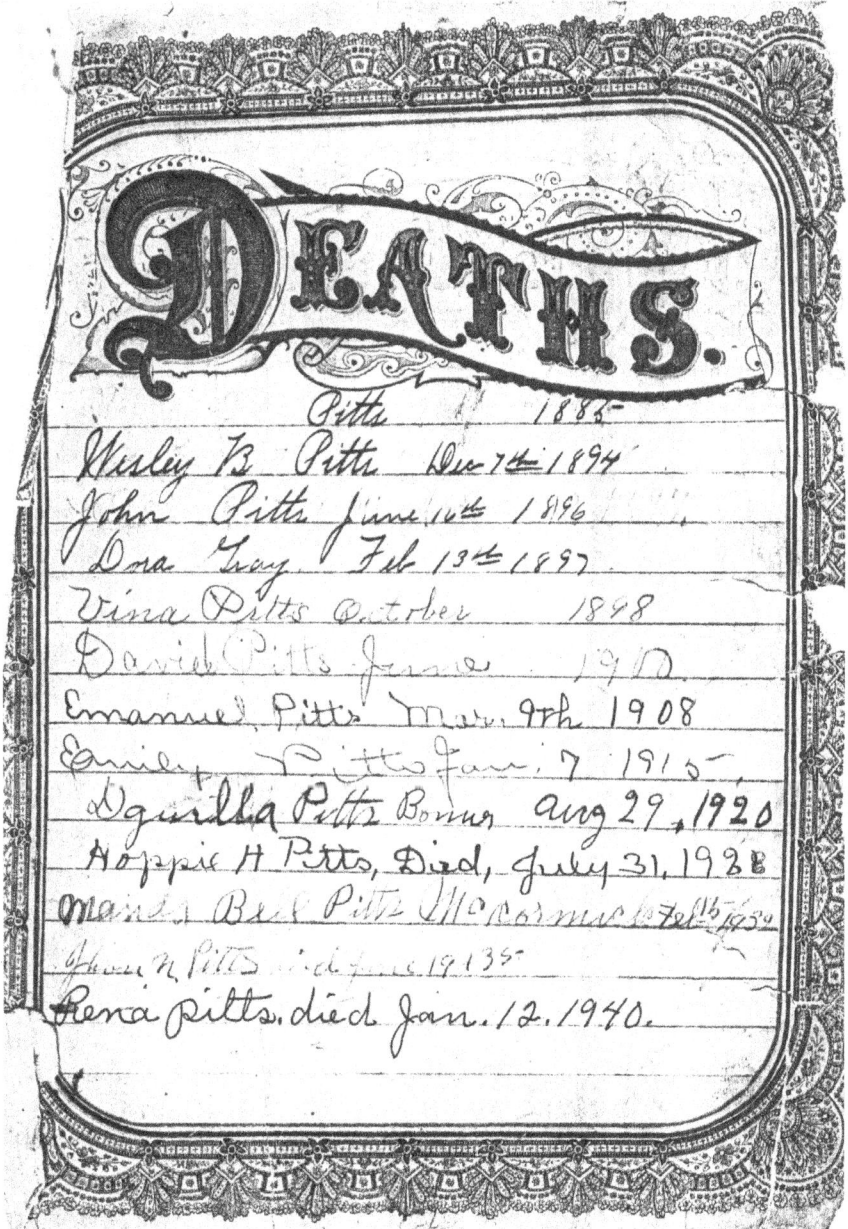

Pitts deaths recorded in an old family Bible; including
Emanuel (1908) and Emily (1915) with their children Dequilla (1920),
Hoppie (1926), Amanda (1932) and John Nelson (1935)

Willis Norman Pitts Sr.

Emanuel's fourth son, Willis Norman, was like his father, a man of uncommon intelligence and ambition. He was probably the only one in his immediate family to achieve a college education, in an era when few blacks completed even the fifth or sixth grade. His life-changing opportunity came when he was about fifteen: he went to live with and clerk for his father's friend Mr. Hubbard, a Macon undertaker. That position gave him the opportunity to attend Lewis High School, because continuing his education would have helped with his clerking. The school also taught carpentry and other manual skills that Willis would use when working with his father in the building and construction trade. Mr. Hubbard's daughter Essie was a Macon teacher, and she encouraged Willis in his educational pursuits. She is thought to have herself attended Tuskegee Institute and, when she saw his intelligence, probably recommended that school to Willis and assisted with his application.

Willis flourished at Tuskegee and, although he concentrated in the practical art of building trades, he devoured as much history and literature as he could possibly take in. The study of history, particularly military history, became his life-long passion. He soon was "Best Boy" in building trades and earned the privilege of working in Booker T. Washington's household.

While at Tuskegee, Willis fell for Roberta Irene Jackson, the equally talented "Best Girl" in home economics. Both were "work-students," paying for their education by living and working at the Institute. Roberta was in the class two years behind Willis, and had similarly been selected by Washington's wife to work in their household as a housekeeper. There the two met and discovered that they had a great deal in common.

Not much is known of Roberta's family. She was the oldest of four surviving children.[1] Her father was the Reverend Daniel Jackson, an itinerant Methodist preacher who later pastored churches in Salem and Birmingham, Alabama. She

---

1 Roberta's brother Walter also attended Tuskegee, and graduated in 1907 with a degree in Dairying. He died in 1969 at Mt Vernon, Alabama. A sister, Florence Jackson, was close to Roberta's age and died in 1947 at Lee, Alabama. The youngest sister, Mittie Cuyler, was born in 1900 and remained close to the whole Pitts family throughout her long life. She died in 1970 in Detroit, Michigan. Other children, listed in census records, included Lucious, Celia, and another Mittie; who all appear to have died in infancy or childhood.

sometimes spoke of traveling with him in his rounds. Her mother was Mary Few Jackson and her grandmother, originally from Virginia, was Minnie Dawkins Few. Roberta, born in Athens, Alabama, had primarily grown up at her grandmother's house in Salem, Alabama. Her mother and father appear to have died relatively young, but her grandmother, the family's matriarch, lived in Salem until she reached the age of one hundred and one. The family also had connections in Tuscaloosa, and Roberta may have lived there for a time as well.

Willis and Roberta both excelled at Tuskegee. They often spoke of the events of December 16, 1898, when then President William McKinley—together with his Cabinet, two Civil War generals, and the entire Alabama state legislature—visited the Institution. Roberta never let anyone forget that, when the students paraded in front of the dignitaries and demonstrated their skills and accomplishments, she was one of the chief exhibitors. Her son, Ray Pitts, wrote about the experience:

It was not unusual for students of Tuskegee to "go forth and conquer..." as each was challenged and encouraged at his graduation by some dignitary. Dignitaries often visited Tuskegee, then one of the most recognized educational institutions in the United States at that time. Contact, however minute, with these visitors and people of importance gave my parents a sense of importance which carried over into their home and community life.

My parents were student participants in two demonstrations of that day which impressed President McKinley most and about which he spoke very highly. My mother was in the parade as a demonstrator of new ways of housekeeping as learned in the Institute's Domestic Science program and my father had done the decorative turn work around the rostrum in the new student-built Chapel in which the President spoke. Both saw to it that we, their four boys, born more than a decade later, knew that they were congratulated by and honored to speak with the President on this important occasion. More precisely, our parents must have gotten the idea that they must be living representatives of the teachings of the Institute; for throughout our lives living conditions in our home, our training for family living, our educational goals, and our plans for growing up and living were constantly discussed and buttressed by the many valuable lessons they had mastered at Tuskegee.

Willis finished a degree in building trades in 1898, graduating with honors. He intended to return in the fall to complete a drawing program, after working at home with his father over the summer. However, he was taken ill. Aware that he could not return as expected to Tuskegee, Mr. Washington recommended Willis for a teaching position in the city of Woodlawn, Alabama. That September he was offered and accepted the eight-month position as teacher and Principal of the Woodlawn Public School. Although he encountered a few difficulties, he proved himself a capable and earnest educator and administrator. In a letter to Mr. Washington, Willis described his experience:

> *I have just closed the school with quite a success, considering the surround-ing circumstances. When I came here the former principal, who for some rea-son had been discharged by the board, tried to make it very unpleasant for me, although he knew nothing of me, nor from what school I came. He had never heard my name, nor had I heard his, still he tried in every way possible to convey the wrong idea. He even went so far as to say I voted the Democratic ticket, and you were also a Democrat. So when I arrived I was given a cold reception by some of the citizens of Woodlawn.*
>
> *After I came he changed and said I was a boy and could not manage the school, and at the same time he opened a private school. There were at the same time two other private schools here also, all in opposition to the city school. Yet, I am glad to say after two months I have succeeded in removing some of my opposition and showing the people they were under the wrong impression. Two of the private schools have closed and the people know I have never voted any kind of a ticket. I am very glad to say now that there is not so much opposition against the city school as when I first came here.*

At the end of the term at Woodlawn, Willis enlisted in the Army to fight in the Spanish-American War. During his last year at Tuskegee, the Civil War Gen-eral William Shafter[2] had come to Tuskegee to participate in a ceremony estab-lishing the former Park High School as the Tuskegee Military Institute for Boys. Willis had been impressed with General Shafter, and his mind had turned to the possibility of a military career. He secured Roberta's promise to wait for him to complete a 2-year tour, and to marry him upon his return.[3] Willis served honor-ably, primarily in the Philippines. He was discharged from duty in August 1900 because of sickness (malaria), but with a "very good" conduct rating. He spoke proudly of his military training for the rest of his life, and always maintained a military polish and dignity. He made sure his sons were the most immaculately dressed and coiffed young men in town, and instilled in them a profound sense of discipline, purpose and accomplishment.

When he was sufficiently recovered, Willis returned to Tuskegee to complete his studies. After graduation, he went back to East Macon to begin a career. Ro-berta had graduated in 1900 and was now an elementary school teacher in the public schools of Alabama. The two were married at Tuscaloosa on December 29, 1904, and then moved to East Macon where, according to the city directo-ry, they initially resided with his parents. At first, Willis taught carpentry and worked with his father as a carpenter and builder. Later, he bought and sold

2   Who later headed the expedition to Cuba.

3   She later told her sons that she nearly refused, because he was asking her to wait 2 years—and two years was a long time!

real estate lots from Thomas Woolfork, suitable for families to build houses. He sought to use his education and experience to improve the Fort Hill area of the East Macon community, which had been settled primarily by Jones and Baldwin County immigrants and included many relatives and friends. Soon, he had started his own construction business, employing two carpenters, one bricklayer, and one painter. Black and white Macon residents alike sought after his skills, and he began to prosper. A leader in church and community, Willis helped to purchase and to build the East Macon School, where he later participated as both a parent and advisor. Despite increasing racial strife in the South, Macon had become large enough to sustain a growing black middle class that was able to create its own version of "normal society," within rigidly prescribed limits.

However, Willis' success did not sit well with Macon's white carpenters. He was growing too popular, and was attracting business that they considered to be their own prerogative. They were able to force him out of business after only a few years—but not before he lovingly designed and built the three-bedroom, plus office, house where he and Roberta planned to raise a family.

Willis was deeply hurt by, and never truly recovered from, the loss of his carefully nurtured business. Nevertheless, owing to his superior education and his military experience, he successfully tested for a position as a senior mail clerk for the Railway Mail Service. Although ordinarily thought of as "a white man's job," this position was open to him because it was a Federal job: subject to the laws of the nation, not of the South.[4] The US Railway Mail Service was his career for the next 20 years.

Building a Life in Macon

The first decade of the 20th century was a time of new beginnings, permeated with a relentless optimism and the assurance that vision, innovation, and hard work would create a better world. Shackleton to the south and Peary to the north thrilled the world with their expeditions to the Earth's remote poles. Ford introduced his Model T sedan, putting the automobile within the reach of average Americans, while the success of the Wright Flyer was turning the imagination of millions to the prospect of commercial flight. America was well on the way to becoming a world power, annexing Puerto Rico, Guam and the Philippines, exploiting new access to Chinese markets, and planning to build the Panama Canal. On the home front, new leisure inventions—such as the cinema, commercial radio, the mass-produced gramophone, and the Brownie camera—transformed leisure hours and captivated the mind.

For African-Americans as well, it was a time of (qualified) optimism, punctuated by disappointing reversals. Despite the nonstop backlash to the reforms of

---

4   With the understanding, of course, that the working conditions of the Railway Mail Service in Macon conformed to the same Jim Crow rules, restrictions, and abuses as everything else in the South at the time.

the Reconstruction period, some things were looking up. In 1901, for the first time ever, a black man—Booker T. Washington—dined in the White House with the President of the United States. In 1905 the Niagara Movement, a black civil-rights organization, was founded. Their purpose was to demand a more active opposition to racism than that advocated by Mr. Washington. And in February 1906, an equal rights convention was held in Macon where W. E. B. Dubois, a renowned lecturer, author, and one of the founders of the Niagara Movement, addressed the gathering. Yet the 1906 Gubernatorial race in Georgia was possibly the most racially charged campaign in Georgia's history. Daily during the campaign, the newspapers carried quotes from the candidates determined to outdo each other in their "contest in denunciation of the Negro."[5] Hoke Smith, the eventually successful candidate, made no secret of his intentions towards Georgia's black citizens:[6]

> *An educated nigger is a curse to his race and a menace to the progress and prosperity of American institutions.*
> *... This is a white man's county, and we are all agreed that not only in the state at large, but in every country and in every community, the white man must control by some means, or life could not be worth living.*

Fueled by the prevailing rhetoric, the renowned 1906 Atlanta race riot was arguably the worst of the several race riots that broke out in US cities during the early years of the 20th century. With their college educations and secure government employment, Willis and Roberta were well placed in a cohesive and mutually supportive black middle-class community, but they could not close their ears to the slurs or completely escape the civil unrest.

Part of the reason for the white backlash in the early years of the century was white anxiety over the growing size and prosperity of the urban, black middle class. Labor shortages had resulted in easily available jobs and good wages, meaning that fewer black women had to work as domestics to make ends meet. And most black children were going to school, even if they did have to pay for private school to ensure a quality education. Successful blacks were not willing to submit to a permanently subservient status, and actively opposed their repression. Willis and Roberta had been taught Booker T. Washington's doctrine that blacks would gradually earn equality as they elevated themselves through industry and usefulness; however, they lived with the reality that with economic gains came even greater racial persecution. They began to shift in their views towards those of the more confrontational W. E. B. Dubois. Dubois believed that black intellectual leaders were critically needed in attaining advancement and equality for their entire race. Those leaders would require a broad, liberal

5   Andrew M Manis (2004). *Macon, Black and White.* Mercer University Press, Macon, GA, p. 29.
6   Ibid., p. 21.

education: equal to that of any white man.

On August 18, 1907, the Georgia Senate adopted the disenfranchisement amendment[7] that had been the signature component of Hoke Smith's platform. Just a few days later, on August 29, Willis and Roberta's first child, Willis Norman Pitts Jr., was born. In March, Willis' father Emanuel died and his mother Emily, with Willis' sister Quilen, moved out of their house and back to Brown's Crossing, to live with Dorsey. The small family was left in Macon with only Willis' Aunt Mary (Marietta) Benford as a boarder. Their second child, Robert Bedford (Bob) Pitts, was born on August 25, 1909, the same year that the NAACP was formally established to channel and amplify black Americans' collective voice. Bob was named "Robert" after Roberta and "Bedford" after Nathan Bedford Forrest,[8] his father's preferred candidate for recognition as "Greatest Civil War General." As if to highlight their community's challenges and hopes, the two boy's personalities took on the two opposite dimensions. Willis was the responsible one; serious, dutiful, and always striving to be an example to his brothers. He was ever conscious of injustice, suffering, and of wrongs to be righted. Bob, like his mother, was hopeful, confident, strong-willed, and determined. And like his Civil War namesake, whose motto was "to get there first with the most men," Bob would be a mover and a shaker, who was always ahead of the game.

Two years apart in age, but just one school grade apart, Bob and Willis were especially close as children and young men. In later life, Willis remembered the young Bob as "a free spirit of buoyant youth" and "one of the spark-plugs of enjoyment," while his younger brothers remembered Willis as "the one to live up to." The boys had a carefree and confident early life, but family troubles would soon bring the weight of responsibility firmly onto Willis' shoulders. The same troubles would turn Bob's energy and enthusiasm into a well-honed talent for survival and an unflagging pursuit of achievement.

Children of a new decade, Raymond Jackson (Ray) Pitts arrived on June 21, 1911, and Nathan Alvin (Nath) Pitts[9] on June 29, 1913. It was a decade of militarism and conflict, even revolution. In the US, now becoming a world power, it was a period of social unrest and rapid change. The white supremacist movement was still very strong in the South. Thomas Dixon's novel and play,

---

7   Almost completely preventing blacks from voting in Georgia.

8   Although Forrest joined the KKK after the war and was likely its first Grand Wizard, by the end of his life he had fully renounced his involvement with the Klan and begun advocating for greater educational opportunities for blacks, and for harmony between the races. This may account for Willis Sr.'s willingness to name his sons, both Robert and Nathan, after the man. Ironically the grandson, Nathan Bedford Forrest II, was significantly involved in the resurgence of the Klan in the 1920s. His son, Nathan Bedford Forrest III was the first American general to be killed in action during WWII in Europe, a war in which both Willis Jr. and Bob also fought for their country.

9   Named, as a compromise, for both Nathan Bedford Forrest (Willis' choice) and Nathan Young, a noted black speaker and Roberta's choice.

The Clansman, and another of his plays, *The Sins of the Father*, received enthusiastic publicity and riveted large audiences to his message of white supremacy. Lynch mobs were becoming common, and a newly resurrected Klan first met at nearby Stone Mountain, Georgia, in 1915. They formed around the rallying cry of white supremacy, nationalism, and anti-Catholicism. The nation's previously insular views of domestic politics and society were giving way to concerns of global importance. With the gradual fracturing of the Ottoman Empire, the Bosnian crisis, and the Balkan Wars, it was becoming clear that the world would soon be involved in a conflict of global proportions. Although the US would not officially enter the war until 1917, it was already apparent that war on such a scale would alter many things, and Macon would not be exempt. Reflecting the times into which they were born, the two younger Pitts boys would know a childhood of greater uncertainty and tumult. The differences would shade their futures, and create a gulf between these two and their two older brothers. Many years later, Willis Jr. wrote:

Individual Differences
(for Ray and Nath)

When a younger brother asked,
   Why didn't you go there?
      The older brother only looked and wondered
         Why this younger could not understand.

When another brother insisted
   That he had talked and met with the other;
      The older brother knew
         He might have answered thus—to both:

Place and time were mine only to decide
And survival train tracks stretched me
   To another side!
      That, my Brothers, is the difference!

Family Life

The young Pitts family enjoyed an affectionate, middle-class existence circumscribed by a close-knit church family and by the local black community. Ray once wrote a letter to a long-time Holsey Temple member about his memories of their church community:

Mrs. Hurley's family that lived on Second Avenue was part of our family. Holsey Temple CME Church was like home. There our first friends were made. Mrs. Hurley was my brother Bob's Godmother, and in the Pitts Collection of family treasures is a beautiful cup given to him at Christmas or at his Christening on his first Easter as a child. That was a custom at the church, you know, and one of the memorable "rights of passage" being forgotten in our families. Mrs. Mary Baker was Godmother to either Willis or Nathan, and Mrs. Sally McCarthy, bless her heart, was mine. We always looked forward to seeing them at Church as we did the other families whom I wish the present Holsey Temple group would remember. Godmothers were SPECIAL.

For us, the four Pitts brothers, their father and mother and their cousins, aunts and uncles, walking from Fort Hill across the Spring Street bridge, passing the Jewish Synagogue and up the hill to Washington Avenue then right to the Church, was both a privilege and an education. We learned, as we walked. Who would be at Sunday school? Who would be our Sunday school teacher? Mrs. Mary Baker was my teacher at one time and one well remembered. Seated in what to my young eyes was the most beautiful open spaced building in my world, we could hear lessons being taught to other classes. Often, I would sneak a look to see where Bob and Willis were and who were their teachers and classmates. These were memorable times for me.

... Mrs. Solomon was our primary teacher and I loved her from the start. She gave me a feeling of importance by letting me take our collection of pennies to the front. Dad would ring the little bell calling for collection from each class. I felt proud walking to the front to add our small bit to the Sunday school collection. In our modern education terms, she was developing our "self-esteem" by letting each of her pupils take turns at this. I learned many lessons like this one in the Sunday school setting. Our teachers taught us cooperation and responsibility.

We did not always walk to Sunday school. Sometimes the East Macon street car took us to Cherry Street and there we transferred to the Vineville line. Often, we would meet a small group coming from South Macon there at Broadway and Cherry, going to OUR church. The Vineville line took us up Mulberry, to Cotton Avenue to Vineville Avenue past the imposing Catholic Church, the white Baptist Church, and we got off just below Holsey Temple. I always remember the Italian Candy Store next-door to our church, which somehow never was a temptation to me. I do remember Mrs. Solomon and Mrs. Baker cautioning us not to go there to buy candy, however.

Our dad, as you know, was the Sunday School Superintendent. Sunday school literature, the beautifully illustrated books and cards, were mailed to our home. This gave us an advantage. We had a preview of the primary, intermediate, advanced and adult literature for the entire Sunday school. Too, knowing where the packages came from and when to expect them became important to us. Geography became one of our specialties. Our father's mail clerk experiences were added to our lessons. We learned to separate out the Sunday school quarterlies for the various levels. We knew that these were mailed from Nashville. We learned our geography from this and from our father telling of transfer points in his work as a railway mail clerk. Too, at that time our mother wrote many letters. All of this coupled with our geography classes at Fort Hill School under the superb and imaginative teachers made us good students of geography.

In my search for written records of early membership, I find very little about the Holsey Temple congregation; but we remember a host of Pitts cousins, aunts and uncles[10] there with us. Our father always attended Holsey Temple, influenced his family to attend there, and gave us, his sons, a family-church experience in our youth which we dearly cherish.

The boys learned history and geography at the feet of their father, who was passionate about both. His chief historical hobby was the battles and generals of the Civil War, and he augmented their education with trips to various Civil War sites.

By the time the boys were in school, Willis Sr. was a railway mail clerk and had hung up his carpenter tools. However, the reminders of his professional past were all around. The boys knew that mysterious tools and blueprints were tucked away in storage, that he had helped to build the community school and develop the surrounding neighborhood, that their very house was of his own construction. They were naturally curious and, by virtue of their being kept mostly out of sight, the tools of that trade took on a special fascination. But their father, who continued to further his own education with the study of history and with correspondence courses in law, discouraged a career in trade. He insisted that they plan for professional careers—in the military; in law, mathematics or science; or at least in the broader liberal arts.

The house their father built reflected the limited city services of the day, but was built with an eye toward the future. His son Ray, recalled:

The home was built on a two acre plot one block within the city limits. At the time there were no sewage or water supplied in that block. Water for the family came from a well especially dug and walled in with brick. The well was just outside the back door and well protected. All of this seemed to have been a part of the design of the house. In keeping with good practice, the toilet was in a fenced in area which we called the "big Garden" and was located about 30 or 35 yards from the back of the house. This three seater was built to accommodate two adults and one child. The child's seat was about ½ as high and on the end. The toilet went through three stages as the city's health regu-

---

10   In addition to their father's siblings and their families, the boys also grew up knowing much of the extended family—especially the families of the youngest two of their Grandfather Emanuel's half-brothers, Oliver and Reuben.

lations and my parents' thoughts about the family's health came into action. It was first an open toilet, then a pit, then a movable can was used. By the end of the first World War it was prevalent knowledge that flies and mosquitoes had a role in the spread of disease. So, the neighbors joined with our family physician to get city water and city sewage lines extended to the city limits. This made it possible for my dad to complete the equipping of the bathroom he had included in his dream house ten years earlier. An indoor toilet did not completely destroy our classic "three-holer." When I left for college in 1928, though unused, it stood as a symbolic relic, a reminder of a family's growing up.

    I write of our family physician: Dr. J. A. Moore, our doctor, delivered the four of us at our home. As far as I know, he was assisted by Aunt May ("Anmay," we called her), one of my father's aunts. Her full name, I learned, was Marietta Pitts Benford. She was married to one of the carpenters who worked with my father in his building business. She was the first of two baby sitters that I knew.

    Dr. Moore aside, my mother took over with care of the children when they were ill. Fevers of many types were quite prevalent throughout the South during this period. Typhoid fever, Malaria fever, Yellow fever had for decades been responsible for deaths numbered in thousands. Dr. Moore prescribed Quinine, for the boys it was coco-quinine, and it was administered regularly by our home nurse and mother. Dr. Moore also recommended screens. My father bought half screens and we used them when the windows were open.

From the time of their birth, Roberta dedicated her life to her sons. According to Willis Jr., "Despite the many physical and emotional stresses which beset her during the depression years, her life was lived as a practical model of hope, encouragement, pride and inspiration for 'her boys.' ... She never wavered in her determination to stand by her sons. In her own words, repeated many time during her latter years, and which she often unconsciously repeated many times during her last illness; 'I want my boys to be good men.' This was her creed."

From their mother, the boys learned community engagement and activism. Roberta figured prominently in the Colored Women's Federated Club and was visited by notable activists of that time, including Mary McCleod Bethune and Charlotte Hawkins Brown. She too considered the boys' education to be paramount, and devotedly put money aside to provide for private school and college, even if she had to go without.

As a youngster, Willis Jr. christened Roberta with the name that they boys would know her by for the rest of her life. He had decided that the family was overloaded with men—four boys and a father to only one mother. He felt that a sister was lacking. His parents were not willing to comply with his request to provide one, and so Roberta became "Sis." He felt she needed to be both sister and mother to make the family complete. From Sis, the boys learned the more practical skills of survival: how to manage their time and resources, how to work and plan for a better future, and how to reap the benefits of hard work, persistence and determination.

Each brother, in turn, worked as a paperboy; and at least Ray and Nathan also worked after school and weekends at the corner bakery. Between school, work and sports, none was ever idle. Ray also discovered that the bakery job came with unexpected social benefits. One day a pretty girl named Kathleen (Kay), whom Ray and Nathan both knew from school, came into the bakery to buy a birthday cake for a party. Ray started a conversation, and Kathleen, not being shy, invited him to the birthday party. That encounter ignited a romance that would last for more than seventy years, and led to the oft-repeated family truism—"Where there's Ray, there's Kay!"

As busy as they all were, the family found time for hobbies and the arts. Each boy was encouraged to learn an instrument. Family chronicler Ray recalled:

> *First, Willis was given a saxophone, an E-flat Alto. Purchased from Williams Music Company store on Cherry Street,[11] it must have cost about thirty-five dollars. I never remember Bro. Willis playing it at all; not even practicing at home. ...*
>
> *Next Bob was given a Violin and lessons by Prof. C. N. Pitts. I do remember Bob Pitts and Bob Saxton coming to the house to practice "Whispering Hope" on their violins and going the next Sunday to play in Rev. Saxton's Church at Bolingbroke, a town near Griffin with a Baptist congregation. Bob and Bob Saxton excited me with their enthusiasm for both the travel to play music and the pretty girls they talked about meeting.*
>
> *On my turn I was given a Mandolin, the egg shaped kind that was considered a "parlor instrument." The fingering was exactly like the violin, So, I would take Prof. Pitts' mandolin lessons and practice them on Bob's violin. Somehow, I did not like playing my mandolin until Mr. Barrow got together the "Bird House Gang"—Albert, Dosh, Carlton, Ezell, Charles Graham— and made the BNS[12] School Orchestra out of us. We considered ourselves very special being invited to play for students to march into Chapel on Friday.*
>
> *Then Nath was given the piano, and piano lessons. I remember that he became quite good at Mrs. Clemons' recitals; but as Sis was later to relate, music lost out to football and baseball.[13] I think we all played one piece on Nath's piano; mine was the waltz, "Silver Moon," which I can do today— with great effort.*

---

11   This saxophone remains in the family; Ray Sr. played it after Willis discarded it. He affectionately called it "Rusty." Ray Jr. played it next; then his sister Kathleen asked for it for her sons Kelvin and Brian.

12   Ballard Normal School.

13   He one day told Sis that; "My hands were made for a football."

Aunt Mittie

Another important female member of the family, and strong influence on the young boys, was Mittie Corrine Jackson, Roberta's youngest sister. Mittie, born in 1900, was only a few years older than her nephews, more like a sister than an Aunt. But, she was not to be the sister Willis Jr. longer for. She moved to Detroit, Michigan, with an aunt when she was only 13. The families remained close, however, and saw each other as frequently as possible. The aura of big city life and of Northern ways made Mittie a unique influence. She was young and hip, and her life looked enticing to the Pitts boys. Remaining childless as she matured, she adopted the boys and their families as her own.

Later in their lives, Mittie's place in Detroit would become the "home away from home" of the young men while they were looking for work in the Great Depression or attending school in Ann Arbor. She was close enough in age for them to trust her to understand their problems, and to listen to her guidance. At the same time, she was the carrier of family traditions and beliefs that made her an essential link with their parents' generation, and an emissary for her sister.

Mittie, like Willis Sr., worked for the Post Office. She was briefly married to Walter McKenzie, but he doesn't figure into any of the family's recollections about their "Aunt Mitt." She was listed in the 1940 Census as "divorced." She afterwards took the name "Mittie C. J. Cuyler," and was still legally known by both McKenzie and Cuyler at the time of her death in 1970. She was devoted to her church as well as to her family, and maintained a faithful membership at Bethel AME Church in Detroit for many years, serving as a senior usher and in several other service positions.[14] She was also active in the Order of the Eastern Star and with the Ames Temple of Elks.

In a letter to his children about this Aunt and her legacy, Ray Sr., said:

> *I had come to think of the address 6870 Boxwood, Detroit, Michigan as our Detroit home in the true sense—a place where Love and Warmth and Affection and Happiness was always found. Our many visits and exchanges of letters, gifts, and phone calls reinforced this as my concept of "home." This human feeling is my interpretation of the little lady's life that I knew as Aunt Mittie.*

School

As young boys the brothers all went to local Fort Hill or East Macon pub-

---

14   Mittie's faith defined her until the end. When she was taken to the hospital in her last illness, she left behind in her Bible a well-thumbed, hand printed paper with these lines:
We seek Thy direction in all things. Be our guide, so that we do not make the wrong turn when we are unsure, nor be led astray by temptation, nor lost in life's confusion. Help us to follow thee faithfully, praying as Thou has taught us to pray.

lic schools for blacks, through the 8th grade. Their parents actively encouraged their academic gifts and love of school. It was in these early years that their academic talents were noted and they were urged by their teachers to continue as far as possible in their education. Ray wrote:

> *Ada Finney McBride was my fifth grade teacher. She convinced me that I was going to be a great mathematician. I have used this often in answer to the question, "How did you happen to choose mathematics as a field of study?" My reply has been, on the most important occasions, "My fifth grade teacher told me that I could be a great mathematician, and I believed her."*

Although it took considerable family sacrifice and expense, all four boys went to high school at the private Ballard Normal School. Ballard, with a student body drawn from Macon as well as the surrounding countryside, offered the best high school education available to blacks in Georgia at the time. It was an American Missionary Association (AMA) school that offered a faculty of both black and white teachers, working together. Such an uncommon environment gave the boys a perspective that was rare, even among the black middle class. In the deeply Jim Crow South, they caught a vision of whites and blacks treating each other equally, with mutual respect.[15] They met white people who were genuine friends of their race and who were deeply interested in their progress and advancement. Despite the outright prejudice and discrimination that they experienced later in life, the four boys maintained an optimism about the possibility of working and living on an equal basis with whites uncommon to those of otherwise-similar backgrounds. Ray wrote:

> *Ballard Normal School gave us a feeling of self-worth that carried us through everything else we had to endure. Having teachers both black and white who believed in us meant that we simply never got the feeling that we were inferior. The student-teacher relationships were so powerful ... and a religious platform that stressed brotherhood, educability and justice—there is nothing like that in the public schools. There is no push for it. Ballard is fundamental to my accomplishment and philosophy.*

At Ballard, there were elementary, secondary and normal school courses, as well as classes in moral and spiritual values. Ballard also served as "a hub for visiting dignitaries and as an activity center for Macon's segregated black community, which in 1920 numbered more than 23,000, almost forty-six percent of the city's 53,000 citizens."[16] The Principal of Ballard for nearly all of their

---

15   Not to suggest that AMA schools were utopias. Black teachers were more often elementary teachers or aides, and were often paid less than white teachers. Whites often carried racist assumptions and attitudes with them into these communities. But, at their best, the schools managed to create environments far more positive than anything else modeled in the Jim Crow South, at least in the eyes of the students.

16   Titus Brown (Summer 1998). *New England Missionary and African-American Education in Macon: Raymond G. Von Tobel at the Ballard Normal School, 1908-1935.* The Georgia Historical Quarterly, Vol. 82,

time at the school was Raymond G. Von Tobel, one of the few notable people in Macon respected by whites and blacks alike. He was loved and revered by the whole student body, and was a significant role model in each Pitts boy's life. Willis Jr. wrote that Von Tobel was "a model of decent living within a spirit of true missionary purpose" and that his wife was a "small woman, soft of voice, but a person possessing those attributes that always symbolize respect for human personality."

The Von Tobels had taken an especial liking to Ray's girlfriend Kathleen, inviting her into their home and into their lives. They had a young daughter Harriet who needed someone to play with, and Kathleen became Harriet's companion. Kathleen was a very light-skinned black—by looks alone, she could easily pass for white—and they recognized that because of this she would always have trouble "fitting in." They tried to give her experiences that would help her navigate that socially difficult line in the sand. She traveled, in the summers, with the Von Tobel family during high school and college, all over the country. They once went as far as the Grand Canyon. They were her second family. Both Ray and Kathleen kept in close contact with the Von Tobels throughout their lives, as did their children for many years.

Willis Jr. (often called Norman in the family, and "Docky" by his father) excelled at academics and at sports, and established a standard for the Pitts brothers that the others found difficult to equal. Although the self-described "runt" of the family, he was on the football, basketball, baseball and track teams, serving as captain of the football team in his senior year. He was an honor student and was especially noted for public speaking. He was his senior class president. Ray remembered:

> Our parents set him up as a model, and he accepted the challenge. I saw him as a model. Willis had talent that was far beyond any talent that we had. I always marveled at the fact that he could capture an audience. When Willis got up to say his speeches at the various school programs, he held the audience spellbound. I can't forget his 7th grade city-wide oratorical contest ...
> It was May 1920. Our parents had taken us to the city hall auditorium. We all sat with our classmates and friends waiting for the contestant from our school. He walked out on the stage like he owned the place, and when he finished there was no doubt as to who would win. ...
> We were expected to fill his shoes as we reached his age level. But, his accomplishment was always far beyond anything I expected to do.

Youngest brother Nathan also recalled:

> I ran into Willis' records both as a scholar and an athlete and, on one hand, the fact that he established certain high records in school tended to

set goals for me. On the other hand, it set challenges that sometimes created problems, in that both in elementary and high school, if I did not respond favorably as teachers expected me to or wanted me to, they would always come back with the statement that "your brother would never have responded this way and we expect you to live up to his standards."

At Ballard, Bob exhibited an early interest in and aptitude for mathematics, but he showed an even greater interest in fun and friends. He was good in sports, and was active in many of the school's social activities. Old photos in one of Bob's scrapbook albums show members of the "Bird House Gang" that he and Ray belonged to, informal groups of Ballard friends, and a number of individual photos of pretty girls—a few inscribed to him "with love." Willis dubbed him "Bob the adventurer," and remembered him as the most fun loving and best socialite among their Ballard gang. Bob himself recalled their early school days as "the age of enjoyment." Several pals from this period would remain life-long friends. One in particular, Judson Howard, would later figure instrumentally in Bob's career.

Bob and Willis Jr. were clearly headed to college. As very close siblings only a year apart in school, they made plans to together attend Talladega College in Alabama. Talladega was, like Ballard, an American Missionary Association sponsored school. The close contacts between Ballard and Talladega made it the college of choice for most Ballard graduates. Willis Sr. and Roberta, well connected in their black middle-class network, advised them about what to expect and provided additional names of contacts who would assist in need, or who could direct them to part-time jobs and lodging. They also gave each of the boys a new trunk for their college journey. They told them they would henceforth need to work, part-time and summers, to finance the bulk of their education— but promised to provide monthly sums for college "incidentals."

Willis Jr. went to Talladega in the fall of 1925 and, as everyone expected, he excelled in this new environment. He pledged Alpha Phi Alpha, the black, inter-collegiate fraternity that all four brothers eventually entered. The friendships made as "Alpha men" became a strong network of social and professional contacts that endured throughout their lifetimes, and helped make it possible for them to prosper and achieve as black men in a still-very-racist society. As he had at Ballard, Willis Jr. continued to excel in athletics and to exercise his passion for speech, writing, and the theater. He came home with stories about college life that fired the imaginations of the younger boys.

The summer of 1926, Willis Jr. and Bob went at the invitation of their Uncle Hoppie to work near where Hoppie was stationed at West Point, in Highland Falls, NY. Hoppie was, at the time, very ill and in the hospital; he probably knew he was dying. Perhaps he wanted to see some family once again, and also to provide the boys their first experience of life outside of the South. Bob came home that fall with a number of photos of himself with a friend, Bob Johnson, at various local sights. Willis Jr. also participated in some of these excursions, although he apparently worked in a somewhat different position and location than Bob. He later spoke of that summer as "the easiest and most pleasant experience that I knew in all of my efforts. At least, I had a place to stay (Uncle Hopy[17]) and a brother to share some of the experience. Elsewhere it was very different." Although in their respective memoirs neither one mentions it, military records indicate that Hoppie died during that summer, so there would be no invitations to return.

In the fall of 1926 Bob also went off to Talladega, where in Willis Jr.'s footsteps he pledged Alpha Phi Alpha. Willis Jr. returned for his second year. Bob, even more so than Willis Jr., began to make the rounds of school athletic and social clubs and, especially, to make the acquaintance of the many pretty girls. Despite his gregarious nature, Bob also excelled in academics. Both boys seemed off to an excellent start. Unfortunately, that blissful life would all soon unravel.

Troubles

In 1917, just weeks after his second election as the first Southerner President since the Civil War, Woodrow Wilson called on Congress to declare war against Germany. The black community in Macon did their part to support the war and, in April, petitioned the city to form a black regiment. Macon was a mobilization center during the war, and its black citizens enthusiastically plunged into fund raising, wartime civilian labor, and relief efforts. In their rallies, public announcements, and letters to the editor of the Macon Telegraph, they also asserted that they expected the black community's cooperation in securing liberty abroad to result in improved conditions at home. Instead, the immediate postwar period saw increased racial tensions. According to one historian, "With little sense of the ironic, the same white Americans who defended democracy 'over there,' redoubled their efforts to deny it to blacks over here."[18] The War Department's "work or fight" rule was applied in Macon largely to stem the black flight to the North, keeping black men working for low wages and driving black women into domestic service. In Macon, one black woman was fined twenty-five dollars for refusing to take a job as a domestic, even though she did not need the money and had children of her own at home to take care of.[19] Georgia led the nation in lynchings, sometimes of black soldiers still in their uniforms. Three lynchings,[20] as well as a rash of attacks by whites on blacks, occurred in Macon

17   The proper spelling is a bit of a mystery. Willis Sr. and Jr. both used "Hopy," the man himself used "Hoppie," but his gravestone says "Hoppy;" and Willis Sr. indicated in one place that his given name was "Hope."

18   Andrew M Manis (2004) *Macon Black and White.* Mercer University Press, Macon, GA, p. 53.

19   Donald L Grant (1993) *The Way it Was in the South.* Birch Lane Press, New York, NY, pp. 306-7.

20   Andrew M. Manis (2004) *Macon Black and White.* p. 60.

between 1918 and 1922. Black flight to the North continued at a steady rate.

Willis Sr. and Roberta were able to shield their boys from direct experience of much of the racism that was rampant at the time. The boys' friends, family, recreation, shopping, athletics and after-school jobs were all in the tight-knit black community. Their only intimate exposure to whites was at Ballard Normal, with its Northern teachers from the AMA who were committed to the ideals of racial equality and cooperation. But the shielded world that the parents created for the boys was not one that they could live in themselves. Continued outright hostility, disenfranchisement and discrimination; lack of community services for black citizens; and the precarious financial environment for even the most prosperous blacks took a heavy emotional toll on the couple and their contemporaries.

Early in 1925 Roberta became seriously ill and was confined to her bed for a significant period of time. Medical care for blacks was sparse and substandard in those days. The black wing of the public hospital was inferior, as was the training of most of the black doctors and nurses who served there.[21] Roberta's situation continued to be serious and the family quickly ran through whatever money the couple had saved. Willis Jr. later wrote:

> *I was midway of my Ballard Normal high school senior year. I remember my mother's long private talk with me at that time, first because it was the first time I had ever seen her really crying while she talked. She did manage to point out that I was her eldest son, and she had to talk to someone. ...*
>
> *Mother was an introvert who kept most of her worries, frustrations, hurts—that were physical, mental—held deep to herself. ...*
>
> *Few people really knew how she fought when our home life broke down, as did her health. My greatest respect for my mother hinges around the deep generous feeling of mine, that "Sis" was a fighter.*

And a fighter she would need to be. Willis Sr. could not secure a loan from a reputable bank to satisfy his creditors, and he eventually felt forced to deal with loan sharks to meet the family's mounting bills. When they insisted on full payment before he had the money, he faced total ruin.

In those days, a black man had essentially no legal recourse in this type of financial matter. Not only were there no "equal opportunity" laws, life had taught the couple that essentially any white man could make a claim against a black man—even with no proof whatsoever—and get away with it. They knew that many authorities acted on the premise that a dubious, or even patently false, testimony of a white man was better than any proof to the contrary offered by a black man. In addition, the abuses of illegal moneylenders and dishonest financiers, although well known, were often overlooked. Willis took what he

---

21   The first private hospital for blacks in Macon, St. Luke's, did not open until 1928.

believed was the only option open to him. Facing the threat of losing his home and all his possessions, he "borrowed" from the mails to pay his debts, hoping to pay it back before the missing money was discovered. According to the newspaper coverage of his trial:

> *Within a short time, he was so entangled with the moneylenders that he could not recover. Pitts then went to a local realtor for help.*
> *The realtor ... agreed to lend the Negro money and "make it all right." The money was advanced, and a mortgage was taken on his home and furniture. Next thing Pitts knew, his attorney said, the realtor was taking steps toward selling the mortgaged property. A usurious interest was demanded, in addition to the money advanced, and Pitts rifled the mails in order to pay it.*[22]

After more than 20 years with the postal service, Willis Sr.'s career ended in ignominy with his arrest in December 1928. One simultaneously tragic and fortunate circumstance did, at least, ease the family's circumstances to some degree. A few weeks before his sentencing in November 1929, the home he had once built with so much optimism burned to the ground. The family lost all their possessions, but the insurance company was able to find no reason to reject their claim. The insurance payment cleared the debt and got the family out from under the shadow of their creditors. The judge, as well, was lenient: he handed down only a three-month sentence, because of the extreme circumstances. Nevertheless, Willis and Roberta were shattered. For the rest of his life, Willis Sr. worked only intermittently as a carpenter, between recurring bouts of malaria and of despair. His sons blamed him and never really forgave him; only Willis Jr. maintained a close relationship with him as an adult.

Roberta soon separated from Willis to seek work, needing to support herself and provide what she could for the boys' educations. Handicapped with the additional challenges of a nation sinking into economic depression, she had few choices. She went into domestic service, seeking work as far as North Carolina. She found a position at Mary Potter School in Oxford, North Carolina, where she served as dining hall matron for several years. Eventually she ended up at Morison Training School in Hoffman, NC, where she was employed as a teacher-matron until she retired in July 1945.[23] She lived in North Carolina for the school year and came home to Macon only briefly in the summers. When she retired, she began living with her sons, moving as needed from one family to the next.

With their older brothers off to college, and later off to seek work, the two younger brothers reacted differently to the family's abrupt dissolution. Ray, closer in age to his college brothers, focused single-mindedly on following them

22   Macon Telegraph (November 5, 1929). *Court Considers Hard Luck Story.*

23   For her approx. 15 years of service in North Carolina schools, she received a monthly retirement allowance of $32.28.

to Talladega. He threw himself into academics and athletics, hoping to win scholarship support, and into his after school job, knowing that he would have to earn the money for college himself.

I didn't really perceive of it as a family deteriorating, my whole goal was getting into college. ... I blocked out anything that did not have to do with my going to college.

For Nathan, the disintegration of the family was the most traumatic. Rethinking the experience in latter life, he said:

The disasters that struck the family hit us at a time when I was just beginning to get into high school. There were two or three years that I had to stop and try to remember even where I lived, because we moved around to three or four places. ... When I finished high school, there was no talk whatever of college. There was no money.

The once tight-knit family had splintered. From that time, each member made his or her way in the world essentially alone.

Roberta (Sis) Jackson Pitts (1878–1959):
Above Left: As a young girl   Above Right: Later in life

Below left: Mary Few Jackson (Roberta's mother)
Below Right: Minnie Dawkins Few (Roberta's grandmother)

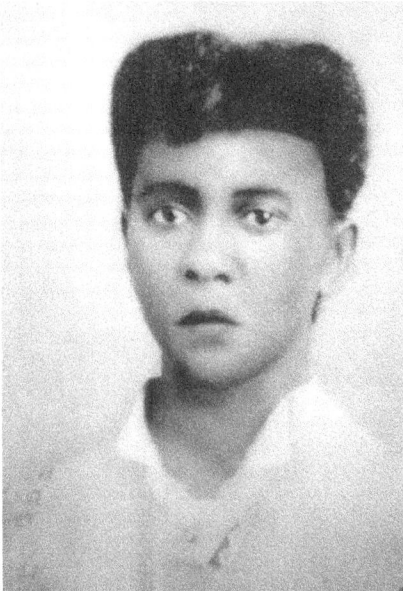

Above Left:
Mittie Corrine
Jackson Cuyler
(a.k.a. Mittie McKenzie)
Roberta's youngest sister

Above Right:
Walter Jackson,
Roberta's brother

Left: Aunt Mittie in Detroit.

Below: Florence Jackson,
Roberta's sister

Willis Norman Pitts
(1877–1948):

Left: In uniform

Right: At the house
on Maynard Street

Above Left: Bob (left) and Willis Jr. (c1910)
Above Right: Raymond Pitts, baptism photo (c1912)

Below: The house Willis Sr. built
at 611 Maynard Street, Macon, Georgia

Photo taken at the baptism of Nathan Pitts (1914)
(l to r) Willis Norman Jr., Nathan Alvin,
Raymond Jackson, Robert Bedford

Above: Bob and Willis Jr. as boys

Below: The Bird House Gang
(Bob and Ray: front row, third and forth from left)

Family Portrait: (front, l to r) Willis Sr, Nathan, Roberta. (back) Robert, Raymond, Willis Jr.

Willis Norman Pitts Jr.

The events that began with his mother's illness in 1925 brought Willis Jr. to a turning point in the summer of 1927. There was no money for either he or Bob to return to Talladega. In fact, they were asked to leave Talladega because they had debts that were overdue. Both, being excellent students and well liked, were encouraged to return as soon as they could pay the outstanding bills and afford to continue.

The depression had come early to central Georgia, in the form of the boll weevil and other factors resulting in the decline in viability of the cotton economy. Faced with the family's financial distress and the poor local job market, the two brothers were forced to look for work "on the road," and went separate ways. Although keeping in touch with his mother as much as possible, at this point Willis' relations with the rest of the family became somewhat distant. They remained that way until much later in his life.

Sis encouraged Willis to get away from what he called the "hellish life experience" of the dissolution of his family. Over the next two years he lived on borrowed money, staying with family and friends or with strangers, taking whatever jobs he could find. He ventured first to nearby Atlanta, but found little opportunity there. Then, knowing his young Aunt Mittie lived in Detroit, he joined the general black migration to the North, and went there to look for work. From Detroit he continued westward to Chicago, where his high school chum Bob Adams now lived and worked. Adams had offered him at least a temporary place to stay. Willis lived with Bob in Chicago from June to November 1927, and then joined the wave of workers headed west, following the Federal project to build Highway 66, linking Chicago with Los Angeles. He ended up in Tulsa Oklahoma,[1] where he found work as a bellboy and as a waiter. Finally, in Oklahoma, he began earning enough to live, pay his college bills, and even set aside funds for his eventual return to school.

---

1   Cyrus Avery of Tulsa, known as the "Father of Route 66," successfully lobbied the government to build the highway, and to route it through his city. In 1928 the Spartan Aircraft Company was also established in Tulsa, and that year the Oklahoma City Oil Field began producing enormous quantities of oil, all burgeoning the economy of Tulsa. However, by the early 30's a glut of oil caused the Tulsa economy to begin to collapse, which might have been a factor in Willis moving back to Georgia and school in the fall of 1930.

Willis was on track to have enough to return to Talladega in the fall of 1929, and he felt optimistic that he was getting his life under control. But just as things were looking up, he received a life-changing request from his mother. Instead of returning to school himself; since he had a good job, Sis asked him to continue working and send home money so that his younger brothers could go to school. As the oldest, and *de facto* head of the household, would he sacrifice his own opportunity to give his brothers a better chance at life?

For one more year, Willis did as she asked. He continued to work in Oklahoma and sent money to the family. The three years on the road during the depression, and his sacrifice for his brothers, became what Willis later saw as the defining moment in his life. Later, he wrote to his brother Ray that he was a "depression victim" and that "most of the 'hell, heartache and heart' which forms the 'essence and substance' of my life seems to have had little to do with academics and academic walls." He went on that the "hellish life experiences" that characterized those years and the "'what and how,' and my size and color, are factors that would furnish you with a better portrait of me than the two years that you knew me as 'Brother Willis' at Talladega."

At various times in his life Willis gave different answers about why he made this sacrifice. To his two youngest brothers, he sometimes insisted that he had been "forced" to work to pay for their education, and occasionally made them feel as though he still resented it. Ray believed that he had never quite forgiven them for the missed opportunities and delays in pursuing his own goals. But at other times, such as decades later in a lay-Sunday sermon to his church in Sherborn, Massachusetts, he talked about his difficult but intentional decision to make a willing sacrifice for the sake of others. The truth probably lies somewhere between the two extremes. Although it was difficult, it was always a part of his essential nature to put the needs of others above his own. This sacrifice was the first in a long series of life choices in which Willis put the hopes and dreams of others first. He ultimately found great pride and joy in seeing others succeed, with the benefit of his sacrifices.

From the perspective of many years, and even though the difficulties and disappointments were often hard to bear, Willis looked back on the troubled years of his early life—and called it all "good."

In Retrospect: The Old Home Town 40 Years Ago

The early years were good—
Two proud Negroes—Man and Wife,—
Educated as first disciples
of Tuskegee's "B. T. W."
Built a home and bred four sons
In a cloistered atmosphere of racial pride.

Early the boys learned
> *The difference between white and black lives*
> *In a deep Southern segregated town:*
> *"Nigger," "Boy," "Stay in your place,"*
> *And, always the threat of something*
> *secretly hovering—the Ku Klux Klan,*
> *Drilled deep into their inner selves—*
> *Racial hatred—nurtured and practiced*
> *In the Old Home Town!*

But the teaching was there
For commonality and decency among human beings!
So, somehow, for these boys—
> *The early years were Good!*

For some, the human spirit, so battered,
Was stunted—remaining segregated
Until this day!
For these boys and others, the human spirit
found help along the way to know, even after
those traumatic shocks—
> *That the early years were Good!*

Return Home

Willis was finally able to return to Talladega in the fall of 1930, joining the same graduating class as his (four years younger) brother Ray. Unlike his brothers, who all studied mathematics or physical science, Willis majored in History and English. He continued to pursue his early passion for speech, debate and theater performance, as well as his talent for team sports (football and baseball). The next fall he was elected secretary of the college's Alpha Phi Alpha fraternity chapter, where his brother Ray was incoming President. Having so missed his carefree college life during the three-year absence, he filled it with activity during his final two years. Editor-in-Chief of the school newspaper, "The Mule's Ear," he was described by that same publication as...

> *probably the busiest man on campus. ... [He] has served efficiently as leader of campus thought and opinion. His method of persuading reluctant undergraduates to express themselves is infallible. 'The Spider' is a writer, an athlete, President of the Little Theatre, Vice-President of the Senior Class, and an active member of the History club.*

Yet, despite their joint service in the fraternity and proximity as brothers,

Willis was often quick to point out that the early "severance forced four brothers with altogether different personalities and perspectives into different paths." In a letter to his sister-in-law Mattalyn after Bob's death, he noted that; "As the elder brother, I recall that when our family became separated, it was a time when our brother relationship became distant. When I returned to Talladega College after a forced dropout of three years, Ray and I became classmates, and during over two college remaining years, Ray and I were practically strangers, rarely communication as 'family.' But, there was the brother link!"

The summer between these final two years at Talladega, Willis made another "brother link"—reuniting with Nathan, whom he had not seen since leaving home four years earlier. He remembered "a small youngster," and discovered Nathan had grown into "a 200-pounder as a new high school graduate." Although living in different households that summer, the two played on the same baseball team and were able to meet each other as adults. Nathan later recalled, "We shared a comradeship that bonded us together as friends as well as brothers."

Willis and Ray graduated together in 1932, ready to pursue careers in a country still in the depths of the Great Depression. They went home to Macon and each tried to survive in his own way. A high point that year was their collaboration on the production of a play/pageant about the history of Ballard Normal School. Willis used the opportunity to put to use, and to further refine, some of the techniques he learned in the theatre club at Talladega.

Although Willis was somewhat more successful than Ray in finding the odd job that paid, he did not find a permanent job until the fall of 1933. Then, he accepted a teaching position in English at the Moultrie, Georgia, public high school, about 130 miles south of Macon. He taught there for two years before accepting a position back in Macon, as Instructor of Social Sciences and English at his *alma mater*, Ballard Normal School.

The move back to Macon, ten years after leaving high school, provided Willis with a chance to reunite with his father on a different footing. He approached the relationship with conflicted expectations and emotions. Writing about that time in a later memoir, he said:

> *I turn to some reflection from the boyhood and youthful "growing up years" of a first-born son privileged, after an absence of some years, to meet with his father once again. There were changes noticed in the man's appearance! The marked features of a once pleasant personality, homeowner and family man, seemed deeper and crossed with some personal loss of dignity that highlighted a slowly deteriorating physical problem. He seemed a man reaching, too soon, the "twilight years" of his life! Too, the son felt in his Father's stooped shoulders and obvious limping footsteps a distraction that challenged his remembrance of a father who once walked with personal pride and a military bearing indicating that he was once a soldier!*

I had been invited to return as an instructor of high school subjects in the mission school from which I had graduated. Afterwards, it was then ten years before renewed contact was made with my father in a memorable way! Together, during my five years of high school teaching, we lived in a different section in my hometown, Macon, Georgia. In the main there were just the two of us from a home that was!

Except for periods when he was forced to return to a veterans hospital in Alabama for needed treatment, the meeting gave us the opportunity to "reach for each other again" as father and oldest son!

During numerous moments of discussion, we often "turned back the clock" to his thoughts of life, including his frustrated hopes and dreams for his four sons. There are several of his expressed sentiments that still remain unforgettably clear in my memory.

But that same father, who had once been so upright and determined, was becoming increasingly fragile. At times, with Sis teaching in North Carolina and the other brothers scattered to the winds, only the intervention of old family friends made the difference between his survival and tragedy. Willis wrote:

When I taught at Ballard, there were two occasions when our Dad fell unconscious in the street around "Middle and First" on Pleasant Hill. A call from a neighbor called me in from Ballard. She had managed to get him to her house and had called in the doctor when I arrived. Twice this occurred, and each time I found her taking care of him as if our Dad was her Dad.

His own words probably best describe the feelings that accompanied this interlude of re-acquaintance.

My Father

Somehow poetry and Motherhood blend together!
But, what can one say—
How can one speak
of a Father!?

I remember—
The stern dignified figure of a man
Who had experienced military
life as a soldier
—and showed it in the erect posture,
and the quick steps of his walk,

I remember—
The large long cabinet box where he
guarded his carefully well sharpened

tools of a carpenter's trade left behind
in his aspiration for a different life!

I remember—
The garden with its vegetables
of different kinds, the cow I learned to milk,
and the hogs kept some distance away to be
butchered in the cold days of the year—
reminding me that my father was born and
bred a farmer!

I remember—
My pride as I watched him
sometimes work with figures and
blueprints as an expert consultant
in the building trades!

I remember—
The "Teaching strap" occasionally
applied to me as the eldest son,
demanding that I know right
from wrong!

And finally,
I remember—
The devastation and loss in our family
as emotional conflicts and the hard
living of depression years set our lives
adrift as our manhood matured—

What can one say
of a Father?

Only this
—*I remember!*

The Long Road to the PhD

During summer breaks from teaching at Ballard (1935, '36 and '37), Willis took advantage of Macon's proximity to the larger city of Atlanta. There he began studies towards a Master's degree at Atlanta University; a historically black, liberal-arts college. Then in 1938, '39 and '40, he spent summers studying at the University of Michigan, Ann Arbor, where his brother Ray had just completed his master's degree in Mathematics. Ray had benefited from the state of Georgia's eagerness to provide black graduate students with tuition vouchers for out-of-state study. The legislators preferred incurring that expense to desegregating Georgia's own educational system. Willis likely took advantage of the same benefit.

The American Missionary Association, grateful for his five years of Ballard teaching, awarded Willis a scholarship to continue attending the University of Michigan, full time, for the 1941–42 academic year. The university had, by this time, become something of a family tradition: in the summer of 1941, Willis joined his brother Ray, Ray's wife Kathleen (Kat), and his brother Nathan—all four there as graduate students. Willis completed a Master of Arts in History in June 1941, and a second Master of Arts in Speech Communication (Drama, Oral Interpretation) in May 1942.

Willis' plans to continue at Ann Arbor for a PhD were, however, interrupted by the impending international crisis. He was conscripted into the Army, and served in the Foreign Service starting in September 1942. He was in anti-aircraft (90th Coast Artillery) and Quartermaster regiments, achieving the rank of Acting First Sergeant. Because of his consummate skill as an orator, he was also frequently called upon to deliver radio addresses to the troops. Although offered the chance to reenlist at a higher rank and with additional officer training, he preferred to return to his graduate studies at the University of Michigan, and was honorably discharged from Fort Dix in October 1945.

Willis initially believed that he was the only member of his family serving in the war. Through an accidental meeting overseas, he discovered that Bob was there as well:

> Conscripted during the first years of World War II, the older brother had been abroad in military service for more than two years. He was grateful and understanding for several reasons that because of rules governing requirements for military service, his three younger brothers had not been required to enlist. Yet one day, while engaged in army routine duty, he heard a familiar voice. Turning around, the older brother was startled to see the familiar smile of his second brother—and in the uniform of a soldier. Thus, again they met, this time near the borderlines of France and Germany. Their much too short meeting was in conversation of shared Army experiences, some bitter, some humorous, as members of the last segregated black Army units of the War era—and of the personal home times still with them in memory. Finally, exchanging a college fraternal handshake reminiscent of enjoyable earlier college days, they parted to go separate ways. Suddenly, from a short distance away, the second brother turned and called to his older brother with an oft-used expression of their boyhood, 'Hi, fellow!' As the older brother turned, the second brother came to standard military attention position, and without a smile, exchanged the Army military salute with his older brother then, without a word, he turned and left his brother's camp. It would be several years

before they met again.

Considering his sensitive nature and superior education, the strict segregation and unequal treatment that was still the rule in the Armed Forces must have been difficult for Willis to accept. Blacks, regardless of their qualifications, were generally relegated to service and support positions in harsh, unfriendly environments. Willis once wrote of his father that:

> *Despite his impressed attitude of the poor treatment afforded black American soldiers in this war effort, his honorable discharge served only to heighten a feeling often expressed to his two older sons that the armed services of that time (Army and Navy) provided a fit opening for manly advancement.*

To the memory of this advice, he now replied:

> *From conscripted military service in World War II, the raw experiences of his two oldest sons caused them to recall the advice—and wonder why!*

Yet World War II also saw the beginnings of desegregation in the military. Blacks and whites trained together even as far as Officer Candidate School. There were some black combat divisions and a very few integrated units. Unfortunately, even this small level of equality in civilian life was still a long ways off.

Willis rarely mentioned his service in later years, and never used it in his resume. He was more forthcoming about how the war and subsequent overseas peacekeeping duties afforded him the opportunity to travel. He served in Morocco, Algeria and Libya early in the war, and later in Sicily and southern Europe. During his final year, he took advantage of accrued leave to see various European cities of note, mostly in Central Europe. He was fascinated by the different lands, but always spoke of his regret at having missed Greece.

When he returned to the States, Willis went back to Ann Arbor and university life. He had applied for and been accepted into a law program while overseas—the career path recommended by his father—but his life-long passion for theater and speech won out. He began work on a PhD in Speech Communication. At that time Sis, who had retired from her position as teacher-matron in North Carolina, was living with Ray and his family. She now came to live with Willis, and primarily made her home with him from then until her death in 1959 (with occasional sojourns to stay with Bob, Ray or Nathan when convenient, or when needed).

Willis remained in residence at the university from that fall of 1945 until the summer of 1948, first working as an assistant in Speech Communication and then supported by the University Fellowship and Honors Award. Then in 1948, although continuing to research and write his dissertation, he took a job of Instructor in the Department of English at Howard University, Washington DC, where he was engaged through the summer of 1949. After completing that job, it's unclear where Willis lived during the 1949–50 academic year; either DC, Michigan, or possibly even back in Macon to settle his father's estate.[2] However, during this time Willis prepared a first draft of his PhD thesis dissertation, which he submitted in early June 1950.

The subject that Willis chose for his dissertation—the speech-making of Booker T. Washington—perhaps reflects some of his lifelong ambivalence toward his father. Willis Sr. had been both a student and personal friend of Mr. Washington. He was, as well, an excellent and successful craftsman whose early career was shaped under Washington's industrial-education tutelage. Yet he turned his back on that path and on Washington's general philosophy. Willis would recall:

> *Despite his valuable educational training in the building trades, my father was never fully oriented to the philosophy advanced by Washington that recently freed blacks in America should concentrate mainly on training of the hands in trades and industry as the best route to truly acceptable American citizenship. Rather, his decided preference was that of the opposite and equally prevailing philosophical approach advanced by W. E. B. DuBois and others, that only training of the mind through exposure to ideas basic to liberal arts was the way toward a more rewarding life.*
>
> *I remember questioning my father about a stern order to me as a boy not to go near his finely oiled tools in the large chest locked away from us. With some youthful pride I had learned that, previously, my father had operated a small but highly reputable building construction business consisting entirely of black craftsmen, with notable success. In addition, a youthful boyhood curiosity had led me to a beautiful set of building blueprints drawn up with what seemed to me, pure mathematical precision, and his name was attached. It all served to enhance a boy's pride in his father!*
>
> *Yet, to my knowledge, very little encouragement to "enter the trades" was ever directed toward his sons. Still, I do recall that my father often spoke to me as a boy of the opportunities which lay ahead for a black race in the fields of law and in military service.*

The subject of Washington was a difficult one for Willis. He spoke of Washington as a man who had upon him "the mark of humility that was not subservient because it was combined with dignity,"[3] but whose perhaps fatal optimism blinded him to the futility of his approach. There would be no equal rights predicated on the black race earning white approbation, nor through proving blacks' goodwill, nor by demonstrating their usefulness to society. Willis must

---

2   Sis did not accompany Willis to DC. After spending a few months with Ray and family in Georgia after Willis Sr. died in June, 1948, she had gone to live for the time being with Bob and Mattalyn in San Francisco.

3   Pitts, William Norman. *A critical study of Booker T. Washington as a speech-maker with an analysis of seven selected speeches.* PhD Dissertation. University of Michigan, 1952. (p. 52)

have remembered his parents speaking their doubts about the man that both had revered as a teacher, but disagreed with philosophically. What was it that made this unforgettable man both so influential and so controversial?

Willis' first thesis attempt was roundly criticized by all the members of his committee. Disappointed and exhausted, he carefully preserved in his files the packet of individual critiques forwarded by the chairman of his committee.[4] Each said, in one way or another, that the thesis was lacking in critical analysis and was not up to the standards set by the Graduate school. It was a major blow for the man who had always been the overachiever, the one his brothers looked up to. His advisor, the chair of the speech department, urged him to revise and resubmit. But at that particular time, Willis felt the more urgent priority was to earn his living and pay some bills. He decided to concentrate, for the immediate future, on his teaching career.

Willis accepted a job as an assistant professor of English with Lincoln University in Jefferson City, Missouri, and moved there in the summer of 1950. He soon proved his excellence as a teacher of speech and drama, experimenting with and perfecting his signature style of group-performance oral interpretation: "a readers group replete with drama costuming, lighting, etc." He used this same basic technique with dramatic groups throughout the remainder of his career. His graduate school advisor, G. E. Densmore, had been an excellent instructor and mentor who instilled in his students his own sense of enthusiasm and engagement. Densmore had once said; "Imagination cannot conceive how utterly crushed the speaker feels when he looks to his instructor for approval and encouragement and sees instead a sleepy, fishy-eyed, dumpy individual with a dyspeptic, sour-pickle expression on an otherwise poker face. If the class in public speaking is dead, bury the instructor."[5]

With Willis at the helm, the students would find no need to hire an undertaker. He continued to excel and was soon elected to Theta Alpha Phi, the national theatre honors fraternity. However, coming into his own as a teacher was not the Lincoln experience that would be his most dramatically life-changing...

A Life Companion

Shortly after moving to Jefferson City, Willis discovered that one of his colleagues, Miss Frances (Fran) Haddock, was an former acquaintance of his brother Bob. Bob had met Fran, a Pittsburgh native, while he was living and studying in that city during the Depression years. A chance comment about their mutual connection served Willis as an introduction to the pretty and vivacious instructor of Physical Education and Hygiene. Fran had obtained her master's degree

---

4   He apparently did not choose to keep the positive comments he received two years later on his final, acceptable thesis.

5   G. E. Densmore (1946) *The Teaching of Speech Delivery.* Quarterly Journal of Speech. Vol 32., No. 1

from Wellesley, and her undergraduate degree in Education from the University of Pittsburgh. At Pittsburgh she was also a successful Olympic place winner in women's track events. Fran was an expert fencer, and was a licensed AAU[6] official for women's sports. Before coming to Lincoln, she had also been employed at Howard University, as an Assistant Professor of Health Education.

Willis fell head over heels in love with the dynamic, talented Fran, and she fell for the studious, dedicated teacher. In later life, Willis would write a "Rhyme-less Ode Shared with F. C. H. P." in which he recounted their meeting:

Was it predetermined—our destiny
That You and I should meet
In that state where it is said,
"The East ends and the West begins"?

There in the "Show me" state, we met,
Somewhere in our youthful middle years,
You, from the rock hills of William Penn's "Good and fruitful" northern
*   land;*
And I, from the peach state of the pine-tree South.

Was it our Fate
Through the ranks of public service
To that campus teaching spot to be drawn,
Where both could feel the steady growing spark
Of sharing with others what we, ourselves, had learned?

Was it Fortune's turn of the wheel
That a chance mention of a Brother of mine
Turned us face to face for a stronger look,
And brought second thoughts twixt You and Me
About each other?

When Willis went to Lincoln he was already forty-three, and Fran was in her late thirties. Certain of their desire for a future together, and seeing no reason to wait, the two were married that December in Washington, DC, after a whirlwind romance.

Was it inevitable
That in that small church of your choice
*   In the "Nation's Capital," rings would bind our hands,*
And the betrothal would end
*   In our mutual vows of wedlock?*

As newlyweds, they finished the academic year at Lincoln University and

---

6   Amateur Athletic Union of the United States

then, resigning their jobs at Lincoln, moved together to Ann Arbor in order for Willis, with the assistance of the Rackham Special Fellowship, to return full-time to the University of Michigan. Fran also enrolled in the graduate school. Sis came to live with them when Ray and family, with whom she had been living since returning from Bob's in California, moved back from Ann Arbor to Fort Valley, Georgia. The next summer Willis completed the requirements for his PhD, successfully defending a significantly revised thesis in June 1952.

Reminiscing many years later, in a letter to his brother Ray, Willis wrote about his graduation day:

> *[With] Fran and our mother sitting up in the stands at the University of Michigan stadium in June 1952 and watching me walk across the platform to receive the PhD degree, it dawned upon me that not since high school graduation had she witnessed my degree reception, and there had been two masters degrees between—when I was not even there to get them myself! ... Anyway, it meant something to her to watch her oldest at least one time getting the degree!*

Capturing the moment in his "rhyme-less ode," he wrote:

> *Was it Fate—or pride—that made me smile*
> *When two women—my mother and you—*
> *Sat among the stadium crowd at our Midwestern school,*
> *And I felt the eyes of both of you*
> *Observing my walk across the platform*
> *With Education's top degree in hand?*

That summer, Willis and Fran both secured teaching jobs at Tennessee Agricultural and Industrial University in Nashville, TN: Willis was offered "Professor of Speech in the Department of Speech and Drama," and Fran "Associate Professor of Health Education." Willis also directed the debate team, and his photo album attests that he, Fran, and Sis often welcomed the team members into their home. They remained in Tennessee until early 1954, when, yet again, their lives would take an unexpected turn.

Camp Whispering Willows

When she was a student at Wellesley, Fran had spent time in the summers working at Camp Whispering Willows, a summer camp and year-round orphanage in the Stoughton area of Massachusetts. The camp primarily served underprivileged black girls, and Fran had been a popular girls' counselor. The camp had been founded in 1933 by Josephine Crawford, an accomplished black New Englander. She had inherited some of the property's 110 acres from a benefactor, Dr. Horace Packard, and used her personal fortune to purchase the rest and operate the camp. The two women became fast friends. Fran had remained in close contact with Crawford even after she left Wellesley, and continued to be a regular supporter of the camp.

In December 1952 Camp Whispering Willows suffered a devastating fire, the last in a string of incidents at the camp that compelled Crawford, whose health was failing, to reach out to Fran for assistance. Both Fran and Willis shared a strong commitment to helping others, and also a deep love of children. Although it would leave their teaching careers in limbo, the two agreed that Fran should go right away and assume the task of co-directing the camp, and Willis would follow when he was able. They both decided to seek local teaching jobs, and to continue their graduate studies in Massachusetts. Willis later wrote in his "rhyme-less ode":

> *Was in the heritage, or the missionary spirit in both of us,*
> *That bade us put degrees (well earned) aside for awhile*
> *And, at your Friend's bidding*
> *Take up the gauntlet of her life-sustained children's camp?*

Crawford did not recover her health, and died in 1955. She left Willis and Fran in charge of the camp, with Fran on its Board of Directors. The couple moved into a house on the property. By this time the camp was racially integrated and served both boys and girls. The first year that they were in charge, Fran and Willis cared for 14 children year-round, as well as numerous campers during the summer.[7] Over time they transitioned the camp to operate as a summer camp only, brought it out of a large indebtedness, revitalized the board, and had the camp fully accredited by the American Camping Association.

Explaining their passion for the camp, their nephew Nat wrote:

> *My father use to talk about how Willis was so talented that he could have been anything, but then he fell head over heels in love with Fran. She was fabulous, beautiful, smart, a Wellesley graduate—and athletic! He gave up all other pursuits to stay and be with her. However, he certainly accomplished a great deal while living in Massachusetts.*
>
> *... Willis loved children! The summer before my sister Frances went off to college (Talladega) she would go to be a camp counselor in this camp, and thus spend time with uncle Willis and aunt Fran.*
>
> *I do not know why they had no children of their own. But they loved children.*

Willis and Fran served as co-directors of the camp from 1955–66, and Fran served on its board for a total of eighteen years. As teachers, they would forgo summer jobs to be at the camp, leaving their house next door and living with the

---

7   Up to 120 campers could be accommodated at a time.

campers on the premises. A 1965 article in the local paper observed,[8] "Directors of the non-profit camp for girls and boys six-to-ten years of age are Dr. and Mrs. Willis N. Pitts of Stoughton, who, in one sense, have no children of their own, yet, who, in another sense, have hundreds of them." For Willis; "Soon as school gets out, I grab a paint brush and become general handy-man. Sometimes I even cook."

Echoing Fran's own early experience at the camp as a counselor, when brother Ray's daughter Frances spent the summer of 1956 with them,[9] it started a tradition of inviting as many of the nieces and nephews as would come.

Ray Jr. spent the summer of 1963 with Willis and Fran. Willis wrote, in a report to Ray and Kathleen, that:

> *Both Fran and I were proud of the manner in which he handled himself as a senior counselor during our six weeks camp session at Whispering Willows. Especially did we appreciate the way in which he took charge of our new swimming pool and supervised our swimming activities. I think he informed Fran that he taught most of them to swim in "the same way Daddy taught me." He helped us to have one of our best summers. ... He seems to have, what is rare these days in so many youths, a pretty good sense and respect for responsibility. ... Too, I might add, he conducted himself like a gentleman—and you know how that affected the counselor ladies—all of them!*

Another niece, Nathan's daughter Mitra, spent at least one happy summer at Whispering Willows as a camper; before the camp's decline. But by the early 1970s, Camp Whispering Willows was no longer viable. It closed and was sold. The board accepted Fran's suggestion that the funds from the sale be used to endow a scholarship for underprivileged youngsters. To honor Willis for all his contributions, Talladega College was chosen to receive the scholarship bequest.

Settling Down in Massachusetts

When they first moved to Stoughton, Fran went back to school at Harvard School of Public Health, where she would earn a Master's of Public Health, with honors, in 1956. She continued on staff at Harvard for another six years, as a part-time instructor. She also accepted a job in 1956 with the Norfolk County TB Association (later the Norfolk County–Newton Lung Association, Inc.). She served the association first as Director of Health Education, and later as Executive Director. Later in her long career, she would also teach Health Education at North Eastern University. She was a member of the Board of Certification of Health Officers, a Fellow of the Society for Public Health Education and

---

8   Lillian Hannon White (July 1, 1965). *Whispering Willows Camp Notes 32 Years of Serving Children*, The Patriot Ledger. Quincy, MA.

9   Willis found her to be "a tall, slim, somewhat lonesome girl."

President of its New England Chapter, a Fellow of the American School Health Association, a member of the American Public Health Association and President of its New England Chapter, Member and President of the New England Health Education Association, a Fellow of Pi Lambda Theta (educational honor society), and Member of the Boston Regional planning Council President's Committee on Health Education. In 1973, she received the 23rd annual "Citizen of the Year" award from the Quincy, Massachusetts, Jewish War Veterans.

Accompanying Fran to Stoughton, Willis accepted a postdoctoral fellowship at Boston University for the 1954–55 academic year, beginning studies towards certification in clinical speech pathology. He later accepted a job with Stoughton high school as an instructor of English and director of the Dramatic Club (1955–1961). He had not taught in a high school for fifteen years, but took to the job with characteristic enthusiasm and compassion; he was soon a favorite instructor.

In particular, Willis took the school's dramatics club in hand. That first year at Stoughton he directed the club in a special Christmas production of *The Other Wise Man*, assisted by the band and Senior Glee Club. This led to incorporating an annual "Verse Choir" performance in the school's Christmas festival, with his actors using his own, signature style of oral interpretation. He established the club as Troupe 1675 of the National Thespian Society during the 1956–57 academic year. The same year, he enrolled the club in the Massachusetts High School Drama Festival's annual competition. In 1958, Willis attended the national conference and play festival of the National Association of Dramatic and Speech Arts, and brought back many additional ideas to try out with his club. They eventually became accomplished enough to perform at the regional-level in the High School Drama Festival competition. For the 1960 competition they staged *The Fifteenth Candle* by Rachel Field, and in 1961 they performed *The Florist Shop*, by Winifred Hawkridge. Over his years as its director, the club generally performed at least one major play each semester, including *Room for One More, The Curious Savage, Our Town, I Remember Mama, Harvey, The Night of January 16th, The Egg and I, Sabrina Fair, Pride and Prejudice*, and *The Family Upstairs*.

While at Stoughton High, Willis continued part-time work on certification in Speech Pathology at Boston University. He became convinced that a speech therapy program was very much needed in the Stoughton Public Schools, and began to advocate for such a program within the school system and to the community at large. When a program was approved in 1961, he became its first director (1961–65). Completing his more than thirty years of quasi-continuous graduate study, he was awarded the American Speech and Hearing Association (ASHA) Certificate of Clinical Competence in January 1965.

Willis was a sought after public speaker in his profession. He frequently spoke to clubs and parents' groups about how to identify speech problems and help their children to overcome them. The President of one of the local PTA associations wrote an "Open Letter to Parents" that was published in the local newspaper, recommending Willis to other groups:

> *He is a man who is concerned with your children, and knows how to talk about them. Here is someone who is dedicated to his task. ... I should like, first of all, to recommend Dr. Pitts to all groups such as ours who desire further knowledge regarding their children.*

Willis and Fran were also active volunteers in the community. He joined the local Rotary Club and, in 1967, was elected to serve as its President. They were active in their local Congregational Church, and Willis was invariably the congregation member who delivered the sermon on "Layman's Sunday." For those sermons, he spoke about growing up amidst oppression and prejudice, but being spurred on by his parents' love. He held up the value of a close-knit church community to build a hedge of hope and protection around children as they set out into the world. He spoke of the value of sacrifice, willing as well as required, and how a life lived for the sake of others was the one he preferred—and the one he recommended. Above all he pointed to his mother's example, the guiding light of his life.

Altogether, they had been very happy in Stoughton. But with his speech certification completed, Willis felt finally able to pursue greater things. In 1963 he had been offered the position of Associate Professor of English and Speech back at Lincoln University in Missouri,[10] but the timing wasn't right. In 1965 however, a position at nearby Bridgewater State University was offered and Willis accepted it, beginning as an Assistant Professor in Communication Arts and Sciences. He worked in that department until his retirement in 1977, by which time he was a Full Professor and past Acting Department Chair. While at Bridgewater, Willis initiated the first program concentration for undergraduates in Speech and Hearing Sciences in the Massachusetts State College system. He also regularly served as a supervisor for Certificate of Clinical Competency applicants to the ASHA.

Having decided that Massachusetts was to be their permanent home, and with a better salary at the university, Willis and Fran decided to purchase land and build the house of their dreams. They moved to a large, sloping, wooded lot in nearby Sherborn, and had a four-bedroom, three-bath home built to suit: moving in during the summer of 1966. The living room featured a large, welcoming fireplace, and thus the property was dubbed "Fran's Fireside" by her "ardent sidekick."

The couple had built the house for entertaining. They immediately set about

---

10   At an initial salary of eighty-five hundred dollars for nine months.

planning a full family reunion at their new home for the following August, as soon as their duties at Camp Whispering Willows were over for the season. In their invitation, they proudly announced, "There are enough nests in the trees on our two acres to have a comfortable sleeping spot for everyone. We'll be ready for you!" Although Willis and his brothers had lived without much regular contact since leaving Macon all those years ago, in later adulthood they were beginning think more often of family, and eagerly wished to get to know each other and spend time with their extended family. The children were one unifying force—the promising next generation—and honoring the wishes of Sis was another.

Since retiring, Sis had lived at various times with each son; often with Ray when his children were younger, as she too adored children. In her latter years, she lived primarily with Willis. She lived for her family and adored her grandchildren. She continually urged her sons to remember that they were *family*, and to stay close. Before Sis died in 1959, the four brothers had been able to reunite at Willis and Fran's in Stoughton, and together visited her in the hospital. Then shortly after her death in 1960, all four brothers and their Aunt Mittie, from Detroit, had gathered to honor Sis and make the necessary arrangements for her estate. Thereafter, they promised to see each other whenever an opportunity presented. But although there had been more family contact, the 1967 reunion was probably the first time all four brothers had been together since 1960, and it was the very first family reunion to include all the wives.

The family dearly hoped to have Aunt Mittie—by this time the only remaining relative of the previous generation—at this reunion as well, but she proved too ill to attend. She was deteriorating rapidly and Willis had already taken over many of her affairs; the brothers were her sole heirs when she died in 1970. Willis, Bob and Nathan all attended her funeral in Detroit, and Ray, who was unable to attend personally, sent his son Ray Jr. in his stead.

Willis and Fran flourished in their new neighborhood. Although childless, and in the process of closing down the camp, they still loved children and were a favorite with many in the neighborhood. Remembering those years one neighbor, Ani Almasian, wrote:[11]

Ever since I was a kid, Uncle Willis has been more than just a neighbor. For over seventeen years, I have shared special moments of my life with him. Although he is not really my Uncle, rather just an extremely close friend of my family, I feel closer to him than I do to some of my real relatives. He has been there through my moments of pride and grief. I remember everyday after school, I would come home and rush over to his house. His paved circular driveway was where I spent most of my afternoons. I just got a new bike and

11   Ani Almasian, "Uncle and Friend." (Unpublished remembrance presented to the family and delivered at the Willis N. Pitts memorial service.)

I was trying to stay on two wheels so I wouldn't have to go back to training wheels. Uncle Willis would watch me try to stay on two wheels time and time again, offering me encouragement and advice. He was like a coach and a fan at the same time. Eventually, with a lot of practice and help, I learned how to ride that bike all by myself. I didn't need for him to run along side me anymore; I could ride on my own. However, without his lessons and support, I would never have been able to do it. Everyone was taking pictures of my big moment and they were all so proud of me. Uncle Willis too, was sharing in that pride, but I think that he was the proudest.

The transplanted Southerner and his wife, however, may have had occasions to have second thoughts about life in New England. During the winter of 1968–69 they survived "the worst snow storm in the Boston area's history"—actually three consecutive winter storms that dumped more than four feet of snow in their yard. Describing the storms that March in a letter to Ray and Kathleen in California, Willis wrote:

We managed to survive the storms—all three of them—in stout fashion. Nevertheless, it was quite an experience!! ... For most of February and up until now, the only entrance way to our house has been through the basement garage doors that we managed somehow to keep clear as a traffic way. ... The "turn-around" near the garage is still about 4'–6' under, as is the lower front "turn-around" section; and the front door is barely accessible after our (all) afternoon effort. But we manage to "navigate"!

Frances managed to fly down to Baltimore between the first and second snowstorms for a 3-day TB conference, and so managed to spend some time with Nath and Mary. I had to call her and tell her not to come in at the end of the conference session because the second storm had everything "snarled up"—so I weathered the second storm alone while she spent another day basking in the Baltimore sun. She managed to squeeze in by airplane just before storm #3 closed down the airport again.

We missed 5 consecutive school days, as did practically everybody else with business and school. ... Anyway, we hope that SPRING is somewhere close!

For nearly twenty years Willis and Fran had spent summers working and living at Camp Whispering Willows. In 1970, as the camp was in the process of closing, they finally took the first true summer vacation of their adult lives: or as Willis put it, "[We are] attempting to 'loaf a summer' for the first time since the marriage vows." That year, Ray and Kathleen hosted them in Sacramento, California. The following year, Willis and Fran went even further afield and took two and a half summer weeks to visit Nathan and his wife Mary in Paris and Geneva. In 1974, Ray's family again came east to visit, this time for Thanksgiving. Ray's youngest child, Nat, recalled that trip:

Willis was a superb athlete. Being small in stature, he still excelled in football and basketball. I have his certificates for lettering in football for two years at Talladega College. He once challenged me to a race while I was in Stoughton. I was about 27 at the time and still refused the challenge. Since he was wearing shorts, I could still see the big quadriceps and calf muscles developed early in life. (He had to be about 70 at that time.) We went bowling instead, for the family competition.

As they increasingly enjoyed traveling, vacations, and reconnecting with family and old friends, Willis duties at the college grew less and less fulfilling. As Frances wrote in a letter to Ray and Kat, "retirement is looking sweeter than ever!" He retired at the end of the spring semester in 1977, and was awarded an emeritus membership of the Phi Delta Kappa (professional educators) Fraternity, in recognition of his many years of outstanding public educational service.

Projects in Retirement

In August of 1977, on his seventieth birthday, Willis wrote letters to all his brothers from the deck of a cottage on Lake Sunapee, New Hampshire, where he and Fran had been vacationing—one week in June and again in late August—for the past several years. Fran had a Harvard friend who allowed them to use the cottage free of charge, in exchange for some painting and general repair work on the property and on some of the owner's boats. Willis wrote:

> *Fran, of course, has been swimming out in the deep. And, like the "Had dock" in her family name, is at home and enjoying it all! ... Today is the 29th, my birthday! ... I suppose I am in good shape—at least I hope so! It is really a bit hard to believe that I am supposed to be as old as the record shows! Say, wasn't there some mistake about this age business, anyway?*
>
> *One reflects a bit about years that have passed—about the family record, and about the Pitts boys! Thanks to some help from "the Man Upstairs," we have been fortunate in many ways—and I know we are grateful!*

By this time, Nathan had returned from his posting in Paris and was living in Baltimore, Maryland, and working in Washington, DC. In 1978, he and Mary hosted another full family reunion, complete with numerous family friends. These friends had been specially gathered from all over and invited to participate in a formal Friday evening dinner held in honor of Willis. One lifetime friend, Ellis Rouses, flew in from Lorraine, Ohio, and another, Jackie Winter, flew from Jamaica, New York, to attend. This social event, involving the four accomplished Pitts brothers with their equally accomplished wives, was significant and drew press attention. The Baltimore Afro-American ran a large photo and accompanying article in the society column:[12]

Highlight of the weekend was the Friday evening dinner party at Cross Keys Inn, when members of the family paid special tribute to the oldest brother, Dr. Willis N. Pitts and his wife, Frances, of Sherborn, Mass., where he has been an inspiration because of his leadership and career as a clinical speech pathologist and community pioneer.

Special notice was made of his service as instructor at Howard University, University of Michigan, Bridgewater State (Mass), and Tenn. State University, where Dr. Pitts earned accolades for his service. The family presented him with a plaque in recognition of his college work and his community service, including his presidency of the Rotary Club of Stoughton, Mass.

Willis was overwhelmed. He sent out effusive thank you notes dated the following Monday morning. Quoting from the one to Ray and Kathleen:

Our family reunion was completely a joyous occasion! I suspect that even our captive audience shared some of the "Pitts Family Spirit" as you three Brothers of mine programmed and executed all of its parts. I even chuckle at recalling how involved our darling sisters-in-law were while watching the expressions on Kat's, Frances', and Mary's faces trying to convince me that I had not seen Ellis' face at the door. Frances' face had the same look on it that I had seen while she was trying to get me to let her have some of the pictures on my desk without really telling me why! I never saw such would be expert secret operators (GRIN)!! Anyway, I think that we "Pitts," as Jackie put it, had a wonderful thoughtful moment in our lives. The salute to me was deeply appreciated!

The '78 reunion offered a chance for Ray (who had also retired) and Willis to confer on their mutual interest in the family's history and their Macon, Georgia, roots. Because all four brothers were distinguished graduates of Ballard Normal School, Ray had decided that he and Willis should collaborate on a special event, in conjunction with the school's annual class reunions, dedicated to recognizing the contributions of Ballard and preserving the school's memory in Macon's historical archives. By the following May, Ray and Willis were heavily engaged in planning two separate but mutually interesting projects: the Ballard history event, and the compilation of a Pitts family history.

The Ballard project was initially Ray's idea, and he wanted it to consist of a book of history and an event timed for the 1980 Grand Reunion of the Lewis High and Ballard Normal Schools.[13] The book was to be Ray's project entirely, and he envisioned that he and Willis would collaborate on the special event.

---

12   Anon. (December 2, 1978) *Pitts Family Reunion.* The Baltimore Afro-American, Baltimore, MD.

13   Raymond Pitts, PhD., Reunion General Chairperson.

Specifically, Ray expected that Willis would write and produce a play about the history of Ballard similar to, but more elaborate than, one that they had produced together as young men in depression-era Macon.

The two—both strong willed and accustomed to being in charge, and both constitutionally uncomfortable with compromise—clashed almost at once. Ray wanted a play, but he had also indicated that he would leave it to Willis to write. Willis wanted a group oral interpretation, following the signature style he had developed and used throughout his professional career. Ray was anxious and impatient. In a letter of February 1980, Willis tried to calm the waters:

> *After our telephone call, it occurred to me that your visit to Macon in February's first week gave you that first "jitters of nervousness" as to the progress of the Ballard Reunion project ... So, let me see if I can clear up your frustration insofar as my promised cooperation with the writing of some form of dramatic script is concerned. ... I ruled out the usual dramatic play. ... My second interest, and minor, in the MA speech work was in Oral Interpretation, as was the first major in Theater. The promise [of previous signature productions] caused me to file the form away for future use. Anyway, I felt that we could use this form for the Reunion audience. ... By the end of March, a set schedule should place (via mail) a script of the "Historical Salute" in the hands of each "Reader" and other responsible Committee members. This is the procedure or schedule I have followed on the basis that it would give us time to do the job! I still think so!*
>
> *Ray, your telephone call also expressed the wish that I should meet with you in Macon sometime in April!? I know that this charge would conflict with plans and appointments here at that time ... However, although I don't favor making two trips instead of one, if it will help you, and ease your anxiety about the venture, let me know the dates of your April meeting in Macon, and I'll see what I can do.*

Occasional clashes continued throughout, and even after, the production: over responsibilities, schedule, how to obtain and use the contributions of former faculty and students, the handling and returning of borrowed property, and myriad other details. Fortunately by this point in their long, close relationship, the brothers had learned how to spar, and reconcile, and spar again another day. The event was an enormous success. Both brothers reveled in the sense of accomplishment, and shared the appreciation and heartfelt thanks of all involved. The oral history Willis created was written, rehearsed, performed at the event, and finally received a copyright from the US Copyright Office on September 22, 1980.[14] In conjunction with the "Grand Reunion," the Mayor of Macon signed a proclamation that Thursday, July3, 1980, would be "Lewis High and

---

14   ©Willis N. Pitts, Registration Number PAU 253-909

Ballard Normal School Day," and called for the citizens "to pay tribute to this fine institution founded in our City, and further call on all our citizens to extend a warm welcome to all the Alumni visiting our City during this Grand Reunion."[15] Additionally, the city placed a historical marker at the original site of the school.[16]

THE BALLARD LEGEND

The years have passed in this hometown;
Yet, there is a tale that is often told.
And the sounds that are still noised around,
Repeated in varied fold,
Voice the muse of a never-ending rule:
The legend of Ballard Normal School!

And so, we graduates together, with thanks
In the native town of our youth
Pausing, "In Memoriam," the blanks in our ranks
As we revel our reflections.—In truth,
Still echoing the muse of a well-timed rule
From the Legend of Our Ballard School!

Share, then, this moment with us!
Hear once more, familiar tunes once sung!
Feel, once again, that strong impulse
Planted, deep-seated, within us, and from us rung—
The impulse
To strive, to hope, and to achieve—
To build a life better than the one we once knew
Instilled, much stronger than we earlier could believe!

Yes, once more, we share the Golden rule
From the Legend of Ballard Normal School!

W. N. P. '25[17]

Some months later, Willis presented Ray and Kathleen with a formally bound copy of his finished product, "The Ballard Legend." It contained brief historical notes, reflections, poems, and the script for the members of the oral interpretation cast. He included a poem of dedication to "the introspective

15   Signed: George Israel, Mayor.

16   770 Pine Street, Macon. It reads, "'A Past to cherish—a future to fulfill.' This marker erected at the original site of Lewis High School in recognition of the contributions of Lewis High and Ballard Normal Schools to the education of black people in the Macon and central Georgia area. 1865-1942."

17   ©Willis N. Pitts, used with permission.

guardians of the legend of a school":

> *Since your insistence was the incubator,*
> *And my "loyalty urge" the responsive activator—*
> *Obligatory, because of your appeal for*
> *This memory-long prospectus!*
>
> *Herewith—this final coalition*
> *From the previously exposed petition*
> *Formulated for you and yours*
> *For your expansive research trust!*

Having successfully completed one project, the two brothers moved on to their second mutual interest—the Pitts family history. When their brother Bob died in 1982, Willis wrote and self-published a reminiscence he titled "Eulogy for a Brother," which he prefaced with a short sketch of the immediate family's history:

> *I am the oldest of four sons of parents of African descent who were born during that era of American history when the issue of legal slavery had been only recently settled, and when successive years marked the first efforts of black people to enter the struggle for full respect as American citizens, a struggle that continues to this day.*
>
> *During the last quarter of the 19th century, my Father and Mother were two human beings who set out to persevere in their pursuit of a rightful share of respect and responsibility inherent in the American dream of democracy. ...*

During the writing of this eulogy and reminiscence, Willis had reached out to Bob's wife Mattalyn, to verify some genealogical data. Writing about Bob's life also stirred Willis to start compiling notes on all his brothers' accomplishments, so that they wouldn't be forgotten. Ray interpreted this action as honing in on his own project of producing a comprehensive history of the Pitts family. Again, the brothers clashed. Willis wrote:

> *I called you on the morning of December 7th, thinking it was a good thing to do, and a good time to talk to you regarding the points mentioned ... it seemed a decent thing to do ... Sorry, if you misunderstood! ...*
>
> *Anyway, I simply remind you that in my heart, I have always had THREE BROTHERS.—and we were all different in personality from the beginning! ...*
>
> *P.S. Gosh! The "Ray Pitts temper" is still there! (Grin.) Take it easy, Brother Ray!*

As before, the brothers continued to collaborate, continued to spar, and continued to reconcile. Ultimately, they remained close and affectionate and con-

tributed to each other's efforts significantly. Ray began in earnest to trace the
broader family history. Willis concentrated on the lives of the four brothers and
their wives, and on documenting their various educational accomplishments
and professional contributions.

Willis also used his retirement years to engage in voluminous correspondence. His letters frequently included original poems and formal tributes, especially, as the years marched on, to loved ones and lost friends. It was during
this time that he wrote the "Rhyme-less Ode Shared with F. C. H. P.," which
concludes:

> *And with passing years, was it fortuity*
> *That handedness, your left, my right*
> *Might symbolize—(North versus South again!)*
> *Our challenging varied viewpoints of life; —*
> *Yet—could find in our lives so much*
> *To blend and bind?*
>
> *Was it only the fortunes of life—Or Fate*
> *That, past the silver anniversary years*
> *Of our lives together, causes us*
> *To still ponder what there is*
> *Found between us*
> *Of Fondness, devotion, affection,*
> *Respect—or love?*
>
> *Oh, "Girl of my Life," what matters now*
> *How we count or weigh the words*
> *In these retiring golden years?!*
> *It is enough that actions will suffice—*
> *Whatever else, tomorrow--!*
> *Our path has been good—*
> *In truth—we have lived well—*
> *This life!*

But life in retirement for Willis was not only writing and research. He set out
to make his "actions suffice" in proving to Fran his penned devotion. Having enjoyed many summer weeks on the lake property of their friends in New Hampshire, he and Fran decided to build their own vacation cottage on George's Pond
in Franklin, Maine. They purchased a plot of land there in January 1982, began
clearing the house site, and commenced to build in 1983. In July 1985 Willis
described his ...

> *... project of the past two year continuation ... attempting to get my dear*
> *"Haddock" near what she has so often wished; to be near—Water! So, we*

strained, financially, and somehow persevered constructively, to dig into rock on an isolated "pond" in eastern Maine made possible by a visit to a one-time neighbor. As a result we managed to spend nearly three weeks, recently, at what we think is, all in all, a beautiful spot—We call it Rock Cove!

The two spent that and the next three summers at the cottage, but unfortunately, Willis did so in increasingly ill health: he had cancer. Although the disease was reasonably controlled for some years, the couple was ultimately informed that it was a terminal case. Through it all he continued writing, telling one friend:

A recently forced hospital stay, following an unexpected health problem last March and April, often made it impossible to relax for sleep. So, I often countered by "body hurt" by sending my thoughts down "memory's trail" to people, places and experiences shared over the years.

In this final time, Willis managed to complete his final project. He had begun to document some of his memories of Sis and his brothers in letters to his "favorite niece" Kathy, who had developed an interest in the family history a few years earlier. Combining that with the research he had done when Bob died, he went on to produce a detailed family record that he called "Beyond Academics." It included specifics of the educational and professional accomplishments of the four sons of Willis Norman Pitts Sr.; some similar information about their wives; thoughts about the family upbringing and genealogy; and his "older brother's comments" and philosophical musings. He had this document bound and printed, and presented it to Ray, Nathan, Mattalyn, and Kathy in February 1988. In it, he noted; "In our immediate family circle of about 17, we have approximately 40 degrees!!!"

Willis and Fran managed to spend some happy times at the cottage that last summer, but he continued to weaken. After a long hospital confinement, he died on November 17, 1988. At his funeral he was remembered by all as a person who had lived to help others:

Even though Uncle Willis is gone, his lessons and advice are still around. He will always be here in my mind; for he was a part of me and my life, and as long as I am around, he will be too. He left us a fighter, and with cherished memories that will never be forgotten.[18]

---

18   Ani Almasian, "Uncle and Friend."

Above: Willis Norman Pitts, high school photo

Below left: Football Quarterback and Halfback
Below right: 1932 Talladega graduation with his brother Ray (left)

Alpha Phi Alpha at Talladega, 1931–32. Willis at left holding banner, Ray in center behind banner

Willis Norman Pitts Jr.
(Army portrait, c1942)

Willis at the mike for a radio broadcast in Switzerland, 1944

Above Left: Willis and Frances Haddock, while dating
(from the Willis Pitts scrapbook)
Above Right: Frances as a young woman

Below: Nathan (left), Frances (in car), and Willis (in PhD regalia)

Above: At Tennessee A&I with the debate team and Sis (1952)

Below: With Aunt Mittie at her house in Detroit, Michigan

The Department of Speech and Theater at Bridgewater State University

Willis Norman Pitts Jr. and Frances Haddock Pitts
Stoughton, Mass.

Below: Willis saluted as outgoing Rotary Club President, 1968

Above: Photo from first family reunion, Sherborn, Mass. (1967)
Seated (l to r): Frances, Mattalyn, Mary, Kathleen
Standing: Willis, Bob, Nathan, Ray

Below: Willis, Bob, Nathan, Ray, at Rotary Club

THANKSGIVING / SHERBORN
NOV. '74

Willis (center) with nephews Ray Jr. (left) and Nat

Above: Willis at Fran's beloved Rock Cove, Franklin, Maine

Below: Ray (left) and Willis, 1987

Robert Bedford Pitts

For Robert (Bob), the summer of 1926 in Highland Falls, New York—what Willis called their "first and only placement together in jobs away from home" and a "baptism in the practice of adjustment to unexpected problems of life"— cemented a singular bond between the brothers that continued during the following academic year at Talladega. They shared many friends and club activities; each played multiple sports, earned excellent grades, and fully enjoyed the college lifestyle that they had so long dreamed of. They did not know it would be their last opportunity to be together as family, or to enjoy a relatively carefree existence, for many years to come. Neither could return to Talladega for another year: the expense proved prohibitive. As the nation sank into the Great Depression, Bob and Willis went separate ways, each determined, as Willis put it, "to keep moving and somehow keep surviving to get back on the track of living." They may not have seen each other again until they met in Europe during the second World War.

Bob was not to complete his bachelor's degree until 1938, the last of the brothers to achieve this milestone. The intervening years were difficult, even brutal. He adapted to the necessity of a nomadic lifestyle, working to support himself and taking college classes whenever possible, using his skills as a "rambler athlete" to secure occasional athletic scholarships. He attributed some of his later health problems to the deprivations of this time, but also his resiliency. He learned that he could face life's worst—and survive.

At first Bob lived with Sis, who had taken a domestic service position at a school in North Carolina, but he soon gravitated towards Pittsburgh, Pennsylvania. He adopted Pittsburgh as both his base of operations and as his new "hometown."[1] Sis contacted a former Railway Mail Service clerk in Pittsburgh, Frank Knight, who had once worked with her husband. Frank promised to keep an eye on her son, and invited Bob to live with the Knight family as a companion for his own son. Bob lived with the Knights off and on for the next several years. Their home was his home whenever he was not residing at one school or

---

1 The disintegration of his family apparently left Bob with unresolved feelings about Macon. When he first met his wife, Mattalyn, he told her not only that he was from Pittsburgh, but also that his father was dead.

another, or was not working too far away. He took a variety of jobs in the vicinity—whatever he could get in the tough depression market—and remained
based in Pittsburgh until finally leaving the area for good in 1935.

One of Bob's first jobs was in nearby McKeesport. He had made a friend
whose father ran a construction site there, and he got a job driving a shovel
behind four mules, cutting out the side of a hill to make room for the new McK-
eesport high school. He made four dollars a day and stayed for three months.
Many years later, Bob recalled that time:

> *I had starved a little since I left Ballard, so at that time I weighed about
> 155 to 160— trying to control that shovel!*
>
> *When I started work, I had only about twenty-five cents. I went out and
> I bought a loaf of bread and a can of pork and beans to keep in this guy's
> refrigerator. I wouldn't get paid until Saturday. So I cut the bread into three
> pieces, and on Wednesday I poured one third of the can of beans into one third
> of the bread and that's what I ate on Wednesday. On Thursday I poured one
> third of the can of beans into one third of the bread, and I ate that Thurs-
> day—and Friday. On Saturday, we were supposed to work a half day and get
> paid at twelve o'clock. And I thought, "I can last until twelve o'clock." —Now,
> I remind you what I am doing; I am riding that darned thing behind four
> mules! Well, fortunately I was in good health, and I just took the darn thing
> as a challenge— Well, on Saturday the guy gave me something like twelve or
> thirteen dollars. Before I could get home, I went to a restaurant and I ordered
> a steak. I was hungry, and I had got some money, and I was going to eat a
> steak! It cost a dollar seventy-five; and I had been so hungry for so long that
> I couldn't eat it. It would have been better if I had gotten a hamburg and
> waited awhile. I remember that!*

Bob next worked briefly in the steel mills. He was willing to work at almost
anything, even though a friend warned him that *nothing* should ever induce
him to work in steel. Later, all Bob had to say was that he was almost glad that
the Great Depression had slowed the steel business so much that the workers
were all let go: the jobs he was able to find elsewhere were significantly more
tolerable.

Bob never stopped thinking of completing his education. By the summer of
1929 he had earned enough to pay his Talladega bills, and wanted to continue
school somewhere in the North. He had, however, been told that the Southern
education for blacks was substandard.[2] Pittsburgh public high schools were free,
so he decided he had better go there and see if this was true. He signed up for a
single quarter of night classes at Schenley high school and found that, thanks to
his excellent Ballard mathematics education under Miss Tuttle, "Those students

---

2   Few teachers in Georgia's black public schools were certified. Many had only a year or two of high school.

didn't know half of what I did."

An opportunity for returning to full-time study came in the form of an athletic scholarship. It happened that Sis was working at a school in Henderson, North Carolina, where the new football coach was Jake Gaither, one of Knoxville College's former star athletes. Sis let it be known that, somewhere along the way, Bob had perfected a "math-figured banked shot," the success of which had provided the high-school substitute basketball player with a degree of athletic notoriety. Gaither suggested to Sis that Bob try Knoxville, and helped to pave the way for an athletic scholarship that fall. A letter from the Registrar at Talladega, dated July 27, 1929, thanks Bob for promptly paying his outstanding bills and says, "I knew that you would do it so that is why I did not hold up your grades. I hope that you will do well at Knoxville and am sorry that you are not able to return to Talladega."

Bob was "not too impressed" with Knoxville, but he stayed long enough to complete a second year of college. While at Knoxville he became friends with another basketball player, Chick, who went that year to summer school at Virginia State College. Chick performed well that summer, and Virginia State offered him an athletic scholarship for the fall term. Excited about his offer, he wrote and invited Bob come try his luck with Virginia as well. Bob also landed an athletic scholarship, and he attended State with Chick that fall. He expected to love this school and was initially delighted with the switch.

Bob found mentors in Dr. John McNeile Hunter, of the Physics department, and his wife. Dr. Hunter was from Cornell and his wife had attended Harvard. The eager and intelligent young student became a regular in the couple's home, and they assisted him in adjusting to the school. That year at Virginia State he was inducted into the Beta Gamma Chapter of the Alpha Phi Alpha Fraternity, which he had originally pledged at Talladega.

While playing basketball for Virginia, Bob once unexpectedly ran into his brother Ray, who was playing for the opposite team. Ray's son Nat recalls;

My father was playing basketball for Talladega College (against Virginia State) when his coach told him he had to guard that left-hander over on the other team. He looked up, and it was his brother! Bob had developed a nice, left-handed bank-shot. When asked how he learned that shot, he told my father it was all mathematics!

Bob would have gladly stayed at Virginia but, once football and basketball seasons were over, he assumed his athletic responsibilities were also over. He expected to take the spring semester to concentrate on his studies. That expectation did not sit well with the Dean, Luther Foster, who told him that the scholarship would have to go to someone who was willing to play baseball as well! Deprived of his scholarship, Bob couldn't even afford the bus fare back home.

He had no idea what to do.

The very next day, Bob got a call from Luther Foster Jr., who happened to be the President of Alpha Phi Alpha on campus. He told Bob that the members had already voted him into the fraternity and, having heard that he lost his scholarship, had also voted to give him a scholarship to cover his expenses for the remainder of the year. When Dean Foster heard what his son and the fraternity had done, he called Bob in and berated him for having the time and funds to waste on a fraternity when he couldn't manage to play baseball to satisfy the terms of his scholarship. Bob—not *exactly* hot-headed but always ready to defend himself—got angry and stood up to him, calling him mean spirited. He marveled that the Dean could, after refusing to help another person himself, then be so unfair as to be angry when someone else did help. And although Bob had loved Virginia State dearly, when he left at the end of that year it was largely this attitude of the Dean's that prevented him from returning.

Back in Pittsburgh, Bob lived with the Knights and worked for the McCloskey family, who were building an apartment house in town. It was going to be a twelve-to-fifteen-story brick building, and this Irish family customarily employed black bricklayers. Bob worked on a scaffold at the site, in extreme hot and cold, for about two years. It was another grueling and dangerous job. He saw one co-worker killed in a crane accident, falling eight stories to the ground, and remembered thinking, "Why not me? Why did he get killed and I survived?" Yet at the same time, this job sparked Bob's lifelong interest in building design and construction. It prompted him to wonder about his father's choice: if he had stayed in building contracting, would their lives have been different?

The McCloskey sons, near Bob's age, were both football players for Notre Dame. Having become as friendly with them as their relative positions allowed, Bob was offered continuing work for the family when the apartment building was finished. He worked first in the receiving room, where he befriended a co-worker who had taught English for many years at Howard University in Washington, DC, and then worked as an elevator operator and in other odd jobs. Still striving to continue his education, Bob also began to take night classes at the University of Pittsburgh.

With each new college experience, Bob saw further evidence that there was a wide range of quality in educational institutions. He developed a compelling desire to graduate from "a good school," and began looking for opportunities to get into a school with a better reputation. Although Pittsburgh's Carnegie School of Technology had, at that time, only one full-time black student,[3] Bob applied and was accepted into night classes in the School of Architectural Engineering. Harboring grave doubts about being accepted for full time study, he nevertheless dreamed of obtaining his degree there, or perhaps from Cornell.

---

3   And he was light skinned, and could pass for white.

However, Bob learned from his co-worker that Howard University, an excellent school with a majority-black student body, was offering $300 scholarships— enough to pay all the tuition and school expenses. That offer was too good to pass up, so he applied to Howard and was accepted.

Bob had prospered in Pittsburgh. Years later as a successful executive in California, he recalled his youth in Pittsburgh as a time "when he could find a job by just walking the streets and popping into a shop and asking the merchant."[4] His scrapbook from Pittsburgh is full of tickets; receipts; and programs of sporting events, theatre, opera, recitals, socials and balls. He was a fond member of a social club called "The Royal Yorkshireites," and belonged to the local YMCA. He saved a program from the 1933 Saratoga Athletic Club annual dinner that lists him as the evening's guest speaker. The fun-loving socialite of Ballard Normal School had, by his mid 20's, accumulated a long list of society friends and acquaintances, including some who were locally prominent and who took an active interest in his career prospects. When Bob finally left Pittsburgh in 1935, two separate "swanky parties" were given in his honor at the home of Alexander D. Graves in the Homewood section of the city. Both parties were written about in a local newspaper's society pages. The articles state that Bob would head next to DC's Howard University, to complete his education in civil engineering.

Distractions

At this point in the account of Bob's life, it should be noted that he, "Bob the adventurer," had one additional "educational" passion. He left ample evidence of avidly pursuing an auxiliary field of study—girls! Tall, handsome, and athletic, Bob had no trouble attracting female attention. His scrapbook is full of their photos, notes and cards; of programs; ticket stubs; and of other testimonials to his active social life. Beginning chronologically with photos of Eva C., Eva P. Fannie, Odessa, and Lil (mostly from Ballard or Talladega), a few of these girls stand out as deserving special mention.

In one album there is a full page, lovingly preserved, undated letter from "Dorothy" that is a detailed message of gratitude for all that Bob has meant in her life; "To Robert, ... I like you because you are helping me to make the lumber of my life not a tavern, but a temple, and the words of my everyday not a reproach, but a song."

From Talladega (1926–27), there are multiple photos of Omily, and a note card with the inscription; "I hold you, in my thoughts, so strong. Oh! Very lovingly and long! My feelings you've not realized; if thoughts were arms—you'd be surprised! Lovingly, your Omily."

Rosalind appears to have been a fond acquaintance for several years. There

4   B. Distefano (March 3, 1970). *Politics and Poverty: A Struggle Within a Struggle.* Oakland Tribune. Oakland, CA.

are photos and notes from 1930, and also an invitation to her graduation from Shaw University (Raleigh, North Carolina) in 1933. A poem entitled "Loves Offering" is inscribed on a card from Rosalind to Bob, with the inscription, "Among your souvenirs, Keep Ros."

Another girl, Evelyn, who signed cards as "Your Evelyn," seems to have been a regular companion during Virginia State College days, in 1931.

Virginia Carter is the name on nearly all of the mementos from 1933–34, in Pittsburgh. Photos of Virginia from South Hills high school, and again from Carnegie School of Technology, sit side by side in the album, surrounded by musical programs of operas and symphonies and recitals—many featuring "Miss Virginia Carter, pianist." However, one memento from 1933 is to a different girl. On the program of the Saratoga Athletic Club annual dinner, Dec. 24, 1933, Bob inscribed a handwritten note: "Sweet memories of 'Gertie' until 4 A.M."

While in Pittsburgh Bob also met a girl named Frances Haddock. Although he doesn't appear to have dated her himself, he did, after the War, arrange an introduction to his brother Willis. Willis knew a good thing when he saw it, and promptly married her.

None of Bob's many early female companions seems to have captured his heart quite like the young Mattalyn did a few years later, but Bob evidently grappled with the seductions and distractions of the female sex. On one page of his photo album, pictures of "Billie, Chink, Martha, Mattie, Ruth, Jan and Theresa" are arranged surrounding this familiar quotation from Milton's *Paradise Lost*:

> *Oh why did God*
> *Creator wise, that peopled highest Heaven*
> *With spirits masculine, create at last*
> *This novelty on earth, this fair defect*
> *Of nature, and not fill the world at once*
> *With men as angels without feminine.*
> *Or find some other way to generate*
> *Mankind? This mischief had not then befallen,*
> *And more that shall befall, innumerable*
> *Disturbances on earth through female snares.*

The Long Road to a Career

With only bus fare and twenty-five dollars in his pocket, Bob moved to Washington, DC, in the summer of 1935, planning to attend Howard University that fall. His first summer job was waiting tables in Silver Spring at a house for retired military; he lived there that summer. When school started, Bob looked up his friend Dick Brown, whom he had known at Virginia State, and the two decided to room together. They ended up sharing living space, occasionally with other roommates,[5] until Bob graduated in 1938.

Bob found a job at an apartment house just across the street from the station in Southeast Washington, working the four-to-midnight shift. He ran the elevator until eight, and then the elevator, the switchboard, and the reception desk until midnight. The job paid seventy-five dollars a month, plus all the tips he could get. He said, "I lived like a king. I never wanted for anything, never missed a meal, the whole time I was in Washington." He kept that job until he finished his degree, with a Bachelor of Science in Mathematics and a minor in Physics.

Bob would bring his textbooks to work and study late in the evening at the reception desk. One couple who lived in the building were from the West Coast; they took a special interest in Bob. The woman often asked about his studies. Bob had planned to go to Cornell after Howard, but she wondered aloud, "Why don't you go to the West Coast, where you don't have to pay to go to school?" Bob had never heard of such a thing, but he liked the idea of a free education. She began to bring him newspaper clippings about the University of Washington, and to fill his head with stories about the city of Seattle and the many opportunities he would find there. Seattle had the reputation as being one of the "best cities on the Pacific Coast in terms of socioeconomic opportunities for ethnic minorities."[6] By the time he graduated, Bob was sold: "There was no question about where I was going." Willis, in his memoirs, writes that this apartment-house job also led to Bob's "chance meeting with a recluse German professor of mathematics" at Howard University that "marked the turning point of the 'serious man' Bob's life." He went on to say that the chance meeting "provoked an interest that inspired him to complete his college degree work and later aided him in a successful bid for graduate work in the western state of Washington."

Bob began saving money for the transcontinental railroad fare. After graduation, he stopped for a week in Pittsburgh, to say his goodbyes, and then purchased a one-way ticket to Seattle. He had never before been further west than Chicago, but when he crossed the Rockies he "just knew" that he was never coming back East.

One of the residents of his Washington apartment building wrote a letter of introduction to lawyer friend of hers in Seattle, asking him to do anything he could to help the young student. The friendly West Coast couple also wrote to some friends in Seattle, who promised to look out for Bob. When he arrived, not knowing where he was going or what he was going to do, the son of that family met him at the station and announced, "You are going home with me."

5   One, for a time, was Bob's brother Nathan. (See chapter on Nathan.)

6   Robert W. O'Brien (November 1945). *Profiles: Seattle. Race Relations on the Pacific Coast.* Journal of Educational Sociology, Vol. 19, No. 3, pp 146-157.

Bob lived with the family for a year, and said they refused to take any rent at all. They insisted he was their guest. He later said, "That experience did more for me than anything: to learn to understand the ways of white folks." Once, the father asked Bob if he ever wondered why the family constantly had so many visitors. Bob hadn't really thought much about it, but was told; "A lot of the people around here have never had the chance to talk to anyone who is black, and you interest them."

Bob got a job at a ready-to-wear business in town, and also worked some nights at the port of Seattle. Sis sent him a little money, and more importantly, she wrote to assure him that she *knew* he would succeed.

You are a lucky young man. You have had a tough time, but you toughed it out, and now your luck have changed. The opportunity is yours to be a great man; use it. I have prayed, and worked hard to see you boys be Somebody. I hope I'll live to see the finish of this.

There were only a very few blacks in town,[7] and nearly all had come there from working on the railroad: mail clerks, porters, cooks, and stewards who got there and stayed, liking what they saw. Bob said that before long he had gotten to know all of them, and they all knew him.

He recounted his experiences many years later to a Seattle Times reporter:[8]

I arrived here in 1938 with exactly $15 in my pocket, hoping to get my master's degree at the University of Washington. I worked at any job I could get to keep body and soul together during the months necessary to establish the one-year residence requirement.

As a Washington resident, you could go to school for practically nothing, $35-a-quarter tuition, as I recall.

I had no credit, knew nobody here and had no Seattle references but, nevertheless, walked into the People National Bank one day and asked for a loan, explaining that I would have to drop out of school unless I got some financial help somewhere.

... Fortunately, the man I talked to apparently decided I was a good risk. Also, he knew that bank's trust department had charge of the Leona Hickman Fund, left in trust by the late widow of a Seattle telephone company official to provide education loans for deserving Seattle or King County college students.

That $300 or $400 loan enabled me to get my masters degree in economics.

Giving credit to the tight-knit, mutually supportive black community in Se-

---

7   According to demographic studies at the time they were about 1% of the total population.

8   John J Reddin (March 16, 1966) *HUD Official Recalls Kindnesses Here.* Seattle Times. Seattle, Washington.

attle, Bob went on to say:

> *The late William Hyatt, who was head janitor at the Port of Seattle, was almost like a father to me. Also, the late Mrs. Minnie Bickford, who worked as a maid at Broadmoor and let me live at her home, 324 23rd Ave., N.*
>
> *I could cite numerous Seattle Negro families who were good to me—Ed Pitter, who worked for many years as a deputy King County clerk, and his family; the late Bernard Squires, former executive director of the Seattle Urban League, and his wife, Melvina, now a social worker for Catholic Children Services; and many, many others.*
>
> *And, that's why I have a warm spot in my heart for Seattle. To me, it will always seem like home.*

While overcoming so many challenges during his twelve-year sojourn of undergraduate education, Bob had developed a knack for forcefully arguing his point. Some even said he'd become argumentative; but this trait ended up serving him well in Seattle. There were only about ten black students at the University, and only two doing graduate work. Once he had met the state's residency requirement and could apply, he was called in for an interview. There he was told that he didn't appear to qualify for graduate school in the Department of Economics. In all the years of his schooling it happened he had taken only two economics courses, and both of them were statistics! Bob was sure he would be fine, so started to argue—and argue—and argue some more. Eventually the man relented; he told Bob to take home a stack of economics books and come back when he'd read them. If he could then pass a comprehensive exam, they would let him in. Bob was back in a week and took the test. The following week he was summoned to come in and instructed to go register. He never was told what he had scored on the test, but at his graduation a few year's later, that same administrator came up to him and said, "Bob, we are glad you came."

Bob worked at a variety of jobs during his master's degree program, but one job, in particular, stood out as part of "the Seattle experience." He knew that he wanted to study "organized labor and the Negro worker." So that first summer, Bob spent a lot of time hanging out at the waterfront talking to people in the labor unions about what the jobs were like, and asking about their concerns. One of them challenged him; "Instead of asking so many questions, why don't you just go to sea?" Bob took him up on that, and for the next three summers that's what he did. He said, "It was a combination of working on my masters thesis and also being paid for it in the process."

At the university, Bob met Robert W. (Bob) O'Brien, a former instructor and friend of his two brothers, Willis and Ray, from while they were at Talladega. O'Brien was now a PhD student in Sociology at Washington, and also served as the minority student advisor. He told Bob that he could offer a position as a graduate assistant in the Department of Sociology, and recommended that Bob add a sociology minor to his economics major. Bob became the first black graduate assistant in the Department of Sociology, and he later found out that he was the first graduate student at the university—of any demographic—to combine an economics major with a sociology minor.

The assistantship was under Howard B. Woolston, chair of the Department of Sociology: a scholar noted for having chosen "world prostitution" as the topic for his PhD dissertation. Woolston was irascible and tough. O'Brien later admitted that he offered Bob the assistantship because he too was tough, and maybe also just a bit irascible. And anyway, none of the graduate students in sociology had been willing to take it. Bob graded papers for one of Woolston's seminars, and the two butted heads over a grade of "C" that Bob gave to a German-Jewish student who had recently escaped Germany over "the Hitler pressure." She had written about Hitler's treatment of the Jews in Germany. Woolston said that Bob, sitting at the University of Washington, couldn't possibly know anything about it. She had lived it. How could he justify giving her a "C"? Bob countered, "How dare you suggest that I don't know anything about the world, just because I am who I am?" They battled back and forth until Woolston eventually said; "I'll tell you what I'm going to do about it. I'm going to send her to you! You two can argue it out." Bob's assigned grade ultimately stood, but he and the girl also ended up understanding each other and becoming good friends. Bob later admitted that he and Woolston, in reality, got along very well: "We *were* very much alike—we would both argue over anything!"

One of the members of the Department, Calvin Schmid, who later established the Office of Population Research in the Department of Sociology, also figures in Bob's tales from his graduate studies. Schmid refused to believe that a black man from the US South could be capable of the work Bob was doing. He insisted that Bob must be from the West Indies, or maybe from Canada. Bob said that they would often go to lunch together and talk about many things. But, he said; "To this day, I don't think he believes that I could be anything but a West Indian." Reflecting on these experiences much later in life, Bob said; "They were willing: they weren't anti-black. They just didn't believe it. What you had to do was get it through their heads that all the things they'd heard, or been taught, were just nonsense!"

While at The University of Washington, Bob was elected to the Alpha Kappa Delta National Sociology Honor Society. His thesis, *Organized Labor and the Negro in Seattle*, was considered "one of the best prewar studies of Negro labor in the western region of the United States."[9] Bob's thesis defense in 1941 was the first time in the school's history that the professors in the Department of Eco-

---

9   Gordon B. Strunk (1946). *Robert B. Pitts—Statistician*. From an unattributed newspaper or magazine clipping held in the Pitts Family private papers.

nomics and Business had ever sat down with the professors in the Department of Sociology for a joint deliberation. He said they quickly stopped asking him questions, and that he sat, quietly, at the head of the table while they debated each other at length. The Chair finally said; "Mr. Pitts, you can go now. I think we're done with you." He was awarded a Master of Arts in Labor Economics, with a minor in Statistics.

Early Career, War, and Marriage

Bob received two offers for teaching positions immediately upon graduating: LeMoyne College in Memphis, Tennessee, or Tuskegee, his parents' *alma mater*. Discussing the options with an advisor, he was told; "Don't go to Tuskegee, that's no place for a young guy to get started in *anything*." So, he went to LeMoyne and, in September 1941, began as an Instructor in Economics. He taught a sequence of courses covering economic principles, money and banking, labor relations, business cycles, business law, and labor legislation. He also participated in the administration of the department. While at LeMoyne, Bob assisted the University of Denver's National Research Institute in conducting a prewar public opinion survey in the city of Memphis.[10] For his contributions, he was later elected to the Academy of Political Science. Although his early teaching career was cut short in December 1942, by his conscription into the Army, Bob would have two fateful experiences at LeMoyne that would determine the future directions of his life.

First, at the request of the college president Mr. Brownlee, he led a faculty committee in a "careful and objective study of the possible services of LeMoyne College to the parents and children who live in LeMoyne Gardens."[11] LeMoyne in the 1930s was, in the words of the committee, an "A-rated Negro college" situated just across the street from an "A-rated Negro slum" known as Shinertown. By 1934, two thirds of the 364 Shinertown houses had leaky roofs; there were only fifteen bathtubs in the entire area; there were more than 300 children with no adequate play space; and ubiquitous cows, horses, chickens and pigs added to the unsanitary conditions. At the request of the Memphis Housing Commission, the college had previously conducted a social survey of Shinertown in 1934, "with a view to determining its validity as a slum clearance project." Although that study clearly revealed the need for slum clearance, delays in government funding and political battles over local funding priorities delayed any action for several years. Finally in March 1941, Shinertown demolition com-

---

10   Ibid.

11   Quotes are from the report of this committee: *LeMoyne Gardens and LeMoyne College: A Survey and a Plan for Community Development.* (May, 1942) A copy is in Bob's archived professional papers, which are held at the California Historical Museum, 678 Mission St., San Francisco, California, and/or at the Armistad Research Center, Tulane University, New Orleans, LA.

92   ROBERTA'S BOYS

menced and, in November 1941, a new low-income housing development of sixty buildings, with 500 living units, had been erected in its place. As a tribute to the efforts of the college, the project was named LeMoyne Gardens. Bob's committee was charged to determine the role of the college in the continued community development of LeMoyne Gardens.

Thus, very early on, Bob was working with public housing agencies, with fair housing and low-income housing issues, with economic justice issues,[12] and with the importance of the arts and the church as instruments of social change—concerns that would come to define his career. Additionally, the committee sought to "instill into the minds (of) the tenants the idea that this entire program is of their own making ... the execution and decisions of each are, as far as possible, placed into the hands of the tenants through the Tenant Association." These values of community participation, pride in ownership, and accountability later became a hallmark of Bob's philosophy at the Department of Housing and Urban Development (HUD).

Second, but most importantly, Bob's life was changed at LeMoyne when he met the beautiful young Mattalyn Coleman, a grocery store owner's daughter from Ennis, Texas. Sent "back East" to begin her college education, Mattalyn caught the eye of the dignified, quiet young instructor. Bob was thirty-two—handsome, mature, and athletic. At last finished with his struggles for an education, and gainfully employed, he allowed himself to look at this new interest with eyes that could foresee the possibility of marriage and a brighter future. Mattalyn said, about meeting him, "I was very young when I met Robert, and so impressed with how gentlemanly he was. Very quiet, but so kind and compassionate, and *always* a gentleman."

The two fell in love, but their romance was interrupted when Bob was drafted into the Army, and had to go to war. His first assignment, in December 1942, was to Ft. Benning, Georgia. He got "a halfway decent grade" on their intelligence test, which resulted in his placement in the induction center. After about three months in the center, Bob had seen enough to know that he needed a different line of work. He "volunteered" to leave the center and his superior officer, with whom Bob had developed a measure of rapport, asked him what part of the service he wanted to go into. At that time, anti-aircraft was the new "big thing." Since it involved so much mathematics, and he was a skilled mathematician, Bob volunteered for that and was accepted. He was sent to Ft. Eustis in Newport News, Virginia, for basic anti-aircraft training. He had been there about two months when then they put him into preparatory training for Officer Candidate School (OCS). He completed the training in about three

12   The report recommended and suggested plans to form a Federal Credit Union to serve both the college and the development communities. Bob was later actively involved in credit union management in California, and his brother Nathan wrote his dissertation on credit unions in North Carolina and their contributions to economic self-sufficiency for Southern black families.

months and was asked to stay on for another three months to teach geometry. Unfortunately for Bob, by the time he was finally due to attend the actual OCS, the Army had determined that they were overproducing anti-artillery officers. Instead, he was sent to Camp Davis in North Carolina to train as a Master Gunner in the Anti-Aircraft Artillery School. He was then sent to Camp Stewart at Savannah—about three months after their infamous "summer-of-1943 race riot." The riot had erupted over the unusually adverse conditions for black soldiers at that camp. Now the camp's standard process was to ship black soldiers overseas as quickly as possible, just to get them out of the way. He was at this anti-aircraft base no more than a month before being assigned to overseas duty.

Bob headed for North Africa in the fall of 1943, on a troop-ship from Newport News, Virginia. He was a Master Gunner with the 492nd antiaircraft-artillery automatic-weapons battalion. The 492nd was one of about six all-black anti-aircraft battalions that had been trained at Stewart—all officered by whites. However, the Army still felt it had oversupplied the anti-aircraft battalions. On reaching North Africa, every black anti-aircraft unit in the vicinity was reassigned to some other kind of unit. Bob was transferred to the transportation corps. Within three weeks they were sent to join the fifth Army in Enzio, Italy. Their supply run was his first exposure to combat conditions. The unit lost two ships to the Germans, and again Bob wondered; "Why not me? Why those two ships and not the one that I was on?"

In the course of his military career, Bob "went through the complete Italian campaign. At the conclusion of the European war, he sailed from Leghorn Italy, with the first troops to be sent directly from Europe to the Pacific Theatre. Landing at Manila, he served through the closing days of the Northern Luzon campaign, and was with the first American troops to occupy the island of Honshu in Japan."[13] Then at the very end of the war Bob, like Willis, took some accrued leave to see a few of the sights of Europe. One photo from Italy, which he sent home to Mattalyn, shows him standing in front of the Roman Colosseum.

While he was away, Bob and Mattalyn wrote faithfully. The two had cemented a strong bond in the brief time at LeMoyne, which only grew during their long-distance correspondence. He faced the war's fear and loneliness by thinking of her and writing love poems.

When Night Falls (To Mattalyn)
R. B. Pitts

Last night I saw a hundred stars, twinkle in a foreign sky,
  And as I gazed above, I felt alone
For through the portals of my mind a thousand thoughts were born,
  Thoughts of the past when the world was free and gay,
    And humanity ran its never ending course in a confused but peaceful way.

13   Gordon B. Strunk (1946). *Robert B. Pitts—Statistician.* .

Then the silence was broken by the tread of marching feet,
And the echo of staccato fire swelled through the valley beneath.
As I slowly turned from the wonders up above
And gazed upon a world at war
I thought of you and love.

Why does mankind seek to destroy the wonders of the earth,
Which gave him life and promise of perpetual rebirth?

Last night I saw a golden moon rise over this valley below and ignoring the
corruption beneath,
Cast its spreading glow of light in a never ending sheath.
A single thought flashed through my mind,
For I saw love and you
Cover the world of my thoughts,
And Faith was born anew.

Released from the service, Bob arrived back in Seattle at the very end of 1945, missing Christmas by just two days. He went back East in early January 1946, to be formally discharged. From there he went to Memphis for two weeks, marrying Mattalyn on January 26. A few months after he returned to Seattle, Mattalyn followed him there[14] to start a new life together.

Bob left behind a series of Army medals that include one from the European/African/Middle Eastern Campaign (which incorporates two bronze stars—indicating participation in two campaigns in this theater, as well as two arrowheads—indicating parachute jumps, glider landings, or amphibious assault landings), an Army of Occupation medal for Japan, a WWII Victory Medal, an American Campaign Medal, an Asia-Pacific Campaign Medal, an Army Good Conduct Medal (given for 3 years consecutive service with good conduct), and a Philippine Liberation Bar.

Although he had served with distinction, Bob, like Willis, downplayed his military service and he omitted any mention of it in his later resumes. His personal notebook of significant career accomplishments contains a single page with the inscription: "Military Record, United States Army, December, 1942–January, 1946." Photos from this period show Bob standing at the far back of groups of soldiers, apparently aloof. Nevertheless, he had been held in high esteem. Once, a Colonel he had served with phoned Mattalyn after losing track of Bob for a time. He said he "just wanted to check up on Bob and see how he was doing." He further told Mattalyn, "Bob was one of the best and most brilliant men I ever served with."

---

14   She traveled early that summer, after stopping along the way in Ann Arbor, Michigan, to meet Sis, Ray and his family, and Willis Jr.

In February 1946, Bob took a job as a statistician in the Washington State Health Department, Hospital Planning and Development Section. A profile of Bob and Mattalyn written at the time indicates that he was poised to make great strides: "The Pittses simply raise a quizzical eyebrow at each stride forward he takes, as if to say: 'Why not? —We expect it."[15]

The Health Department position was short-lived, however.[16] He soon decided it was not the job for him, and made tentative plans to go to Harvard Business School, at the recommendation of a former professor. But before he could do so, in early 1947, that same professor, Jesse Epstein, made Bob another recommendation. Epstein was by then the Regional Director of the Federal Public Housing Authority in Seattle. He talked Bob into taking the Civil Service Examination and joining his agency as an economist.

Bob passed the exam and went to work for Epstein as Assistant Regional Economist at the Public Housing Administration[17] (PHA) in Seattle. In this position, he once again became concerned with the urgent challenge of housing for low-income families. The population of the area had boomed after the war: it experienced an increase from 1940–46 of forty-two percent for the total population and 300 percent for the Negro population.[18] Perhaps in part due to the efforts of Epstein and his young protégé, the public housing situation in Seattle continued to be relatively fair to Negro families:

> *The policy of the Seattle Housing Authority toward racial minorities is democratic, practical, but somewhat unique in these United States. It is the one public housing authority on the Pacific Coast which has consistently refused to either set up segregated housing for Negro workers or to place Negro in-migrant workers in racial "islands" of segregation within the existing projects. Negro tenants are integrated not only into the living program, but also into the educational and recreational program of the projects. Negro personnel [are] employed by the Authority in various capacities on the basis of individual merit. Jim Crow practices aren't in evidence in either the project restaurants or in the recreational centers.*
>
> *By contrast the Bremerton Housing Authority follows a policy of both segregated all-Negro projects, such as Sinclair Heights, and of mixed projects with segregated racial "islands" as exist at View Ridge.[19]*

In March 1947, Bob completed a major study of income changes and housing costs, 1940–46, for non-agricultural workers in Bremerton, Washington.

15   Gordon B. Strunk (1946). *Robert B. Pitts—Statistician.*

16   In Bob's notebook, it also rates a single page with only the title and relevant dates.

17   The Federal Public Housing Authority was renamed the Public Housing Administration in 1947.

18   Robert W. O'Brien (November1945). *Profiles: Seattle.* pp 146-157.

19   Ibid.

The detailed analysis established new recommended figures of average family income limits for the population to be served by public housing programs, and it supported community requests for low-income housing projects. He loved living in Seattle and was off to a good start at the PHA, but later that year he had to choose between the two. Regional PHA offices were being consolidated. Bob was reassigned with Epstein to the San Francisco office, where Epstein was named West Coast Regional Director.

Bob chose to stay with the PHA, leaving Seattle. He would remain in the housing field, employed by one of its many relevant government agencies, for the remainder of his long and influential career.

Climbing the Ladder

Effective July 27, 1947, the Public Housing Administration became a constituent unit of the independent Housing and Home Finance Agency (HHFA), a reorganization that involved the consolidation of the West Coast regional offices, and Bob's relocation to San Francisco. With this move, the San Francisco Bay area became Bob and Mattalyn's permanent home.

When they first moved to San Francisco, the young Mr. and Mrs. Pitts moved into a public housing project called Codornices Village in the Berkeley area. They lived there until the mid 1950s, and Sis lived there with them for a some months in 1949–50. The Codornices Village was a wartime public housing project of barrack-like apartments that was largely, but not exclusively, African-American. Although Bob and Mattalyn found the experience of living in public housing beneficial to his career, they saw their time in the Berkeley project as simply a temporary interlude. Once they felt sure that San Francisco was to be their permanent location, they set their hearts on owning their own home. Their aspiration lay across the Golden Gate, in one of the most sought after San Francisco suburbs. Bob wanted to design and build the home of their dreams.

In 1948, Bob was asked to move into the position of Racial Relations Officer for the regional PHA office, a position he would hold until 1953. Racial Relations was a newly created position: the necessity of proactive race relations having become evident after the War. The minority population of California had ballooned and the too-rapid changes resulted in economic and social segregation and racial conflict. As the region's sole Racial Relations Officer, Bob had to establish the guideposts and pioneer agreements. A Berkeley Daily Gazette[20] article from 1950 lists Bob as the Berkeley Community Chest's one "Male Major" in the residential division that included Cordonices Village. There is a letter in Bob's files from the director of the San Francisco Field Office (J. G. Melville) commending Bob for taking on this "extra-curricular activity, at my request." In

20   Anon. (November 2, 1950). *Chest's 1 'Male Major', Codornices Effort Cited.* Berkeley Daily Gazette. Berkeley, California.

addition, throughout his stint as the agency's Racial Relations Officer, he also supported the PHA as an economist, another skill that was in short supply. For larger projects, he was detailed back to the Office of the Chief Economist.

In 1953, Bob left the PHA to become the Racial Relations Officer for the Federal Housing Administration (FHA), an organization Bob called "the untouchable" because it was so closely tied to private enterprise. The FHA had never had a racial-relations position before or, in fact, any black professionals at all in their West Coast office.

As Racial Relations Officer, the reports Bob prepared and the public lectures he delivered were dignified and technical, well organized, and presented in a logical and persuasive voice—but Bob was no retiring bureaucrat. Without ever crossing over the line, he could be scathing in his criticism of racial inequality and of those who fought to maintain the segregated *status quo*. He was biting in his assessment of the "unconcern of government, lulled to sleep by that which, for the moment, is most expedient."[21] Yet, he also emphasized that progress would come only through application of the tenets of democracy: people hammering out their differences with understanding and good will. "There is no place in this area for the bigot, or for the reckless agitator." In a report from the early 1950s that analyzed the political arguments behind California's Proposition 10 (of 1950),[22] his discussion of the "battle of words" that raged over the controversy sounds remarkably contemporary:

> *These slogans made an appeal to certain concepts which are current in the minds of the public. "High Taxes"—"Big Government"—"Socialism" (implying communistic influence)—"Political Influence" are ideas to be abhorred. While "individual rights"—"American rights"—"have your say"—"let the people speak" are all points around which people can be made to rally.*
>
> *Implied here is the Two Valued Orientation. The "All Good" (individual rights—have your say—etc.), a yes vote, and the "All Bad" (socialism—high taxes—big government), a no vote. The case here is simply a matter of choice. There is no question of degree. In short, the proposition as advanced sets up an "either—or" relationship in addition to the "Good—Bad" concept. ...*
>
> *These illustrate the nature of the appeal made by the supporters of Proposition 10. Simplicity—directness—and an appeal to high-level abstractions. Little effort was devoted to informational matters. The entire appeal was to "self-interest." These patterns gave their opponent little to attack, while, at the same time, made it necessary for them to be continually "explaining away" the charges implied in the slogans.*

---

21 Copies of several of his articles and speeches may be found in his professional papers.

22 Proposition 10 was submitted by opponents of public housing. It sought to amend the California constitution so as to require a majority approval by the voters in each community before any new public housing project could be developed in that community.

Similarly, Bob did not mince words in numerous speeches to civic groups or religious organizations (including an address at Berkeley Divinity School). He freely labeled "vicious" the controls that result in the creation of a discriminated housing market, and excoriated the restrictive practices within the real estate and financing fields that "create and maintain the racial ghetto." He called for sacrifices to be made in abandoning those "cherished concepts which facilitate our own selfish ends at the expense of a challenged democratic concept." He stated that the "inevitable consequence of segregation is discrimination" and that the existence of the ghetto...

> *buttresses the racial myths and fallacies which characterize our thinking.*
>
> *...We must be ... unafraid of carrying out the logical conclusions of democracy's meaning, regardless of how much these conclusions may invalidate the framework of prevailing mores.*
>
> *...The real test of Human Rights in our society lies in the reaction of the majority of the to the rights of an unpopular minority.*
>
> *...How much longer will we be hide-bound by the old clichés which blind us to the fact that so-called 'minority groups' are made of individuals?*

In 1957 Bob applied for a position as an FHA Market Analyst, but had quite of bit of difficulty convincing the agency's leaders to consider him seriously for the position. Qualifications weren't the problem; he had far better qualifications than most of the potential applicants. Being *black* was the problem. A head of Market Analysis from DC called him and spoke with him for about an hour. He said; "Bob, do you think you could walk into a bank and get from them the kind of information you would need to do the job?" To which Bob said; "I would like to *try.*"

Bob had George Snowden, the head of racial relations for FHA in DC, behind him on this promotion effort. The two had met earlier and agreed that the agency would never progress if it kept all of its black professionals confined to racial relations positions. Snowden advocated for Bob's promotion with the agency Commissioner, N. P. Mason, and Bob was finally selected—over the objections of several who persisted in saying, "It can never be!" From 1957 to 1961, he served as an FHA Market Analyst. In this position he participated, for the first time, in the world of privately financed housing policy. It was his responsibility to devise measures whereby privately financed housing could be brought into the reach of the working class and of racial minorities.

Without the moral authority stemming from direct Federal funding, the diplomacy required in this new position was even more exacting. There were two Market Analysts in the West Coast office who divided the region between them. Bob was assigned the inter-mountain area, which included Wyoming, Montana, Arizona, Utah, Nevada and Iowa. He learned about the analysis of communities and of building sites, economic and market conditions governing real estate, legal and political considerations, and dealing with private and public individuals and institutions. He loved getting to know the area, but what he found most extraordinary was the experience of going as an agency representative into these states and being *black*. Most of the people he met had never worked with a "real-live black person" before.

Bob told of going to Provo, Utah, during a major steel strike, to advise the local bank about the status of FHA commitments in the area. He stayed for about a week, and in the process had to go to visit the steel company. He had an appointment with the vice president in charge of public relations. The receptionist phoned to let the VP know that Mr. Pitts was coming and, in the habit of getting up to meet and greet visitors, the VP came walking down the hall:

He's coming this way, and I was coming that way. We both got to the corner at about the same time. He almost passed me, looking for Mr. Pitts. I could tell he was going to keep walking, so I said, "you are Mr. So-and-So?" He said, "yeah." So, I said; "I'm Mr. Pitts."

You should have seen the guy. I thought he was going to fall! But, he worked his way through it, shook my hand, and showed me into his office. I have never in my life so enjoyed a conversation. I saw a guy who was influential in a big operation really admit that he had missed something. He said to me; "I've been in the steel business all my life, and this is the first time that I've ever sat down in my office with a black man and talked about my company and about the steel business. You know, if this kind of thing happened more, we wouldn't have all the foolishness." And then we talked for another hour.

By the time I left, this guy had done a lot of thinking—about himself—and he had the feeling that he had really missed something. In fact, we talked so long that I was kind of anxious to get out of there! But, every time I went back, he would take me to lunch and we'd talk some more. It was that kind of encounter that made me so happy to be assigned to that inter-mountain area.

At the time, housing was the biggest industry in the country. People were anxious to buy—and everybody wanted to live in California. It was also a time when the race question became very important. Bob learned fast on both fronts, and was respected enough to be asked to lecture on "Housing Market Conditions and Integration" at the National Conference of Social Work in San Francisco (1955). Then in 1958 the International United Automobile Workers (AFL-CIO) presented him with an award for contributions toward the development of a model planned community. He was admired by all types of people, whether they were for or against the programs he promoted. This earned the notice of his peers and superiors, setting the stage for further advancement in the housing agency. Mattalyn, meanwhile, became a teacher of Kindergarten in the San Francisco Public School District at Hunters Point, a predominantly minority, industrial neighborhood in the Southeast portion of the city. Judging from the numerous letters and testimonials of former students and their parents kept among her things, she was well regarded and much loved.

Bob and Mattalyn weren't satisfied to simply speak out, excel at their jobs, and wait until the laws and society changed around them. Bob began to study real estate at the University of California at Berkeley, and earned certification in 1955. Drawing on the added strength of his real estate certification, he addressed the Alameda County Board of Realtors in 1957 as one of their peers. His speech was on the housing industry and minority groups. He challenged the thinking behind restrictive covenants and asserted that his agency, the FHA, had pledged itself to "assuring to all Americans the right of free choice and the opportunity to satisfy their housing needs." Meanwhile, having learned the ins and outs of the market, he and Mattalyn purchased property in exclusive Mill Valley, located just North of San Francisco at the edge of the beautiful Muir Woods. They finally began to plan the construction of their permanent home.

Mill Valley had, according to the 1950 census, a population of about seventy-three hundred, of whom 99.4 percent were white. Only seventeen African-Americans resided within the city limits. A family member recalls that Bob had to purchase the land through a front, because no one would have sold land to a black man.[23] But this didn't stop the young couple. Drawing on his early engineering training and his newfound expertise in real estate, Bob designed and had built his dream home—three bedrooms, two baths, and large windows looking out into the woods. The house, 345 Montford Avenue, was completed in 1957.[24]

Despite the difficulties in purchasing land and establishing themselves as residents, Bob and Mattalyn throve in Mill Valley. She was active in the League of Women Voters, the Consumer Cooperative, and Marin Aid to Retarded Children. He served at various times on a host of civic organizations, including the Bay Area Urban League; Bay Area Social Planning Council; San Francisco Council for Civic Unity; American Civil Liberties Union, Northern California Branch; Planned Parenthood Association of San Francisco (Board Member); Marin County Fair Play Committee; Men of Tomorrow, Inc., Oakland, California; Homestead Valley Improvement Club; Marin County Conservation League; United Bay Area Crusade; the Rotary Club; and the Commonwealth

---

23   In 1955 William Byron Rumford, the first black to serve in the California State Legislature, introduced a fair-housing bill; but it was not until 1963 that California passed the Rumford Fair Housing Act, which outlawed restrictive covenants and the refusal to sell property on the basis of race. Even so, when Bob's brother Ray tested the law that fall in Los Angeles, the owners refused to sell a black man the property in question.

24   Although Bob and Mattalyn felt at home in the neighborhood, the demographics did not change much over the years. The 1960 census lists only nineteen African-Americans living in Mill Valley, although the total population had grown to more than 10,400. Bob and Mattalyn may have been the only two blacks to move into that city during the entire decade. Mill Valley, in 2010, remains less than one percent black.

Club of California.

Although Bob formally converted to Roman Catholicism at some point, perhaps at the time of his marriage,[25] he attended and was active in Mill Valley Community Church. This church was a socially active non-denominational church that, over time, became associated with the United Church of Christ. The congregation had, in the 1950s, actively supported freedom riders for civil rights. In the 1960s, by which time Bob had become a church leader,[26] the congregation was, probably not coincidentally, agitating for fair housing in Marin County. Bob also served as a member of the Board of Directors for the Northern California Conference of the United Church of Christ.

In addition to community service, Mattalyn and Bob became quite active in the Bay area social circuit. Over time they became well-known fixtures at concerts, theatre and opera, and were frequently featured in the society pages of the local newspaper. One such photograph labels them "perpetual first nighters" at the San Francisco Opera.

Regional Administrator

By the early 1960s, Bob's dedication, expertise, and diplomacy, plus the recognition he had won as a Federal administrator and community leader, paid off with a series of significant promotions. "Those who worked closely with Mr. Pitts during this period ... remark on his intelligence, his negotiating ability in difficult situations, and his constant concern for people. It is important to point out that he gained the respect and admiration of an amazingly varied spectrum of people during this time. They included laborers, bank presidents, the Federal officials with whom he worked, and a remarkable number of people who were opposed either in principle or through what they considered economic reality to what he was trying to do."[27] In July 1961 at the Regional Administrator's request, he was named the Assistant to the Regional Administrator of HHFA. He was subsequently named Deputy Regional Administrator in November 1962 and Regional Administrator in October 1964, the first black ever to be appointed to a regional administrator position. Lest one forget how uncommon this level of seniority was for a black man in 1964, it is worth noting that the San Francisco News-Call Bulletin announced his selection using the headline "West Housing—Negro Chief?"[28]

25   His funeral service was in Mill Valley's Our Lady of Mt. Carmel Catholic Church, which would have been unlikely if he was not a Roman Catholic communicant. Pastors of both churches were participants in Bob's 1970 retirement party.

26   He chaired the church's 1963 study on its mission and future in the next decade, and at some point served on its Board of Trustees.

27   The quote is from a letter written in support of Bob's nomination for the Rockefeller Public Service Award (1967 or 1969). Copies of the nominations are in his archived professional papers..

28   Anon. (August 8, 1964). *West Housing—Negro Chief?* San Francisco News-Call Bulletin.

The Regional Administrator's Office, with a staff of 300, coordinated all agency program operations in eleven western states[29] and the Territory of Guam. The time that Bob spent as Regional Administrator of HHFA "was one of increasing Federal activity in the whole immense field of housing and urban development. Active urban renewal projects in his region jumped from 422 to 555 in the first fifteen months of his incumbency. Public works programs on the books increased from 1248 to 1390. Program activity in his first full year alone increased twenty-three percent."[30] The nation as a whole "had gone through and was still undergoing a period of breakneck urban growth. Metropolitan areas were strained to the utmost to furnish services and a decent living environment to millions of new urban dwellers. Central cities were undergoing inordinate pressures as middle-income citizens moved to the suburbs, and the rural poor, many in racial minority groups, poured into what were to become slums and racial ghettos in the cities. ... Under the impetus of this broad and rapid general awakening, the Congress in the 1960s passed a large body of housing and urban development legislation."[31] Bob would be responsible for achieving an almost encyclopedic knowledge of the agency's programs, coordinating the construction of thousands of projects, and making decisions affecting the lives of millions of urban people. All the while, he would be learning how to manage and direct a large Federal office and communicating both up and down the administrative chain, as well as with congressional overseers. Despite his busy schedule, Bob also found time to contribute a chapter to the University of California's book *Race and Property* (John Denton, ed., 1964). At least two printings of this book had sold out by mid-1966, at which time the editor sent Bob a check for his share of the royalties—a whopping five dollars.

The new Regional Administrator found the fall of 1964 a challenging time to engage with California's public housing sector. By the 50s and 60s, most blacks in California's cities found themselves pushed into segregated housing and excluded from the real estate market, but they were increasingly unwilling to accept the status quo. They had achieved a measure of success with the passage of the Rumford Fair-Housing Act. The Act had been introduced in 1955 by William Byron Rumford, California's first black legislator, and finally passed in 1963. It outlawed discrimination in housing on the basis of race, ethnicity, gender, marital status, or physical disability. However by early 1964 conservative groups, equally unwilling to abandon the *status quo*, were pushing for Proposition 14, a ballot referendum that would amend the state's Constitution to give any property owner the right to rent or sell "only to such person or persons as he, in his absolute discretion, chooses."

29 Washington, Oregon, California, Hawaii, Alaska, Idaho, Nevada, Arizona, Utah, Montana, and Wyoming.
30 Nomination, Rockefeller Public Service Award.
31 Ibid.

The same month that Bob took office, the Agency's Washington, DC-based Administrator, Robert C. Weaver,[32] while on a campaign visit to Sacramento, announced that HHFA funds would be cut off if Proposition 14 were to pass.[33] Less than one month later, on November 3, 1964, Proposition 14 was adopted by Californians with a margin of two to one—regardless of warnings that violence would be the probable result.[34] Most HHFA aid to the region was subsequently cut off.

Bob's office coordinated sixty-eight urban renewal projects in California, involving nearly 270 million dollars of Agency funds. Faced with the task of an orderly shut down of projects that would not again see Federal funds until the Supreme Court ruled Proposition 14 unconstitutional in 1967, and with his agency the target of anger and frustration from all sides, one might forgive the new Regional Administrator for wondering if he had landed "the assignment from hell."

Nevertheless, Bob "handled the Proposition 14 imbroglio in exemplary fashion. By carefully extending what legal financial help was permitted, he helped maintain the professional staff of various redevelopment agencies,"[35] and he did whatever he could to assist them to mothball projects until funding could be restored. He kept essential lines of communication open between community groups, state agencies, and the Federal government. In fact, Bob told an Oakland Tribune reporter that the passage of proposition 14, in his personal opinion, "was not without benefit to the state. It destroyed the myth that there is no racial discrimination in the state. ... Prior to the election there were many persons involved in housing who insisted there was no discrimination. ... 'Many of us in the housing field were aware for some time of the tremendous undercurrent of opinion opposed to fair housing ... the vote brought it out in the open.'"[36]

At least partly a response to the passage of Proposition 14, the "Watts riots" broke out in Los Angeles the following summer. They significantly exacerbated the already difficult situation. Over a five-day period in August 1965, more than 30,000 adults participated in riots that left the Watts community looking like a war ravaged battle zone, with nearly 14,000 police and national guardsmen called in to quell the destruction.[37] Civil rights activist Bayard Rustin said of

---

32 Who was also black.

33 Anon. (Oct 21, 1964). *US Housing Official Calls Proposition 14 Disease*. The Modesto Bee, Modesto, California.

34 Anon. (Dec 1, 1964). *Proposition 14 Approval Cancels US Renewal Aid for California*. Milwaukee Sentinel, Milwaukee, Wisconsin.

35 Nomination, Rockefeller Public Service Award.

36 Anon. (Jan 24, 1965). *Peralta Project Fund Grant Held Up by Prop. 14 Puzzle*. Oakland Tribune, Oakland, California.

37 Statistics from Casey Nichols, in *Watts Rebellion* (August 1965). Retrieved on June 12, 2012 from www.blackpast.org.

the riots, "the whole point of the outbreak in Watts was that it marked the first major rebellion of Negroes against their own masochism and was carried on with the express purpose of asserting that they would no longer quietly submit to the deprivation of slum life."[38]

Then in September 1966 race riots broke out in the San Francisco neighborhood of Hunters Point. It was another five-day conflagration that mobilized the National Guard. This one was of special concern to Bob, as it was the neighborhood where Mattalyn worked as a kindergarten teacher. He used all his diplomatic talents to create an environment where city-government leaders and the activists could try to come to an understanding and negotiate possible solutions. Rioting also soon broke out in the Fillmore district, and also across the Bay in Oakland.

The riots did not, in the end, significantly improve the lives of the black population of these communities, and much of the promised action from local, state and Federal governments was quickly forgotten, Bob, however, threw himself into meeting the communities' needs in whatever ways he and his agency could contrive. In Los Angeles, Bob's old friend Judson (Jud) Howard[39] was then field deputy to City Councilman John S. Gibson Jr. His close friendship with Jud greatly facilitated the agency's collaboration with the city government. Bob came to LA weekly during the aftermath of the riots, coordinating strategy with Jud (nicknamed the "Mayor of Watts" for his many health-education and community-organization activities in the neighborhood) to negotiate and maximize the effectiveness of the combined community/municipal/Federal response to Watts' needs. Bob refused, as always, to impose Federal solutions from above. In their analysis of the Watts community, they sought to first determine what the people perceived as their problems, and then to recruit them to lead the implementation of their own solutions.

Vice President Hubert Humphrey charged Bob, through HHFA chief Robert Weaver, to find a group of alienated Watts youth and try to do something to provide Federal assistance to them. Jud introduced Bob to the Watts' Happening Coffee House, which was (and remains today) a vital center for minority youth engagement in the city. The young board of directors of the coffeehouse helped with developing the plans for a new neighborhood center and, under the guidance of Bob and Jud, undertook for themselves the processes of applying, fund raising, site selection, architect selection, and design—as well as all other necessary tasks for the center's development. "Former Assistant Secretary Dwight Ink of HUD,[40] remarked on one of his later visits to Watts and the

38   Bayard Rustin, (March 1966). *The Watts*. Commentary Magazine.

39   They were Ballard Normal School classmates.

40   HHFA's successor agency, the Department of Housing and Urban Development (HUD). The programs Bob coordinated in Los Angeles, San Francisco and Oakland, after the riots, spanned the transition to the new agency..

Coffeehouse, 'If the building is never built, the changes I see in the manner, confidence and respect of the Board Members is worth whatever investment HUD has made in the past two years.'"[41]

As part of his response to Watts, Bob recruited Emma McFarlin to HUD from a classroom in San Francisco. He sent her to LA with the charge; "live in the Watts community—open a one-person HUD office on 103rd Street, determine what the people perceive as their problems, and find a way to get Federal assistance for them." She said that he "admonished me not to impose HUD's will on the community, nor to seek media nor public exposure for what we were doing—that's not how the building got built."[42] Honoring his efforts years later in 1985, the building was renamed named the Robert Pitts Westminster Neighborhood Center. City Councilwoman Joan Milke Flores, in a tribute to Bob at that time, said:

The Watts Neighborhood Center ... was the first new building in Watts following the 1965 riot, and was the result of [Bob's] commitment to the community. ... Mr. Pitts' leadership and sensitivity to the needs of the Watts community in the late 60s gave the community new hope and a vision at a time of frustration and discouragement. Among other things, he helped bring facilities for services and care into the community; including the Neighborhood Development Center, the Economic Resources Industrial Park, the Multipurpose Child Development Center at Locke High School, and some 2,000 new housing units. He was also instrumental in achieving modified transportation routing and scheduling so that residents could reach jobs within reasonable travel times.[43]

Concerning Bob's handling of the racial strife in San Francisco during this period, colleagues had this to say:[44]

As the city, however, attempted to utilize the program [HHFA-HUD public housing] in the 1960s, a dramatic confrontation occurred between the local officials and the militant residents of these areas, with HUD caught in the cross-fire. Mr. Pitts' behind-the-scene leadership brought a harmonious ending to a dramatic confrontation between the city government and activists protesting plans for an urban renewal project. In less skillful hands, lengthy lawsuits and lasting bitterness might have resulted, but with Mr. Pitts' quiet help, the city government and the activists were more clearly understood by

41 Nomination, Rockefeller Public Service Award.

42 Quotes from a speech Dr. McFarlin gave in Bob's honor at the dedication of the Robert B. Pitts Neighborhood Center on Feb 20, 1985. Copy in R. Pitts' professional papers

43 Joan Milke Flores (Feb. 8, 1985). *Press Release: Ceremony Honoring Robert Pitts Slated Wednesday in Watts.* Copy in R. Pitts' professional papers.

44 Nomination, Rockefeller Public Service Award.

each other. Confidence was restored and improved housing programs are now underway for low- and moderate-income families sponsored by nonprofit organizations indigenous to the area, employing professionals and craftsmen with strong neighborhood identity.

Only a handful of San Franciscans know the key role played by Mr. Pitts, but those who do will testify clearly that he was indispensable in achieving the solution.

At HUD

In August 1965, President Lyndon B. Johnson signed into law the Housing and Urban Development Act that would result in the creation of the new and vastly expanded Department of Housing and Urban Development (HUD). Bob's DC boss at the HHFA, Robert Weaver, was chosen to head the new agency, becoming the first African-American elevated to a cabinet-level position in the US government. Having worked with Bob and learned to respect his abilities and value his advice, Weaver petitioned the President to appoint Bob to the position of Regional Administrator for the Western region.[45] In addition, Weaver asked Bob to chair the task force to lead the reorganization plan for the entirety of the HUD regional offices.

There were some who insinuated that Bob's selection as a regional administrator was primarily motivated by the politics of placing an African-American in a high level position. What few realized, outside of the agency, was that he was one of only five or six people in the entire country who had broad experience in almost every agency that was being collected under the HUD umbrella, and that they had planned for some time to ask him to lead the departmental-offices reorganization. Not only did he now run a regional office that had grown significantly in its responsibilities, with a staff of over 2000, he spent fully half his time over the next six months in Washington, DC, leading this task force. In his "spare" time Bob enrolled in and completed the Brookings Institution *Advanced Study Program in Public Administration.* He also reconnected with his brother Nathan, who was then working in DC for the Federal government's Office of Education.

The reorganization of the regional offices "was not one that resulted only in a movement of little bosses on an organizational chart. It consisted of re-directing the functions and operations of whole major operating units into new and more efficient patterns. ... It is a testimony to his stamina and executive ability that he administered a heavy operational program at the same time, and then returned to San Francisco to re-structure his own regional organization."[46] Speaking to

---

45   The same geographic region that he had overseen as Regional Administrator for HHFA.

46   Nomination, Rockefeller Public Service Award.

a Conference on Intergovernmental Relations at Berkeley in the fall of 1966, Bob presented a paper titled *Designing the Regional Office Organizational Structure: Department of Housing and Urban Development*. He said it was "the first attempt to reshape a Federal bureaucracy from top to bottom since the New Deal days." For Bob, the essence of the reorganization was "rooted not so much in terms of organizational structure but in the direction in which the structure is pointed ... a new role for Federal programs in the field of urban development."

Bob was not shy about noting the problems of bringing Federal executives, particularly across multiple agencies, together to work on new directions. In his paper, he noted that:

> *I listened with a great deal of interest to the diversity of opinions expressed by representatives at various levels of government. The duet of 'whatever you can do, I can do better,' the counter charges that 'if you would just clean your own house, the thing would work,' and the assurance that 'I know more about this than you' are all familiar tunes. And we continue to sing while our cities and towns grow and decay and explode around us. ... May I further suggest that if we give this self-examination a 'real try,' we will find that we have been 'off target.'*

Bob detailed four primary goals of the reorganization effort: 1) to form a structure such that formerly disparate agencies and sub-agencies could come to know each other and work together integrally; 2) to decentralize the decision-making process and put more funding authority in the field, where operational responsibility resides; 3) to create a closer working relationship between the Federal agencies and local authorities, community agencies and community representatives; and 4) to shift the Federal approach to urban problems from a "project approach" to a "problem-solving approach."

President Kennedy, and after him President Johnson, had the vision that a consolidated HUD would encourage urban growth and successfully tackle the problems of inner-city decay and racial-minority ghettos. In implementing this "vision of the Federal government's participation and cooperation in providing adequate housing and urban development that protects and promotes opportunities of diverse ethnic populations and the poorest families in the country, HUD made significant strides during its first three years. It made the Federal Housing Administration a key part of HUD's mission to develop low-income housing, initiated cross-communication between programs so that related issues could be addressed in a coordinated way, involved neighborhood groups in spearheading inner-city rehabilitation through the Model Cities program, and looked for innovative ways to fund private housing for lower-income families."[47] Under this vision, Bob's activities as Regional Administrator took on

47 Gale Encyclopedia of US History: *Department of Housing and Urban Development*. Retrieved June 25, 2012 from: http://www.answers.com/topic/housing-and-urban-development-department-of

even greater prominence, and demands for his time and talents increased. He also used his professional contacts and his various civic memberships to further the goals of HUD, and to extend the effectiveness of the Federal government's investment in local communities, especially through enhanced intergovernmental cooperation.

In Oakland, a city with severe racial tensions, Mr. Pitts undertook efforts to coordinate Federal programs. Using the tact and patience for which he is so well noted, he succeeded once again in making Federal programs an important key to solving problems involving a skeptical city administration and skeptical racial groups.

As he worked diplomatically with the city, through its officials and residents, he challenged the Critical Urban Problems Committee of the San Francisco Federal Executive Board, of which he was the Chairman, to set up a Task Force to identify the massive Federal inputs into that community, and to devise a means for measuring the effectiveness of the investment. Exercising extreme patience and persuasiveness, he finally succeeded in garnering the support of his Federal colleagues in undertaking the endeavor. This was followed by a year of negotiating with the Washington office to get funds to carry out the work of the Task Force.

Under his guidance and direction this Task Force carried out a project to its final conclusion that was recorded in a two volume report entitled An Analysis of Federal Decision-Making and Impact: The Federal Government in Oakland,[48] *which has already become a major guide for intergovernmental approaches to urban problems. ... Oakland has become one of the largest users of HUD and other Federal programs in the West, a feat which would not be possible without the quiet perception and determination of the Regional Administrator, serving as Chairman of the Critical Urban Problems Committee.*[49]

Bob's contributions during his years as HUD Regional Administrator were not confined to the more developed areas of California, Oregon and Washington, nor were they confined to navigating through the racial strife between the white and black communities. Another notable accomplishment was his extensive guidance and direction to state leaders for comprehensive planning towards the economic and social development of Alaska and Hawaii. In both states, he advised and encouraged regional governments to deal pragmatically with a fast developing area. He drew upon his analysis of the failings and mistakes of other portions of the country, particularly the more populous states of the West.

Bob's extensive involvement in Los Angeles after the Watts riots, and the

48   (1968) Published by the Economic Development Administration, US Dept. of Commerce, for the Oakland Task Force, San Francisco Federal Executive Board.

49   Nomination, Rockefeller Public Service Award.

suite of intergovernmental programs that resulted, had become the blueprint and testbed for HUD's Model Cities Program and Block Grant programs, which he administered throughout his region. In Honolulu, Bob won the confidence of Senator Inouye, who featured him as a speaker in a 1969 housing policies conference. There, Bob assisted in the implementation of a Model Cities program that was considered one of the best in the nation.[50] Other models and policies that were demonstrated successfully in Oakland were effectively put into practice in urban areas of Arizona and Nevada. A public tribute presented to Bob from the Western states reads; "The beauty, wealth and newness of the West often masked the poverty and needs of these states; Bob saw them and the developing patterns, [and] used his position to become the foremost advocate for the Urban West in national urban policy."

There were many other important contributions. In early December 1969, Bob led a Federal deputation that conducted negotiations with the American-Indian activists who had been occupying Alcatraz Island since November 20, in protest of their treatment at the hands of the government. Unfortunately for the negotiators, Bob's deputation had been charged to investigate whether Federal programs could be focused on some of the problems highlighted by the protesters, while the protesters expected immediate concessions and felt a fact-finding meeting was a waste of time.[51] They were unable to come to an understanding.

Bob was also heavily involved with the Mexican-American community of Los Angeles. He worked tirelessly to resolve some of their critical issues—in particular, the problem of transporting willing workers to areas where there were thriving industries in need of service. He spearheaded a Transportation Demonstration Project that virtually eliminated what had been almost insurmountable commuting obstacles for this worker community. He established HUD's Southwest-Area Office in Los Angeles and "installed Ignacio Galindo to serve as its director, thereby providing the Hispanic community with its first Federal leader of such stature."[52]

While he was still in office, numerous cities in his region—including Honolulu, Los Angeles, San Francisco, Oakland, Portland, and Seattle—issued formal resolutions commemorating Bob's contributions in the field of housing and urban development. Also in recognition of his many contributions, he was awarded the Bay Area Howard University Alumni Award, in 1966.

Bob was nominated for the Rockefeller Public Service Award[53] on three sep-

50   (1979) *An Evaluation of the Effectiveness of the Neighborhood Boards and Neighborhood Plan*. Prepared for the Neighborhood Commission City and County of Honolulu by PAC West Community Associates, Inc.

51   Anon. (Dec. 3, 1969). *Indian Chiefs of Alcatraz Pow-Wow With Palefaces(?), Vow to Remain*. The Modesto Bee, Modesto, California.

52   Nomination, Rockefeller Public Service Award.

53   Given by the Woodrow Wilson School of Public and International Affairs, at Princeton University.

arate occasions—in1967 by the Department of HUD, in 1969 by a coalition of West Coast mayors led by San Francisco Mayor Joe Alioto, and again in 1970 by HUD together with the mayors' support. The large monetary award was presented annually to a single outstanding civilian employee in the Federal Government. In 1967, the award was given to Wilber Joseph (Joe) Cohen, the founder of the Social Security system. The rumor around Washington was that, if Joe hadn't been in the pool, Bob would have gotten it. In fact, he'd been informed he was a "shoe-in" for the award. It would have been the first time in the history of the Federal government that a black man had won it.

The April 4, 1968 assassination of Martin Luther King Jr. prompted President Johnson, who had been advancing fair housing legislation for some time, to urge Congress to pass the Fair Housing Act. The US Supreme Court had, in 1967, finally ruled California's Proposition 14 unconstitutional, and the Fair Housing Act was intended to introduce meaningful Federal enforcement mechanisms. The Act was passed that April 11, but the power of HUD to realize the promise of the Act was much weakened by "the Dirksen Compromise." This congressional compromise was that the law's enforcement would be at the discretion of the Attorney General, rather than the Secretary of HUD; and that sale-by-owner homes would be exempted from compliance.

With the election of Nixon in November 1968, the writing was on the wall for significant changes that would further reduce the impact and effectiveness of HUD. Nixon was a fiscal conservative and not, in general, a strong advocate of HUD's goals or programs. He installed his political rival, George Romney, as HUD Secretary. The two neither liked nor trusted one another. Romney proceeded to put in place new housing programs and policies in good faith, but did so without the political backing and support of the President. This put the agency on a collision course with the Administration that eventually culminated in Nixon's 1973 moratorium on Federal housing and community development assistance.

Bob served as Regional Administrator through 1969 but, as expected of any Presidential appointee, he offered his resignation to make way for the President to ask him to continue or to appoint a new Regional Administrator. In addition, the agency had changed so significantly that Bob began to wonder if he could not contribute more effectively from outside the government. His resignation was accepted, and he announced his retirement effective January 1970.

Bob's professional involvement in the Western Region already extended beyond his HUD position, and he would continue to be influential in the field. He was, and in most cases would remain, an active member of the Western Governmental Research Association; the Academy of Political Science; the American Academy of Political and Social Science; the American Society for Public Administration; the California Real Estate Certificate Institute; The California

Real Estate Association; the National Association of Housing and Redevelopment Officials; The International Fraternity of Lambda Alpha (Land Economics);[54] and the Federal Executive Board (San Francisco and Los Angeles). But Bob hoped that retirement would also give him time for private pursuits.

When they had each been finishing graduate school and establishing careers, the Pitts brothers saw and heard little of each other. There were early years during which Bob and Mattalyn were only minimally aware of the details of his other brothers' lives, and that only because Sis never flagged in her determination to keep the family together. As they all relaxed into mid-life and into distinguished careers, however, the brothers began seeing more of each other. In retirement, Bob and Mattalyn hoped to invest even more time in family, as well as engage in hobbies and travel.

Raymond [Ray] had moved his family to the Pasadena/Santa Barbara area in 1956 to work with the Los Angeles State College. This afforded the two brothers not only a chance to catch up personally, but also to work together on certain projects. In Ray's words, "Bob and I collaborated on several projects during the period when Federal and state efforts were concentrated on the inter-related problems of housing [and] education in our state. It was both an inspiration and a joy to work with my brother in a professional realm after many years of separation. As I reflect on those years, we were responding to a long remembered phrase in one of our father's prayers, that God would '... give us the strength to make the world a better place by our having lived in it.'" Nat, Ray's son, recalls a more personal side to the distinguished public administrator:

> We rarely went out to eat while I was growing up ... but when Uncle Bob would come to town, he would always take us out to dinner. I remember the first time I had a T-bone steak in a restaurant. I was about 11 years old. Uncle Bob took us to dinner at his hotel, the Hilton, in downtown LA, where he always stayed when he was there on business. I did not know what to order and was looking to my mom for guidance. But, before she could steer me towards something reasonably inexpensive, Uncle Bob says, "I think you need a good T-bone steak young fellow." Since Uncle Bob did not have children, he would splurge on us from time to time. He came to my junior-high school, high school and college graduations, and he always gave me money (usually a $20 bill) every time he came to town.
>
> I can remember playing baseball in my neighborhood street ... and my Uncle Bob was due to come over for dinner one night. My mother told me to be on the lookout for him. In those days he would take the bus to Pasadena and come up to our house on the Los Robles bus that would let him out on the corner just up the street. I first saw him walking tall, down the street with a paper under his arm. Uncle Bob was a very proud, very black, very

---

54   He was elected one of their three Vice Presidents in 1972.

distinguished looking man. And, when he spoke, you were forced to listen.
He measured his words carefully. Bob went first class wherever he went. He
drove a gray/brown Mercedes.

When I got to know him later in life, through visits to his house, by being
nosy I found him to be very picky about how he dressed, how he looked, how
his hair was cut, what color of clothes he wore, etc. In his closet of suits, I found
only gray, dark blue or black suits, and of course a couple of tuxes—and, only
white shirts. Once for his birthday I bought him a present of an orange-ish
mock turtleneck short-sleeve sweater, the type the college kids were wearing
at the time. He laughed at it and wondered out loud, "Now where would I
wear that?" His house was made mostly of wood, and the acoustics were great
for the music that would play on his stereo. He played mostly symphony mu-
sic, but I would always bring over something new—jazz, like Roberta Flack,
Donny Hathaway, Nancy Wilson—that he would like. When I asked him
about his favorite song from the "good old days" he did not hesitate: Stormy
Weather, *by Lena Horne (who was from his hometown of Macon, GA).*

I attended his retirement party in 1969–70 where representatives (some
governors) from all these states [the 11 in the Western Region] were present
paying tribute. I saw Senator Inouye there for the first time. I recall going to
Bob's office in downtown San Francisco as a college student. It was big, as it
should be, with the US flag behind his desk. He did not show me around the
office suite; we were going to a ball game—something we always did when I
was in town and the Giants were playing.

When I was at college at Whittier, he would come there and give lectures
to the sociology department. He was connected to Dr. Bob O'Brien, chair
of the Department. They had known each other from old times. Uncle Bob
would come to Whittier and sometimes I would get a chance to go for lunch
or dinner with him. But in any case, other students on campus would tell me
about his talks. It let them know that I was "somebody," and that made me
feel good.

When Bob announced his intention to retire, the Department pulled out all
the stops to fête the popular and respected leader. A testimonial dinner was held
on February 7, 1970, at the Kabuki Theatre Restaurant, Japanese Cultural Center, San Francisco. Just the organizing committee alone for this dinner consisted
of more than sixty people. The full event involved more than two hundred individual and corporate sponsors. Speakers included the mayors of San Francisco
and Honolulu, as well as the Under Secretary of HUD from Washington. A
second and equally elaborate event, a testimonial luncheon, was held on February 14 at the Hilton Hotel in Los Angeles. Bob's longtime friend Jud Howard
served as the Toastmaster, and the luncheon included presentations from the
mayors of Los Angeles and Compton, the President of the Los Angeles City

Council, and the Chairman of the County Board of Supervisors. Along with a lengthy acknowledgment of Bob's many accomplishments during his professional career, the program for the San Francisco event included this tribute:

All of us, on this happy occasion, ask only that our honorees enjoy themselves ... Bob has earned the gratitude of this Region for his unselfish and constructive service in the field of Housing and Urban Development.

People, from the very young to the senior citizen, in the activities ranging from the physical to the cultural—in every walk of life and with divergent interests—have all benefited from his twenty-two years of service with the Federal Government.

In all of these years his gracious wife, Mattalyn, has likewise contributed to this success by her counsel, patience and helpfulness.

We, their friends, offer this small tribute tonight in appreciation of their friendship and for what they have done to make this nation a happier place in which to live.

Retirement

Retirement, in Bob's case, did not involve slowing down. Bob took a part time position at the University of California, Berkeley, School of Business Administration, lecturing in urban economics and real estate, conducting studies, and authoring papers on urban affairs. Simultaneously, he founded his own firm, Urban Consultants, Inc., with offices at the Berkeley Marina. He also continued to be in demand on the public lecture circuit. Over time, Bob became Vice-President and a member of the board of Applied Urbanology, Inc., in San Francisco, and a member of the board of the Twin Pines Federal Savings & Loan, in Berkeley.

Bob expanded his community and charitable involvement. He served on the Marin County Redevelopment Agency, and was one of the founders of the Marin Co-op in Corte Madera. He helped to create the Bay Area Black Fund and worked with the United Crusade[55] and as a consultant to the Buck Foundation[56] regarding Marin City. He was also a significant contributor to a citizen's committee study of San Francisco's juvenile justice system for the Bay Area Social Planning Council.

As generous and gracious as Bob was with his time, talents and resources, he was mindful of his dignity and constitutionally opposed to being coerced or cheated. Once, a tree on his property fell due to a heavy rain, causing damage to the sewer pipeline of the local sanitary district. The sanitary district removed

55   Forerunner of the United Way Campaign.

56   Which became part of the San Francisco Foundation in 1975, and eventually became the Marin Community Foundation in 1987.

the tree to prevent further damage to the municipal system, and only after the fact called Bob to request that he share a portion of the removal costs. Bob's insurance determined that he was not liable, and refused to cover the claim; but the sanitary district pressed the claim on Bob and asserted that he had a "moral responsibility" to share the costs. Bob—still his customary, argumentative self—replied emphatically, via his lawyer, that by referring the claim to both his insurance and to his attorney for their guidance, he felt that he had discharged any "moral obligation" in the matter.[57]

One of Bob's first post-retirement activities in his new business was performing market analysis for the Organization of American States (OAS) on a housing study for the Republic of Trinidad & Tobago, West Indies. For the first few months of 1971, he and Mattalyn resided in Port of Spain on Trinidad. There Bob assisted in carrying out a housing demand survey, and did an analysis of the housing environment and market on the islands. While in Trinidad, they became close friends with Otway (Sonny) Prevat, a national housing official, and despite chaos both within the OAS and within the Republic that resulted in an early demise of the effort (Bob had hoped to be able to return to Port of Spain the following year to continue his studies), the two continued, as friends, to exchange letters and plan mutual family visits for many years.

At another juncture, Bob represented the Regional Planning Committee of the Association of Bay Area Governments (ABAG) against the Department of Housing and Urban Development over HUD's withholding of full funding for many ABAG programs. He was "turned to 'in desperation' to draw up a housing work program acceptable to his former employers."[58] The relationship with the planning committee lasted until 1973, through several additions to the original contract, until HUD's moratorium on housing and community development assistance left the Planning Committee with essentially no programs to plan.

Bob continued to work on housing development, urban environments, and land use studies until his death in 1982. He was a chief consultant to President Jimmy Carter's transition team on housing and development, and regularly served as a consultant to his old employer, HUD. At the request of the Department of Transportation and in support of the impact study for the Bay Area Rapid Transit System, he conducted an extensive study of the social factors (particularly as affecting minority groups) of significance in the planning, development and operation of mass transit systems in urban areas. He conducted an major economic analysis of the housing market for Visitación Rancho, a proposed development in San Mateo, for the Crocker Land Company. He collaborated with a friend on the design for a potential condominium complex

---

57   Another time, Bob again engaged his lawyer to strongly contest what he felt to be several "extraordinary fees" charged by the estate agent in settling the estate of his Aunt Mittie McKenzie.

58   Mark Trautwein. (Sept. 3, 1971). *ABAG Retains Pitts to Help Battle HUD*. Berkeley Daily Gazette, Berkeley, California.

in San Fransisco, called "SealRock," and "his last determined effort was to find a source to finance the Jones Memorial [senior citizens'] apartments at Post and Fillmore in San Francisco. He was successful in doing this the week before entering the hospital."[59]

Bob used his retirement to reflect on his work and career. He was particularly interested in understanding what he called "the philosophical concept of cities": the history of cities, how they develop, how they grow and change, and how they serve mankind—or fail to. He developed, lectured on, and wrote about theories of good urban planning and the principal rules for city growth.

He also reflected on lessons life had taught him. Bob often thought back to what he called "the Pittsburgh period," which he felt was the defining period of his life. He was in Pittsburgh when it was a one-industry town, and during the depression he saw that industry all but destroyed. He saw men in long lines looking for work when there was none to be had, stood in those lines himself, and went hungry as often as not. In Pittsburgh he developed a resilience that served him well. He told his brother Ray; "It was a depressed and hopeless city and I learned not to allow it to make me like that." Even at the worst of times he had managed to find work, survive, and eventually prosper. "I learned that no matter what happened I could somehow make it, but that just making it was not the issue"—to do more, to achieve, to accomplish something! Out of adversity, he developed three steadfast rules for life, rules that he then lived by:

—*First, never follow the crowd. If a crowd is going one way, you head the other.*
—*Second, don't stay in one place too long.*
—*Third, get out there where things are unknown. And when you get there, do your damnedest to make them known.*

Yet retirement was not all work or serious thought. Bob kept busy, but he enjoyed the freedom of setting his own schedule and of taking breaks whenever he wanted or needed to. Both Bob and Mattalyn suffered from prolonged illnesses in the early 1970s, Mattalyn in 1971 after their return from Trinidad, and Bob in 1972–73. But after a long recovery, Bob wrote to "Sonny" in Trinidad that he now felt better than he had in years. He and Mattalyn took frequent trips to visit the brothers, including to Paris to visit Nathan at his posting to UNESCO. From this base they continued on to explore other parts of Europe. In Rome, both succumbed to the mystique of Italian leather and of fine Italian shoes. They purchased three pair to be shipped home and, thus, also discovered a common bane of the traveler's existence—the delayed or lost package from

59   Lindajoy Fenley (June 21, 1985) *Marin Man Honored by Watts.* Marin Independent Journal, Marin, California. p. A5.

a European retailer.[60] Bob also enjoyed several hobbies—he created a Japanese garden in the yard at their Mill Valley home, and took up an interest in Bonsai—and encouraged Mattalyn in hers.

Although Mattalyn continued to work in the San Francisco school system for several years after Bob retired, he worried about the stress she was under in the increasingly marginalized neighborhood of Hunters Point. He encouraged her to retire and to turn her passion for fashion, design, and decorating into a new career. Thus the businesses *Mattalyn of Mill Valley*, and later *Interiors by Mattalyn* were born. In 1978, she discussed her job transition in an interview.[61] "A dinner guest in our home, who is a decorator, liked the way I decorated our house and asked me to join his firm. I've already completed my first job." She was soon quite successful, branched out on her own, and was sought after as both a fashion and home designer. Her gowns were featured in the 1983 Couturier Collection at Neiman Marcus. She once forwarded Nancy Reagan a dress she had designed especially for her: making the connection through Senator S. I. "Samurai Sam" Hayakawa, a mutual acquaintance. Her nephew Nat tells the following story about "Aunt Mattalyn":

> *Aunt Mattalyn loved the MG car, so she bought one for herself one Christmas, and had it delivered to her home in Mill Valley. She had no idea that it was a stick shift: there were no automatic transmissions available. So, Aunt Mattalyn would only drive the car down the hill to the bus stop in Mill Valley, and then take the bus to work. ... San Francisco is full of hills that anyone would be uncomfortable driving on with stick shift, and so she would never drive this car outside of Mill Valley.*

Then, after twelve good years of retirement, Bob's health began deteriorating in the early 1980s. It soon it became clear that he would not recover. Nat recalled his last visit, knowing that it was for the last time:

> *Uncle Bob always held his head high with dignity. I recall the last time I saw him in the hospital before he died. His kidneys were failing. From the hospital bed, he still said; "Hi there, fellow!" and spoke to me as if nothing was happening. ... It was clear to me he was dying.*

Remembering Bob

Bob died from kidney failure at 10 P.M. August 30, 1982, at Kaiser Hospital in San Francisco. He was 73. His Mass of Christian Burial was celebrated at Our Lady of Mr. Carmel Church in Mill Valley, and he was buried at Fern-

---

60   A copy of a letter in his files acknowledges the receipt of only one pair, and pointedly asks when the other two might be expected?

61   Rubye Cadison Coffman (Feb. 25, 1978). *Stunning Visitors in Our Town*. Tri-State Defender., Memphis, Tennessee.

wood Cemetery. A second memorial service was held on September 26 in Los Angeles, at Lincoln Memorial Congregational Church. His three brothers all attended the burial, and Willis described the scene in his self-published *Eulogy for a Brother* (1983):

> *There is an interesting, picturesque, panoramic view from one of the mountainous California hillsides partly surrounding an arena-like valley. Glimpsed below in this nearby San Francisco area, and dotting the slanting slopes below, are built varied modernistic types of house structures centered around the small town called Mill Valley. ... At one point on the often-found steep slopes surrounding the region, some farsighted commercial entrepreneur has laid out plots designed as future burial lots. ... At one of the highest levels of his burial ground where only a few scattered closed graves were marked, there was one quite recently prepared. ... On a bright, clear midday morning of September 1982, a number of us were gathered at that open site, having walked a climbing, twisting path from the roadside ... We watched down below as the coffin with its burden was taken from the hearse, and a gathering of pallbearers, bearing their burden, began the difficult task of bringing that silver-gray coffin up the tortuous hillside path to the open grave. Finally, the task was complete with a proper placement of the coffin over the open grave, and the ministration of last rites for the dead man began.*
>
> *His wife of 36 years, half of his lifetime, sat at his graveside in a final public farewell to her husband. ... I recalled that, just a few days prior to this service, I had accompanied the wife to this grave-site selected by her. And I had heard her murmur in a torn, sorrowing voice, "Don't you think this is a beautiful spot? Bob would have liked it here."*

Numerous laudatory obituaries were published in San Francisco, Los Angeles, and even Macon, Georgia newspapers. "The notices served to make readers more aware of this black man's achievements." The accounts, according to Willis, "revealed a man who had left his personal compassionate imprint upon his accomplishments, which appeared to link, inextricably, race relations and equal opportunity in public policy."

There was an additional outpouring of condolences, testimonials, and remembrances that appeared in the newspapers after Bob's death, or were sent to Mattalyn, his widow. The effect of this was to fuel a determination among several of Bob's colleagues and friends to see some permanent memorial made to Bob in the two cities that had benefited the most from his passion for practical, community-led urban renewal—Los Angeles and San Francisco. Mattalyn, in particular, was tireless in her letter-writing campaign, securing the support of US Representatives Sala Burton, Barbara Boxer, and Ronald Dellums; Mayors Lionel Wilson (Oakland), Tom Bradley (Los Angeles), and Diane Feinstein

(San Francisco); and numerous other Federal executives and prominent colleagues Bob had worked with for all those years.

In Los Angeles Mayor Bradley, who had long been a friend of Bob's, together with many in the city government and in the community of Watts, still felt indebted to Bob for the enormous effort he put into the redevelopment of that area after the riots of 1965. They wanted to demonstrate the city's gratitude, and through their efforts the Los Angeles City Council, in 1985, authorized the renaming of the Watts Westminster Neighborhood Center to be "The Robert B. Pitts Westminster Neighborhood Center." The Neighborhood Center was the first new building built in the Watts neighborhood after the riots, and was built with funding directly resulting from Bob's involvement as the Regional Administrator of HHFA/HUD. Bob was one of the speakers at its original dedication ceremony in 1968. In 1975 the center's main tenant, the Mafundi Institute, vacated, and the building was taken over and renovated by the city of Los Angeles to be a center that would house both public and private agencies serving the greater Watts community. Bob was invited as a special guest to the dedication ceremony of the renovated neighborhood center in 1978. On Wednesday, February 20, 1985, yet another ceremony, the renaming ceremony, was held to permanently associate the building with its benefactor. The Pitts Neighborhood Center continues to serve the neighborhood, and is currently home to the Watts Happening Coffee House and to a charter high school operated through the LA Conservation Corps.

On August 28, 1986, the city of San Francisco followed suit with a resolution that the new Yerba Buena Plaza West development under construction by HUD be named, upon completion, the Robert B. Pitts Housing Development. The development was considered a landmark for its innovative design. Every unit in the Victorian-styled complex was a private space with clear visual separation from its neighbors. Each had private access to a common inner court and play areas, features that enhanced security and as well as aesthetics over the previous generation's high-rise developments. Extensive community participation was a part of the entire redevelopment project, which was one of the hallmarks of Bob's leadership style and thus made the choice of memorial to Bob particularly fitting. The project was once considered a showcase of successful Federal-city partnership in public housing.

Since 1947, Bob had lived in and loved California—and California loved him back. But, perhaps the greatest memorial to Bob Pitts is simply the memory of a man who believed in himself and in his ability to make a difference. Some of the friends who knew him best offer this conclusion:

Mr. Pitts exemplifies the best of American life; the hard-working American who, by virtue of his own efforts and dedication overcomes handicaps to become one of his nation's most effective leaders. Entering the Federal civ-

il service virtually at the bottom, working for many years at a time when advancement for Negroes was difficult at best, Mr. Pitts demonstrated the qualities of patience and dedication that have made him one of the outstanding Federal administrators. It is typical of Mr. Pitts that he has sought no glory or prominence for himself; he is satisfied to let others take the credit; his satisfaction comes in seeing genuine improvement in the lives of Americans, particularly the poor.[62]

---

62   Nomination, Rockefeller Public Service Award..

Above Left: With Bob Johnson (left), West Point, NY
Above Right: Ballard graduation (Bob; top middle)

Below: Talladega Sphinx club. Bob: back left
Willis: front row, center

Left: Bob in Italy, during or just after the war, in a photo he sent home to Mattalyn: ("Hello 'Little Girl'")

Below: With his regiment. (back row, second from right)

Bob, atop Mt. McKinley in Alaska

Above: Bob, early career in Seattle

Below left: Bob and Mattalyn at home in Mill Valley (Mattalyn in a dress of her own design)
Below: Bob with Sis, while visiting Ann Arbor, Michigan

Mattalyn and Bob,
at Ray's house in Sacramento, California

Bob, at his desk as HUD Regional Administrator

Bob, left. Weaver, center: with other HUD Executives.

Left: Bob, with
Hawaii Senator
Daniel Inouye

Below: Bob, with
San Francisco Mayor
Joseph Alioto

Bob, awarded Los Angeles City Council Resolution in his honor.
l to r: John Gibson, Bob, Emma McFarlin, Gilbert Lindsay, Judson Howard

Bob (post retirement), with nephew Nat

Mattalyn (center) accepts a posthumous resolution
naming the Robert B. Pitts Westminster Neighborhood Center.
Pictured with Los Angeles Mayor Thomas Bradley
and City Councilwoman Joan Milke Flores

Raymond Jackson Pitts

As the third of four sons, Ray was strongly influenced by his older brothers and their prior experiences. In a personal memoir, Ray gave the following account[1] of his early family life:

> I, Raymond Pitts, was born in Macon, Georgia, June 21, 1911, the third of four sons. My home life was happy, as I know it, and shaped by my parents' upbringing of two older brothers. They went to church; I went to church. They were christened in church and had a Godmother; I was christened in church and had a Godmother. They went to East Macon school; I went to East Macon school, and had almost the same teachers. They learned to take care of the "Boy's Room;" I learned to take care of the "Boy's Room." They became paperboys, carriers of the Macon Telegraph; I became a paperboy and carried the Macon Telegraph. Our parents, both graduates of Booker T. Washington's Tuskegee Institute, taught us well the reading, writing and arithmetic skills that satisfied our teachers at school. They also taught well how to earn money for baseball bats and gloves, books, and dimes for movie theater fares—and all of the extra things that growing boys want and need to make life enjoyable.

But the family troubles of the late 1920s affected Ray differently than his older brothers. In a taped conversation with Nathan about their early lives, he related:

> I was in the setting, but I didn't perceive of it as a deteriorating setting. At that time, I was headed for college and my whole goal was to get into college. When Willis came back from college, I would go through all of the things he had from college—his yearbooks, his notes—and I knew most of the people that he knew because he'd talk about them. That's' how I got to be an Alpha. I knew those people; knew who to contact when I got there. But at home, I just blocked out anything that did not have to do with my going to college.
> It is difficult for me to put in perspective the deterioration of the family.

---

1 Because Ray was a prolific writer who left voluminous records—as well as four children—wherever possible this chapter is told in his own words or those of his heirs. Ray's professional papers are preserved at the Amistad Research Center, Tulane University, New Orleans, Louisiana.

What I do remember is that Willis and Bob were each bought a wardrobe trunk to go to college. I didn't get a new one, but one of theirs was given to me when I planned to go. I recall Sis said to me, "You have the money [from the paper route—about seventy-five dollars] to stay in school. If you get through the first year and still have some money, stay there." So, I didn't come home the first year. The new man coming in [to teach Physics] gave me a job in the Physics lab, and on the bases of that[2] I was able to stay in school, with Sis sending me five dollars a month for "incidentals."

One other difference for Ray was the presence of a steady girlfriend, through both the latter years of high school and during college. About this sweetheart, Kathleen Lenora (Kay) Cook, he wrote:

Kathleen Cook was born in Soperton, Georgia the fourth of nine children. She was the oldest of the four girls in the family. Kathleen came to Macon in 1921[3] and entered grade four at the Pleasant Hill school. She lived with her brother James in East Macon for one year, and entered Green Street School to finish grade seven. In 1925, she enrolled in the eighth grade at Ballard Normal School. Kathleen too had been well schooled in "the three R's;" and in the Macon setting in which she lived, a seamstress taught her the skills needed to earn money for activities of a young high school girl.

It was at Ballard, during our high school days, that we first became friends. I was grade ten and not too interested in the groups of girls that my friends, my younger brother Nathan, and I walked past while making our daily four mile walk across the Ocmulgee River's Spring Street bridge to Ballard Normal School. My best friend, Edinburgh Hubbard, became interested in one of Kathleen's friends. Kathleen and I were purposely introduced so that four of us could "double date." From that point on our relationship grew and we became high school "sweethearts."

When he arrived at Talladega, Ray looked up the Alpha members he knew so well from his older brothers' tales. He immediately joined the Sphinx Club, the club for those planning to pledge Alpha Phi Alpha. He pledged Alpha in 1929, served as its Secretary in 1930–31, and as its President in his senior year. Maintaining an honors GPA during his entire time at Talladega, Ray also played on the varsity basketball squad, belonged to the Little Theater and various other clubs, and enjoyed the college social life. Lonely for his high school sweetheart, he occasionally wrote to ask if she minded if he took another girl to some event. But more often, he wrote to encourage her to also come to Talladega when she graduated:

---

2   For at least some of the four years, he also received financial assistance from the college. For the 1931–32 school year, his student aid was $100, paid in three installments.

3   Living with extended family in order to attend school, and returning to Soperton in the summers.

You must come over and spend a year before you know what TC really is. After you've spent your first year here you will not want to leave. ... I fell so deeply in love with the college that I didn't want to leave for fear I would stay out as my brothers did. ... What is stressed more here than at any other college, I believe, is scholarship. ... Scholarship, however, is not the only side of the college life. ... I was lucky enough to attend the Inter-Fraternal dance. It was the best dance I've been to in my life. ... We have movies and lectures to which a young man may take his lady friend. ... We have all kinds of athletics. I was lucky enough to play on the varsity basketball squad. The men's gymnasium has a swimming pool and just about all one could wish for. Just everything we have here I can't mention. You must come over next year when you finish. You couldn't go to a better place.

Another time Ray sent her an entertaining essay he called "A Day in the Life of a Talladega Sophomore." Apparently the constant encouragement and pleading letters did the trick. Kathleen, together with three of her Ballard classmates, arrived in the fall of 1930.

One of the things Ray loved about Talladega was traveling with the varsity basketball team. In addition to the one surprise encounter with his brother Bob playing for the opposing team,[4] he once met a family hero, George Washington Carver, when the team played at Tuskegee:

It was my second year traveling with the Talladega College basketball team. Our two cars carried a squad of ten players, five in each car with coach/driver. Traveling as we did in those days, we left our College Campus around 10:00 A.M. on Friday and would travel for 4 or 5 hours to reach Tuskegee by mid-afternoon. On this day, the last Friday in January 1930, our basketball schedule called for us to play two games, Friday night and Saturday afternoon, at Tuskegee. We would live in the men's dorm for two nights and leave Tuskegee on Sunday after breakfast.

I played sports in college because I liked playing; but at college, it gave me the added advantage of visiting other college campuses and meeting people, both teachers and students. Visiting teams, in those days, were considered as guests and were given campus tours and Saturday evening socials, usually dances. Assigned students and selected faculty served as our hosts. It was during a campus tour that I met and talked with George Washington Carver, one of the great scientists of that era. ... Dr. Carver had been at the institute when both my parents were there, and two certificates bearing his signature adorned the walls of the living room of my childhood. ... Dr. Carver [looked] much older now than the science teacher described by my parents ... but he still wore the collar and tie and the rose in the lapel of his threadbare coat.

---

4   Related in more detail in the chapter on Bob.

His apron was soiled with the dirt and chemicals of his trade; but he greeted us by shaking our hands and expressing appreciation for our visit to his "work place."... He said many things. I was both amazed and surprised at his high pitched voice; and it suddenly dawned upon me as I stood there listening; here was the same man whom I had seen seemingly "horsing around" with several students in the dorm as we were finding our rooms ... they appeared to be loudly debating some issue; and he, definitely the older and less well dressed, with his high pitched voice, seemed to challenge each statement; ... always smiling, but always challenging his younger colleagues. ...

Riding back to Talladega on Sunday morning, I hardly remembered the scores of our basketball games. But, my meeting with Dr. Carver helped me to be more determined to get back and really "hit the books" and work in the labs, to become more like the scientist I had just visited.

Ray drove himself and his girlfriend hard, convinced that the secret to life was to work to one's highest potential, and that education was key. In the summer of 1931, he wrote to Kay:

I have a chance to finish with an honor average if I work. If I make two more A's and no C's, I can do it. Nobody can beat me working when I want to, so I'll work like everything the first and second quarters. "K. L.," I don't want you to become discouraged because you made low marks last year. You can work and make up for all of that and I am sure you will, won't you? You have a schedule which is quite difficult and you must study to keep up. I don't want you to dodge difficult subjects, no, but take all that you can and do more than your best. You will do that for me at least won't you, "K. L."?

That summer, neither Ray nor Willis, who was again studying at Talladega, managed to find a job, either at the college or anywhere else. Returning home to Macon, Ray became discouraged. In his senior year, he renewed his efforts and was determined to find a way out of Macon and away from the depressed South. At the suggestion of his Physics professor, he visited Howard University in Washington, DC, and applied for a graduate fellowship in Physics. He was assured of his acceptance into the graduate school and that the stipend would be forthcoming. Now confident, he graduated Talladega in the spring of 1932 with a degree in Mathematics and Physics. He was then devastated when the promised graduate stipend at Howard did not actually materialize.

The Difficult Years

Ray and Willis did not find full-time jobs at all that year of 1932, in the midst of the depression.[5] They kept busy with athletics, and Ray began what

---

5   He did, however, relate that he had refused to write insurance for Atlanta Life in 1932—"I'd die first."

would become a life-long addiction to tennis. Trying his hand at freelance writing, Ray had least one article accepted by *The Congregationalist.*[6] (He does not mention being paid for it, but said that being published encouraged him during what was "a low period.") He was often disconsolate, fretting over the delay in beginning his envisioned future. For the first of several times over the next few years, he wrote to Kathleen intending to break-up with her:

> *You will never know how much you mean to me and how well I appreciate your friendship. ... Tomorrow I see you again. I shall not say that it is the last time, for events happen strangely. ... I love you very much but you are free to do whatever you wish—one exception, you must be something worthwhile. ... Although I love you dearly, I could not stand in your way. There are many reasons why I am driven to say this. You know that financially I am at a very low ebb and I cannot get along without money in anything. Also there is my ideal for which I am always striving and always will be. That, above all things, will be the outstanding thing in my life. So I must sacrifice something. I have very many things to do in this life and I will try to make each one better than the other. If I should set out to make you happy then I could not half do the job. Then you see why I say that. Believe me sweetheart. I do not feel that you should go without boy friends even this year just because of me. I shall expect you then to do what will make you happiest.*
>
> *For me, I think I can become very hard-boiled. As long as there are other things to think of, I do not have to think of love. So that athletics and other things can be used during my periods of diversion.*

That year, Willis and Ray collaborated on a play/pageant: *The Story of Ballard.* This first "Joint Pitts Bro. Act," was produced in May 1933 to a good audience and deemed "amazingly beautiful" in the newspaper review—although netting very little as a fund-raiser for the college. He wrote afterwards to Kathleen, "I shall feel lost without my regular work. Bro. Willis and I worked hand and hand on this. We have almost fought over some of the scenes and arrangements. He is a genius at handling people. Some of the characters don't think I am as friendly because I didn't humor them. I can only tell them what I think." Reminiscing years later about that difficult year in Macon, and working with Willis, he said, "The year after we graduated was when I really got to know the *quality* of Willis."

In his own words, Ray picks up the story of his years after Talladega:

> *The four years at Talladega, 1928–1932, had been "breakaway years" for me. In this ideal academic atmosphere, I had been literally shut-off from both family, and the world of work, and the economics of living. I didn't know how*

---

6   The denominational magazine of Congregational Churches, supporters of the American Missionary Association that founded Ballard Normal School and Talladega College.

competitive and sometimes cruel the off campus world could be. It had been my hope to continue my studies by going directly, either for a degree in engineering or for the PhD in physics. The five years between graduation in 1932 and admission to a graduate program in 1937 were the only real "downside" of my pursuit of a professional career. This period in my life requires a complete chapter in this story. During these years, I learned much about the people around me, about the American economic culture and climate, and more importantly, I learned much about myself.

My earnings during that down period were outweighed by my learnings nearly ten-fold. During that first year, without a position of any kind, I earned exactly 7 dollars, and that was for refereeing two basketball games in towns nearby. At one of these games [in Forsyth, GA], I learned from a Talladega Graduate teaching there that the Athletic Coach/Social Studies teacher was leaving. I applied for the position, landed my first contract for $50.00 per month for 9 months, and later found out it was cut to $45.00. This cut was for room and board as this was a "live-in" college—Forsyth State Teachers and Agricultural College. My teaching assignment was Social Science, a general studies course for freshmen; General Mathematics; and Geometry. Additionally, I was to coach Football, Track, and Basketball for men. Living and working at this school, one of three "Colleges for Negroes" operated by the state of Georgia during the period of "Separate but Equal," gave me an opportunity to observe the philosophy of Southern education for Black citizens in the State of Georgia, first hand and for the first time. For me the lessons learned at Forsyth in the year 1933–34 convinced me that I should not and could not work within the philosophy then existent in the State of Georgia.

With a brother in College at Florida A&M at Tallahassee, and my college roommate principal of a small rural high school, I wrote them about teaching positions in Florida. In the summer of 1934, I went to Tallahassee to satisfy the Florida teaching credential requirements, and in the fall I began teaching in the high school of DeFuniak Springs with the same teaching assignment but with a salary of $60.00 per month. After two years of teaching with a wonderful group of students and two area championship basketball teams, I went to Pensacola, principally to coach basketball—salary $80.00 per month.

At Pensacola, I took a hard look at myself and where I was going—farther and farther away from my chosen field [of] mathematics and engineering. Too, I had been able to save enough money to get to Ann Arbor, where I had former Talladega College schoolmates. In 1937, I made the decision to enter the University of Michigan, with the view of studying engineering, and leave the southeast forever.

In fact, Ray's desire to go to Ann Arbor for graduate school dated back to at least the spring of 1935, when he wrote to his "Dearest K." encouraging her to think of graduate study and attending there with him. The school had become a Mecca for black scholars from the state of Georgia. The state, not wanting to integrate their own graduate schools, offered financial assistance to black scholars willing to enroll elsewhere. Kathleen was then teaching at Lincoln Normal School in Marion, Alabama, and traveling in the summers with the Von Tobels on fund-raising trips for Ballard. Although Ray supported the opportunities this gave her, he sometimes complained that she seemed to have no time for him. That summer, able to visit together briefly in Macon between her trips, he secured her promise that they would have a future together—and he gave her an engagement ring.

Ray's early teaching career was at times discouraging. He wanted desperately to continue learning and to share a vibrant "life of the mind" with equally passionate friends, and with his "dear K. L." in particular. From Forsyth, he wrote to her of reading Eugene O'Neil and James Weldon Johnson, and remarked; "Life is interesting but I am greatly puzzled over many things ... I often wish I were around some very deep thinkers so that I could hear them express themselves on certain things. That is one of the reason I wish to study further, so that I might be able to think deeply; to puzzle out this thing called life." Later, at DeFuniak Springs, he despaired of fitting in with his peers and wrote:

> I try to be efficient, personally. I try to be straightforward in all of my dealings. Whenever I am given [a] job to do, I strive for perfection. More and more I am finding each day that very few people admire such qualities. In fact they discourage such qualities. I am wondering if I should continue to strive for perfection in my work or become carefree as most of my colleagues? In teaching I shall be a failure—at least in this type. I am not flashy enough. I shall never be. Personally, I think I shall stick to the course that I've chosen. If I loose out trying to be perfect then I'll just lose.

Possibly to substitute for his lack of sympathetic company, Ray took seriously to writing poetry, and reading the well-known works of others. He kept a journal in 1933–35 that remains carefully preserved in the family's archives. In it, he quoted Pasteur, Shakespeare, poets from the classical repertoire, and many of the era's great black poets. In his own poems, he explored girls, beauty, despair, questions about life, his dreams for the future, and his sense of duty.

To a Young Lad Dreaming (8/20/35)

Dream, Lad,
Dream of heights, unbounded—
Of hills, of mountain tops
Of far, far away stars;

Dream that you are among them
Rising – ever rising
Higher, and higher, and higher;
And then
Come down to earth,
And scale the hills
The high mountain tops.
And by your dream path
Soar on and up
To the stars.

By fall of 1935, Ray was feeling much more positive about teaching, yet he was still was anxious to move on and better himself. He wrote:

I think I am falling in love with my students here. I hope that I won't become so attached that it will be impossible to leave. ... My class work is getting along just fine. If you should step in my classroom one day you would be surprised at what goes on. I know that most of the things are going over.

He took a few graduate education courses at Atlanta University during the summer of 1936, where Willis was also enrolled in graduate study. He worked in Pensacola that fall, and for nearly a year he and Kathleen took a "vacation" from writing. The Pensacola job appears to have been more to his liking than DeFuniak Springs, at least in the beginning. He made a number of good friends and several of his colleagues, who had themselves attended graduate school in Ann Arbor, encouraged him to pursue that dream. The school at Pensacola even guaranteed him that a position would remain open, should he wish to return.

Thus, in the summer of 1937 Ray found himself at the University of Michigan in Ann Arbor. After enjoying the summer session, he decided for full time enrollment in the fall. He was again writing to Kathleen, and was enthusiastic about new opportunities. He was far more optimistic about his future than at any time in the past several years. Although asking her if they must take another mutual break from each other, he argues strongly for the opposite:

Interesting though life is, I want you more than ever. I had a girlfriend this summer who was very understanding, but that is not like Kay and I am tiring of substituting. Each day I wonder how I can get you here and keep you. Personally, as long as it is not too much of a loss, I want to remain here. So you must be here somehow. If things work out well you shall.

Instead, Kathleen accepted a teaching position in Fort Valley, Georgia, and again Ray found their communication sporadic and disappointing. In January of 1938, he wrote:

Last Christmas – no word from Kay; this Christmas – no word from Kathleen. I go on expecting them; yet there is none. ... I find myself becoming very indifferent and in some instances very intolerant towards the girl I once thought so much of. Even distance can shatter what I once thought was infallible. ... I shall not write again for a long time. In that time I shall forget—at least try to—that you exist. I shall continue to work for what I've always hoped to be mine. And knowing that like all other things for which I work it will be disappointing when I reach that goal, I shall set them higher. As is often said, the joy is in the striving. ... You will do me a kindness of not answering this and just forgetting for a time that I exist. ... So, best wishes for 1938 and every other year thereafter.

Marriage and Family

Ray completed his Masters degree in Mathematics that spring of 1938. He, of course, had not forgotten his Kay as he had threatened, nor did she forget him. Rather than follow his dream of leaving teaching and the South forever, he chose to accept a teaching position near where she would be teaching in the fall, and set about to rekindle the romance.

Ray's Alpha Phi Alpha brother from Talladega, Waldo E. Blanchet, was now Dean and Head of the Science Department at Fort Valley Normal and Industrial School. Blanchet recommended Ray for a summer teaching position in rural Baxley, Georgia, and then for a faculty teaching position at Fort Valley in the fall, as "Instructor of Physical Science and Mathematics, and Coach of Women's Basketball and Track." As he told it to his family later in life, Ray agonized that summer about Kathleen: thinking of her enjoying summer school classes in Atlanta, perhaps making new boyfriends, and truly forgetting about him. He poured out his troubles to his best and most constant advisor, his mother, and she told him—"Well then, go up there and marry her!" So, he did.

In his memoir, Ray wrote:

Kathleen L. Cook and Raymond J. Pitts were married in Atlanta, Ga., at historic First Congregational Church. Reverend John C. Wright, the father of one of our Talladega College schoolmates, Peggy, was the officiating minister. Naomi Lucas, a Ballard schoolmate of both of us, and Robert N. Perry, a friend of ours, were the attendants. The ceremony was performed July 20, 1938 at nine o'clock in the evening.

Getting married on July 20 required fast movement on the part of both of us. There had been little time for preparation. Ray had come to Atlanta University on Monday to visit with Kathleen during her summer study. On Tuesday we discussed getting married and found that the County Offices in

Atlanta were closed on Wednesday; so we could not get a marriage license. Learning that we could get a license in Cobb County, Kathleen borrowed Mrs. Xenia Ray Stephens' car and we drove, with Naomi, to Marietta.

Obtaining the license at that quaint Cobb County Courthouse was a significant initial experience for both of us. We often laughed about the scene; three old, white, gray-bearded bench sitters gazed curiously at us as we approached, and followed us inside. We think they were all "professional witnesses." The clerk inside was startled but curiously courteous as we filled out the application. Then Alfred Blackwell, one of our former bench sitters, played his role as witness. His signature with that of Naomi made the application legal. We were of the legal age and could be married as of "today" as we indicated on the line, "date of contemplated marriage?"

The wedding ceremony was simple but profound. There were no guests. The attendants, Robert and Naomi, were well aware of the long friendship that had developed into a full and mature relationship. Kathleen had kept the wedding ring, along with an engagement ring, since 1935 when we had visited briefly in Macon. They were used in the ceremony. Reverend White must have been briefed about us, for his words to us were meaningful and we have remembered them for these fifty years. ... Following the ceremony, the four of us had our first dinner at Black Atlanta's "Cat and the Fiddle." The food was good Southern Fried Chicken with all the trimmings and we followed it with a night ride through Atlanta City streets.

Ray returned to his teaching position and Kathleen to her summer school. The separation was difficult, but the tone of Ray's letters changed dramatically:

With you now it will be different. There will be the inspiration of you there, and I'll probably do more. You have always embodied all that was good and beautiful and true for me; so much so that I thought too much of you. These recent years caused me to be very bitter at times only because I began to loose faith even in you. With you now I can, perhaps, accomplish the dreams of my youth. Someday I'll tell you the whole story of the little boy who has been thinking, dreaming, planning, and working all his life and will continue to do so.

The two finally moved in together as a married couple that fall, living in Ohio Hall, the college men's dorm and faculty housing, and eating in the dining hall. Both supplemented their teaching positions by teaching Saturday extension classes, and with the extra income provided, immediately began studying house plans. They hoped to build as quickly as possible because, by the fall, Kathleen was already pregnant with their first child.

When Ray had accepted the position at Fort Valley Normal and Industrial School (at that time a two-year junior college), negotiations were already underway to sever ties with the Episcopal Church and combine that school with the State Teachers and Agricultural College of Forsyth, to become a four-year college under the University System of Georgia. Horace Mann Bond,[7] an experienced college administrator, was brought in to lead the transition. Mr. Alva Tabor Sr., who as supervisor of Vocational Agricultural programs in the black Schools of Georgia and had an office at Fort Valley, deeded a lot near his own home to Ray and Kathleen "to pay for at your convenience." Eldest son Ray Jr. recalls that "the transaction was confirmed with a handshake. Even though Mr. Tabor died unexpectedly [several years later], Dad paid his dept in full to the Tabor family."

Securing an FHA-backed loan,[8] the newlyweds began construction. They proceeded to build quickly, and hoped to move in by Christmas. The new home was a necessity, as Frances Irene Pitts had been born at the college infirmary on the morning of May 25, 1939. Kathleen and Frances were welcomed back to Ohio Hall with a beautiful baby shower, but the faculty housing was much too cramped to accommodate a baby.

Considering the new baby to care for and the home construction underway in Fort Valley, Kathleen did not teach that fall. She and Frances moved to Macon to live with her sister Josephine Bell. There she planned furniture and fixtures for the new home, and visited Ray often using "Bro. Jim's Dodge." Thinking of the upcoming move, Ray wrote to them in December 1939:

> *Moving in our home means more than just another family moving. All through my life I've felt that always I should like to live in a community and be a decent community citizen. To me we must move and live there—live in the fullest sense of the word. Here are some of the questions that arise for us. We shall answer them with our lives—you, Frances and me.*
>
> *What shall be our attitude toward our neighbors both white and Negro? Shall we be a campus bound family or know the people who live around us? I think we ought to get to know and love our neighbors. ... What shall we do about the institutions in our community? Shall we go to church in the community? Yes. Shall we work on projects in the city like the nursery school? Yes. As taxpayers, shall we vote and take part in elections as far as we can? Yes. ... In our home, shall we develop religion as a real thing? Somehow, my idea of religion must be a bit different. It is put into practice, without show, without fanfare, without noise. I should like to get to know the real meaning of the life we live. ...*
>
> *I'm thinking of the books we must write, the flowers, vegetables and chickens we must grow. Of the sewing and upholstering we must do. Our lives will be rich after we've completed some of our projects. But there are years and*

7 Father of civil rights legend Julian Bond.
8 It was the first FHA-backed home built in Peach County, Georgia.

*years ahead of us and the more we do now the more we shall find to do as
the years go by. We shall have a beautiful home and we shall have real joy in
keeping it beautiful.*

For Christmas, Ray presented Kathleen with the keys to their new home, although the move in date had to be postponed until late January due to flooding.
Until they could move in, Ray, Kathleen, and little Fran were welcomed into
the home of the college President, Horace Bond. The college community took
care of its own. And tiny house though their new house was, when they finally
moved into it they invited fellow faculty member William Hale Jr., with his wife
Helene, to live with them until they too could move into a home of their own.
Even before the house was completely furnished, Ray and Kay began hosting
major parties and campus events, earning an enduring reputation as the premier
campus party-givers.

Under Bond's leadership, the college focused on teacher training, grew sub-
stantially, and doubled its annual income. As was common in those days, Bond
had taught in numerous academic institutions while studying for his PhD,
working up the ladders of academics and administration simultaneously. He
encouraged his ambitious faculty to do likewise, and Ray jumped at the chance.
In the summer of 1940, Ray returned to the University of Michigan, seizing the
opportunity to live with brothers Willis and Nathan, who were also studying
there. Kathleen returned with Fran to her former teaching position in Adrian,
Georgia, and the house (now fully furnished) was rented to friends for nineteen
dollars per month, enough to cover the mortgage.

Ray wrote faithfully from Ann Arbor, encouraging Kathleen to "practice
her writing," exercise faithfully, improve her tennis, and think about coming to
Ann Arbor for the summer session. He also related much about Michigan and
what the campus life was like, mentioning his surprise at the Northerner's lack
of fashion sense: "The people here do not make as much over their clothes as we
Southerners." It was a time when the inevitability of the US joining the war in
Europe was becoming apparent, a war that would carry both his elder brothers
into the armed services. He worried about his own chances of being called up in
the draft, and about what war might do to his little family. The prospect of war
was already changing life on campus.

> *There are many people here who I think are war refugees. I am taking
> a class under one Dr. Eilenberg, a young Jewish mathematician (very bril-
> liant, incidentally) whose clothes make me wish I had brought along that
> brown suit. He escaped from Poland before the Nazis got in. ... In that class
> is a young lady who must be a very recent comer. She is the wife of one of the
> new professors. ... She says she is taking the course so that she can talk with
> her husband, who is incidentally another Jew named Kaplin. She is quite*

intelligent but looks rather homely—I think that is the way you would say it. Her clothes have made me wish I had brought some of yours along. Her hair is always flying.

Ray was sympathetic with the war refugees, but unfortunately for him and the other black graduate students, he also found that teaching assistantships and choice campus jobs tended to be reserved for the refugees, and for German intellectuals being wooed away from their troubled country. The North was not like the South, but segregation and discrimination were still the rule of the day. The black graduate students were consigned to work in the dining hall, to domestic service, or to manual labor.

Ray was disappointed, when he returned home for Christmas, to find out that his little "Dadoo" (that is, Frances; alias "Sugar Doll") did not remember him, even after daily being put to sleep while looking at his photo. Ray certainly never forgot his little daughter while he was away. Being an avid reader and learner, he peppered his letters home with advice on child rearing:

> *I am particularly glad to hear about Frances and her development. I am not sure that I can find any information on her word count; but I am happy to know that you are keeping up with it. Teach her more sounds, and teach her to tell stories. ... The more interest you take in her the more she will develop. I saw in Look [magazine] the picture of a two year old who could dress and undress herself. How is Frances coming with that?[9] She should be learning that, to wash her face and hands, and some few other things. ...*
>
> *She must look sweet in her little apron. Let her wash her own socks, pants, etc. She will appreciate doing it. I am sure that you know how many things she can learn and that you will teach them to her. Do teach her many things. No one else will.*

Ever the academic, Ray studied marriage as well as child rearing. In February of that year he sent Kathleen the book *Personality and Family* by Hornell Hart and Ellen B. Hart. He wrote:

> *I am having sent to you a book for us. It is one of the best I have seen here. Later we shall discuss it. Tell me what you think of it when it arrives. I read a few pages every day. Some parts of it I read over and over. There is so much [in] it that we must discuss. I'm learning to be a good husband. Maybe someday I shall be. At least I think I'm on the right road.*

And later:

> *I hope you will read the whole book; but tell me what you think about the chapters mentioned. ... I find it very inspiring and quite helpful, especially the*

9   She was 21 months at the time of the letter.

chapters on "creative relations between husband and wife" and "parents and children." Read them carefully.

Ray was counting the days until Kathleen would join him for the summer in Ann Arbor. Somewhat reluctantly, she had enrolled to take summer graduate classes in elementary education. He wrote, "I have not been myself this year. My work has suffered accordingly. ... That is why I say we shall not be apart again, not for any length of time anyway." And another time, "I wish I were there to bid my sweethearts goodnight. They don't know how much I miss them." However, it was not just loneliness that motivated Ray to bring Kay to Ann Arbor. He always believed that she should take advantage of the opportunity to develop her full potential, just as he did. He wrote, "I like to think of having you here because your further development will add so much to both Frances and me, and I'm sure you will enjoy your stay here. I will see to that." He also informed her that she should practice her tennis, as he was playing tennis every Tuesday with his brothers and was getting quite good. "When you are here we might get in some good sets. That is why I want you to be good."[10] Succumbing to his pleas, Kathleen left Frances in the keeping of her sister, Josephine,[11] and lived for the summer of 1941 with Ray, Willis and Nathan at 1005 Catherine St., Ann Arbor, Michigan. However when Frances did not recognize them or want to go home with them when they returned in the fall, Ray vowed he would never again leave his children behind.

When the young family returned to Fort Valley, Kathleen took a position teaching in Peach County schools; but the position was not to last long. She was out on maternity leave the following February, and gave birth to the family's second child, Raymond J. Pitts Jr., on March 4, 1942. In the fall, she started employment as a mathematics teacher at Hunt High School; a position that she kept for the remainder of the time the family lived in Fort Valley. Ray, who had been saving American Home magazines for some time, began to implement many of his decorating and home economics ideas around the property. He started a side business that spring selling chickens and eggs[12] "to the college dining hall at top prices." And true to his vow to be an active citizen and involved in the community, he petitioned with Mr. Tabor to have the name of their road changed from "Shuffletown Road" to "Carver Drive."

Proud of his two children and the home he and Kay had made for them, Ray

---

10   Considering his constant instructions to train Frances, study the book on marriage and family, and learn tennis—together with her responsibilities of teaching full time, caring for an infant, and managing Ray's business affairs in Fort Valley while living in Adrian—one cannot help but conclude that the ever "sweet" and patient Kathleen was a true saint!

11   A difficult decision for both. Ray wrote; "Perhaps she knows her Daddy is thinking of her. I know we both shall miss her and I wish she might come. Don't make me say bring her."

12   While in Ann Arbor, he had written to Kathleen, "I wish that she [Frances] had some chicks for the spring. Next year I must get her some to play with. I think I'll teach her to feed them. She will like that."

was eager to show it all off. The little family traveled to Macon frequently to visit family members of both who lived there. But that year for Father's Day, despite their somewhat estranged relationship, Ray invited his father Willis Sr. to visit them in Fort Valley. Sis came, in turn, to visit over the Christmas holidays.

By 1943 the little family was well settled into the routine of the college and the social life it afforded. Ray purchased a Chow as a pet for the children, and named it Lin Yutang after his favorite author. They had an excellent garden (tomatoes, beets, okra), and Kathleen canned peaches and pears, becoming noted for her green and pink pears in glass jars: green and pink were her Alpha Kappa Alpha sorority's signature colors.[13] Ray continued perfecting his tennis game and played in the Georgia State Tournament. Kathleen became pregnant again and, on February 25, 1944, Kathleen Norma (Kathy) Pitts was born at their home on Carver Drive. That fall, Ray was promoted from Assistant to Associate Professor of Mathematics.[14]

Then in the summer of 1945, the little family moved to Ann Arbor where Ray, on a year's leave from his teaching position, was to again study at the University of Michigan. Kathleen took a teaching position there at Kambly School for Special Children, and also took classes at the "U of M," in special education. Sis, who had retired from her teaching position in North Carolina, came to live with them. Kathleen packed up children and dog, and the whole family moved into a house they rented from the grandmother of Ray's tennis partner. A friend who was a pre-medical student also lived with them. When Willis Jr. got out of the service, he moved in as well. Their Aunt Mittie from Detroit came to visit that fall, and early the next spring brother Bob came to visit, after he too had been discharged from the service. Bob's new bride Mattalyn came two months later, on her way to join Bob in Seattle.

In August 1946, the family returned to Fort Valley, minus Sis who went to live with Willis in veteran's housing in Ann Arbor. Although by this point Ray had completed the coursework required for the PhD in Mathematics, he was not allowed to take the preliminary examinations nor to enter into the dissertation phase of the degree program.[15] The family traveled home via train from Chicago, where an influential friend had managed to get them smuggled into a family Pullman car (at the time, blacks were not allowed in the premier cars). The porters smuggled them meals and other necessities, but daughter Frances remembers how they could not leave the car for the entire trip, for fear of being caught.

Once at home, the family plunged into Fort Valley home-life and commu-

---

13   Also to honor Kay (and because Ray would have wanted it), this book's cover design is in green and pink.

14   He was awarded Full Professor in 1946 and also served, for a time, as Chair of the Mathematics Department.

15   He was told, "We've never yet given a PhD in Mathematics to a black man, and we're not going to start now."

nity activities. Frances, who remembers her parents as an elegant, affectionate couple, reminisced about those days in Fort Valley:

Our life in Ft. Valley revolved around the intellectual atmosphere of a college campus. Everything we did was connected to that. We basically lived on the campus and were members of that community. The dinner bell was rung to tell the students to come to dinner, and that was our cue to come home. On Friday nights they had a Lyceum program, with famous artists, opera, drama, etc. We would go over to the campus and sat with the other faculty families—all the faculty children were brought there. That group of faculty kids still all like art, opera, museums, etc. We have another way of looking at life than our contemporaries. In this sense we were very different from the community outside the campus.

Our parents and our friends' parents were college educated in elite black colleges (often times having been taught by Northern white missionaries who came South specifically to educate Negroes). We knew we were different from the rest of the community. The expectations for us were different. College was a given—where we went depended on where our parents went, but we knew we were going. We were ostracized in the public schools because our family circumstances were so different: we were the privileged teachers' kids. But Mother and Dad were seen by others as kind and generous, and we were expected to be polite, kind and empathetic to the "others" around us. However, we were also expected to be better, and to achieve more. I had little additional exposure to the town kids I went to school with, but when I did see them, we were all aware that there were obvious class differences that kept us from more closely relating to each other. The differences are still there.

When I was a tiny girl, we got our eggs from the Tabors, who were just across the field. I would walk across the field to go and get eggs, milk and butter, which seemed like a long way to me at the time. Later, we raised chickens in our backyard and traded eggs and chickens for other things with farmers coming down the road to town. Even when we no longer had chickens the farmers would remember their "good friend" and sometimes leave excess produce on our porch.

Mother and Dad were the only faculty who owned a house. Some of the administrators did, and Mr. Tabor had a house, but most of the faculty lived in faculty housing.[16] Mother was accustomed to giving big gatherings. All over campus, they (mostly Mother) were known for their parties. Mother did it—Dad went along. Theirs was "the party house": even though it was a tiny house, it was more than the others had. They also went to parties. They were always getting dressed up and going to parties, leaving us at home. They would bring us party favors, but we didn't go with them. Sometimes someone

---

16   Generally called "the barracks," because of the brick construction reminiscent of Army barracks.

stayed with us but often we stayed alone, since the college was really just next-door. We always tore the house up when they were gone. One time they came home and the bed was broken down, because we'd been jumping on it. They were exhausted that night so they just slept on the floor, but we heard about it the next day!

One of my favorite memories took place just after the war. They used to give dances at the college for the black soldiers.[17] Mother noticed how Ruthie Merriweather and her group enjoyed entertaining the black soldiers. Ruthie was a basketball player that dad coached. She met and fell in love with Sergeant Chester Hodges at these dances. After they dated for a few months, they wanted to "run off" and get married. Mother said, "Don't do that! I will give you a little luncheon and you come have the wedding in our back yard." It was supposed to be just a "small gathering," but Mother mentioned it to the head of the college food service, who promised to make a wedding cake. Word got out, and when it happened they had a gigantic party. Everyone—nearly all the faculty—came trudging across the field to the house for the ceremony. Mother was pregnant with Nat at the time. I remember Dad running across from work, alarmed at seeing Mother, pregnant, standing on a ladder decorating the house! I met the Hodges again as an adult when we moved to St. Louis. Ruthie told me that party lived forever in their memory.

With a fourth child on the way, home remodeling was in order. They converted the existing dining room into a master bedroom, making the other two bedrooms a "boy's room" in the back and "girl's room" in the front, and converted the breakfast room and screen porch into a new dining room with glass walls. A piano was also added, for Fran to continue the lessons she began in Ann Arbor. Then on April 2, 1947, Nathaniel Gilbert [Nat] Pitts, the couple's fourth and last child, was born at St. Luke's hospital in Macon.

The Fort Valley Days

As the little family grew, life took on a rhythm of work, study and family. Ray and Kay resumed their regular jobs at the college and at the high school across the street from it. When Willis Sr., Ray's father, died in the summer of 1948, Sis came for the funeral and then stayed with the family to help out with the children until Christmas. The following summer, after completing summer school in Library Science in Ann Arbor, Ray purchased the family's first car in Detroit, while visiting Aunt Mittie. He had to hire a friend to drive it home for him, as he had never yet learned to drive.[18] The children were all active in school, church,

---

17   Fort Benning and Robins Air Force base are both nearby..

18   Kathleen, the farm girl, had previously done all the family's driving: knowing how to drive was a necessity on the farm.

athletics and summer camp, and when Macon got a new swimming pool, open to colored people, all the children except baby Nat took swimming lessons.

In June 1950 the whole family, minus the dog Tang, left for a year of study in Ann Arbor, renting a place at 924 Woodlawn. Barred from the PhD program in Mathematics, Ray had entered the Mathematics Education program in the summer of 1948; still intent on eventually obtaining education's highest degree. Sis came to them that year, from living with Bob and Mattalyn in San Francisco. She continued to live with them until they left Ann Arbor to return to Fort Valley the following summer. Then she moved in with Willis and Frances, who had just returned to Ann Arbor so that Willis could finish his PhD. Ray's children recall that Sis was always welcome with her other sons, but she preferred their household with its noisy brood. Sis, by then, was frail, with high blood pressure, "sugar diabetes," and an essential tremor that left her voice "wobbly." Nevertheless, both girls remember her fondly, and talk of having to comb her hair and take care of her wigs. Although she pinched when they were naughty, they describe her as "affectionate but not interfering."

That year of 1950–51, on the trips both to and from Ann Arbor, the family took the time to travel together and visit friends—Washington, DC; Cambridge, Massachusetts; Cranston, Rhode Island; Niagara Falls, New York; Chicago, Illinois; and Louisville, Kentucky were among the stops. They returned to find Tang, who had been left in the care of friends, old and broken down. He had to be put to sleep. But, their cherished little house and garden were in good condition and waiting for them to resume their normal Fort Valley life. Ray had completed the coursework for his degree and passed the preliminary exams. He had hoped to remain in Ann Arbor, solo, to finish his dissertation, but the necessary leave from Fort Valley and financial support were not forthcoming. He would not return until September 1955, ultimately completing the degree in August 1956.

Asked about their family life, daughter Kathy recalled:

> *Mother and Dad were a great team. Neither was dominant, and they worked together. It was a strong family. Dad didn't know what to do with girls, I don't think. They boys grew up mowing lawns and having paper routes. We girls were expected to work, but he wasn't sure what things girls did. I was not a classic "Daddy's girl," but I think I was closer to Dad than Fran was. Fran was closest to Mother.*
>
> *Dad brought us up to think for ourselves and to make good decisions. He trusted us—to a point—but if he thought we made a bad decision he made a different decision for us. But he usually didn't so much give advice as give his commentary on life. There was always a good message in it. He wasn't upset if you didn't take his advice or think his way, unless he thought it was important. Then he didn't hesitate to make the decision for you.*

Dad was a quiet influence. He expected the best out of himself and out of those closest to him. He wanted us to do the very best we were able to in school and in life. We were expected to be involved in the community and church, to volunteer, to take music lessons and be in clubs and sports. Music was important in the house. Mom sang and played piano. She had been a soloist as a girl and traveled all over the country with the Von Tobels, both as a singer to raise money for the school and as a companion for their daughter Harriet. Dad sang and played Mandolin or Ukulele. He was not really a musician, but that was what folks did back then. Music was our entertainment. I remember the piano was important in our house. We often sang Mocking Bird Hill. There are 6 verses and there were six of us, so we each had our own verse. I have a photo of us all in front of the piano that brings back those memories.

Ray was building a prominent role for himself in Fort Valley, both at the college and in the community. He especially enjoyed exposing his children to the cultural and athletic opportunities afforded by the campus. Ray Jr. recalled being recruited to assist with the basketball team:

As long as I can remember, we were good friends. Dad was someone I enjoyed being around. He seemed aware of my pleasure in interacting with people of all ages and backgrounds, and he appreciated the magnetic pull athletics had for me. With these shared interests as a base, our friendship flourished. He carefully guided me toward activities that gave me access to people within a college town setting. There I would meet students and educators who had traveled the world and returned with a variety of understandings and experiences. Dad carefully geared me toward energies and programs that were likely to instill his own character of personal responsibility, and his own conviction that people can seem very different and yet have similar basic needs.

The simple joy of traveling from the small town of Fort Valley to Macon on the team bus with his university basketball teams became the focus of my adventures. I had the additional responsibly of passing out the sandwiches and sliced oranges, which I was charged with picking up from the dining [service] prior to each game. I grew into relationships with many of the team members, and I was always on time for practices at the end of my school day. I was proud to know that the players themselves were proud to call me "Little Pitts."

In 1948 a young Catherine Hardy had joined the basketball team Ray coached, and he had noticed unusual talent. He encouraged her to try out for women's track, which he also coached, and she was a natural. For several years, Ray coached and counseled her, and even helped with financial support for her athletic pursuits. She went on to anchor the women's 4 x 100 relay track team in the 1952 Olympics (Helsinki, Finland). Hardy also set records for the 50-meter and 100-meter dashes, in earlier AAU[19] meets. The Olympic team came home with the gold medal, and Frances recalls that even the white people from town showed up for the parade that they gave Hardy in Fort Valley—a rare occasion indeed.

Ray started the first Georgia State High School Science Fair.[20] He established the Fort Valley State College statistics laboratory, which used ten Monroe electric calculators. He developed Fort Valley's College Mathematics and Teaching Secondary School Mathematics program for the qualification of future high school teachers, and extended his ideas for teacher education through establishing an annual meeting of science and mathematics teachers in black colleges at Fort Valley, under the auspices of the National Institute of Science.[21] He also organized and taught the first course in the home economics program on Marriage and Family Living. Ray was influential in obtaining scholarships, fellowships and teaching positions for many of his qualified students, and occasionally for fellow teachers and administrators. He assisted in establishing undergraduate and graduate chapters of Alpha Phi Alpha at Fort Valley, and a graduate chapter in Macon. He also served the campus on numerous committees and in other professional activities. He published research papers and participated in meetings of the American Mathematical Society, Mathematical Association of America, National Council of Teachers of Mathematics, American Educational Research Association, National Institute of Science, and the academic honorary societies Phi Delta Kappa (Education) and Beta Kappa Chi (Science).

For the community, Ray worked with his neighbor, Alva Tabor, to get sewers, water, lights, paving of the streets, and police protection for the growing college neighborhoods. The Pitts family had the neighborhood's first TV, and the house was always filled with students and faculty who wanted to watch it. Daughter Frances recalls that the TV store either gave it to him or sold it at a substantial discount, because they knew if they put a TV in the Pitts house, soon everyone would come in wanting to buy one. Asked what she remembered most about her father during this period of their lives, Frances recalled her father as "fearless":

When we were kids, the road to our house was unpaved. I remember whenever it rained it was just mud, good red Georgia mud. And Dad wanted it paved. Cars slipping off the road in the mud were a daily occurrence.

When Dad wanted something done, it usually got done. He went, uninvited, to a meeting of the white town fathers. He would have had to go in

---

19   Amateur Athletic Union of the United States.

20   In the black schools, leaving the white schools to establish their own science fair in order to keep up.

21   An organization established in 1943 to promote the professional growth of black mathematicians and scientists at the nation's historically black colleges and universities (HBCU). Ray served as the Institutes's President in 1955–56

the back door: he wouldn't have been allowed to go through the front door of the Town Hall. He went into the meeting and sat in the back where Negroes were required to sit. When the meeting was over, one of the men said to him, "Pitts, what can we do for you, tonight?" They would never have addressed him as "Mr." It was not done. Mother said he answered, "I want my street paved. I pay taxes in this town, and I want my street paved." Few Negroes at the time would have felt that they had a right to go and speak. On the other hand, the town fathers had a grudging respect for the college and those who worked there. I don't know much else except that our street was soon paved: to the end of our lot.

Another incident happened at church. We always sat on the left side, two rows from the front. This church had altar dressings made of brocade satin cloth that reached from the altar itself, up the back wall to an overhang that extended out over the altar. I sang in the choir, so my other teen aged friends and I were seated close to the altar and this overhang. One imagines that this decoration was essentially permanent. I don't know if they ever took it down to clean it, or when they dusted it. Anyway, one Sunday we were in the middle of the service when we watched a small fire start up the overhang. If you know anything about Episcopal Church services, they are very quiet. And everyone sat quietly, as if spellbound by the flames climbing up the wall. After a few moments Dad got out of his seat, genuflected at the altar, climbed onto part of the altar itself and put the flames out with his white handkerchief. Then he quietly climbed down, walked back, genuflected to the altar and sat down. The service went on as usual. I vaguely remember something about his hand being burned, but there was no big hoopla about it all. It just happened. We all expected Dad to do this sort of thing in various circumstances.

In the early 1950's, Ray started the Pitts, Rutland & Thompson Corporation (PRT, Inc.) with two Alpha brothers, intending to build homes similar to his own in the immediate neighborhood. They eventually built five homes, primarily intended to be faculty housing. He also was involved in the establishment of Fort Valley Community Builders, Inc., another business focused on real estate interests. They ambitiously intended, according to the articles of incorporation, to "carry out the business of establishing and conducting a general department store business, ... to operate a barbershop, beauty shop, cleaning plant, laundry, gasoline station, drug store, hotel and restaurant, and ... to operate a funeral home and ambulance service." The builders did invest in some houses, an apartment building, and a delivery service, but the corporation never grew to meet their original expectations.

Ray and his partners learned the hard way about business, and his idealism suffered over the realization that, even in close-knit communities, people's self-serving ways can derail promising projects. After generations with passive resistance their only tool to fight the economic subjugation of the Jim-Crow South, some blacks could not bring themselves to treat even the members of their own race any differently. Of the first three houses PRT, Inc., built and financed, two families were excellent partners who paid their mortgages regularly and on time, but the third family gave exactly one payment, in 1953. Even by 1959 the builders had neither been able to dislodge the family from the property nor extract any additional payments.

Contractors were difficult to work with, delays were a rule rather than an exception, funding was difficult to come by, and obtaining payment for services could be even worse. Even securing a clear title to the land on which they were building was a challenge. One series of letters with a building contractor, Nathan Pearson, is worth recounting. It provides a glimpse of the home construction and ownership realities of the time, and also shows that, while Ray had not lost the temper that once made the actors in the Ballard Normal pageant call him "difficult," he was not alone in his tendency toward either bluntness or taking offense.

Pearson (Nov 7, 1953): I regret very much that I could not finish the job in its entirety. ... I would have finished if I could have gotten the material. I was working under a great physical strain the last two weeks I was there.

Pitts (Dec 3, 1953): Your leaving left us in a very bad situation ... I, personally, seemed to have inherited a situation that I would have not agreed to in the first place. Among the many things, I would like to point out two that I feel is your responsibility to this group and for which you have been paid. ... Leaks are still persisting and I suggest that at your earliest convenience you ought to come here and stop them. This, any contractor would do on the job for which he is paid. ... Yesterday, I went under the Allen house and to my surprise every piece of bridging supporting the floor joists was not nailed at the bottom. Seemingly, it had been cut too long, and rather than cut them correctly and nail them they have been left hanging with the nails stuck in them. This should not be. ... My suggestion is that you owe it to this group to compete these things for which you have been paid.

Pearson (Dec 22, 1953): I plan to get by there some times during the holidays and see what your worries are all about. You numbered things to rake me over the coals about. Now I shall do the same for you. ... It is your best bet to always get a straight contract on your jobs. People with any kind of mechanical ability these days don't have to put up with a man like you. ... I am just as amazed as you were about the timbers hanging down under the house but, I'm amazed at you being that ignorant. For your information, those are left like that until the building has settled. A smart homeowner nails those him self after about three months. ... The largest mistake was made when they picked you for a partner. .... I'll be over there as soon as possible and do what I can at no cost to you. I also got more than I bargained for. I deal with men. I'm not an eighteen year old. ... Don't get me wrong now. I'm not angry but, I had to let you know you aren't dealing with those students in your class-room. Season's greetings to you and your family.

Presumably, the construction on the three PRT, Inc., houses was eventually completed satisfactorily, but Community Builders had more problems. In 1958, after several years of annual losses, his partner in both businesses, Stan Rutland, wrote to Ray (who was already living in California). "Community Builders has flopped. ... I guess we will soon dissolve the corporation. That is my guess." Ray replied, "When my autobiography is published, this story will be one of the documentation of the conflicting philosophies among Negroes and the consequences. The loss we suffered with Community Builders is totally unnecessary."

Life at the college was, as well, not always satisfying. When the family first moved to Fort Valley, it was a small Episcopal school in the early stages of transition to a four-year state college. President Bond wanted to emphasize teacher training and excellence of education. But Bond left in 1945 and the new President, Cornelius Troup, changed the emphasis from education to agriculture, started numerous graduate programs, and began heavily recruiting from the Northern black population as well as from the South. It changed the atmosphere of the campus drastically. The Northern black students didn't have the rules of the segregated South written in their veins, like their local counterparts. They didn't know how to behave, or understand the dangers of behaving differently. There were more conflicts with the town's white population who, being generally poor and not very well educated, already tended to resent the elite community of educated blacks.

Troup settled for less than what Ray considered to be "excellence in education," and the two clashed frequently over Ray's proposals for new classes and new laboratory services in mathematics education. Although they were joint investors in Community Builders and managed to maintain cordial personal relations even after Ray left for California, the two clashed frequently over Troup's college administrative methods. Troup was a "by the book" administrator who required faithful attendance at all faculty meetings, required proper forms filled out at the assigned times, and rarely admitted deviations from the rules for any purpose. Ray was impatient with what he considered to be arbitrary and inessential paperwork, form-filing or deadlines; and he preferred yielding to common sense and good reason, as opposed to following rules written in stone.

At times, the conflict grew intense. In April of 1948 Troup deducted eighteen dollars from Ray's paycheck for dismissing classes on two days without approval from the administration. He noted that it had been deducted for "spring vacation." Ray did not protest the deduction itself, but insisted that he had taken no "vacation" and that the notation be changed to "unexcused absence" on the college records before he would cash his paycheck (likely so that the record would become ammunition to complain, if he discovered that other faculty were treated more leniently). In June of that year, Troup wrote asking for Ray's signed employment contract, which was by then two days late: "In the event I do not hear from you immediately, I shall be compelled to consider your place vacant and take the necessary steps to fill it."

The following year, they engaged in yet another formal conflict through inter-office mail. This time the offense was Ray's failure to attend a faculty meeting, and again he archived the exchange for future reference:

Troup: For some reason unknown to me or to the Administrative Dean, you were absent from our professional faculty meeting Thursday, Feb. 10. Perhaps you will recall that it was pointed out in our first faculty meeting of this academic year that all faculty members are expected to attend all faculty meetings unless excused by the President or the Administrative Dean.

I am therefore requesting that you submit to me in writing on or before Monday, Feb. 14 your reason for failing to attend the meeting yesterday. In the future it is expected that you will either attend all faculty meetings or abide by our request that excuses for absence be obtained in advance.

Pitts: I wish to state that my absence from the meeting on Thursday was due to an oversight on my part. I checked the calendar on that day and either did not see the meeting listed or overlooked it. I shall become informed on what went on in the meeting and be present at the next.

The last year he was employed at Fort Valley (1955–56), despite his intent never to leave his family for an extended period again, Ray returned to Ann Arbor alone. He knew he would need to push himself in Ann Arbor to finish the PhD dissertation within the year, while also serving as a research consultant in their curriculum laboratory and as a research assistant in their examination division. He felt he could not disrupt the family with another short-term move. It would be Frances' senior year in high school and the children were all deeply involved in school, and in community clubs and programs.

Kathleen had gotten a fellowship to study at Howard University for the summer of 1955, so Ray stayed with the family and did not leave Georgia for Ann Arbor until September, after she returned. That year he completed all the requirements for the dissertation, defended, and then graduated in August of 1956, recipient of the university's Clifford Woody Award for Excellence in Education Research.

Left in Fort Valley as the "man of the family," eldest son Ray Jr. tells this story:

There [had been] much excitement in the small town when the first drive-

in movie theater was built in the all-black neighborhood less that a mile away from the college. The only street leading to this venue was right in front of our home. On several occasions, people would trespass upon our property and look through the house windows after the drive-in closed. Once, I remember hearing someone at the elevated bathroom window as I took a bath. Another time, we suddenly realized that someone had come into the screened in porch and was standing at the door. I can still hear my mother's screams as she tried to frighten the "peeping Toms" away. Fortunately, no one was ever harmed in these ordeals.

In the spring of my 7th grade year, Dad came home from Ann Arbor for a visit. I remember being pleased and more relaxed when he was at home. He would bring baseball caps for my brother and me, and we would have fun wearing them around the house. During this visit, he suggested that we go to a neighbor's farm and learn to shoot a rifle he had purchased. I was thrilled to once again do something with my dad, and I thought only of the fun we would have together as I became an accurate shot. After several sessions Dad told me that he would be returning to the University of Michigan to complete his work, and that he wanted me to take care of the rifle and use it to protect the family, if necessary. Suddenly I knew that Dad had very thoughtfully positioned our discussion, and I realized the magnitude of the responsibility.

That was my initial step towards becoming a man—a position that I quietly accepted with solemnity and insight. There was no fear or confusion. I was focused on the family's well being. Dad further instructed that the rifle was not to be shown or discussed with my friends. His words were not in the form of a directive, but more as a necessity that he thought I could handle. In the years ahead, he continued to prepare me for manhood, as we discussed many things. At one point, I asked him why he didn't introduce himself as Dr. Pitts, using a title that signifies status symbol in the academic setting. He explained that it was not necessary; he used the title only professionally, and only if appropriate. That I was only thirteen never entered our talks. He and I both understood our relationship. I was no longer an innocent child. As we drove home on the night Dad gave me the charge of the rifle, there was total silence. Dad was a pensive person; often deep in his own thoughts, and I had learned to be comfortable with his silence. I began to imagine a situation in which I would have to grab the rifle and dash out the back door to confront an intruder. My confidence would never waver. I grasped the mission clearly, with the exception of one last question for my dad. "Dad, should I shoot over his head or into the ground?" He answered with a thoughtfulness that left me with my courage intact, and my new responsibility squarely on my shoulders.

"That will be your decision."

I was relieved that there was no need to use the family rifle while Dad was

*away. And we never spoke about the rifle, even though we both understood
that we had come through a journey together.*

The disagreements about the direction the college was taking under Troup
were not the only factors troubling Ray and Kathleen in Fort Valley. By the
end of his final year in Ann Arbor, they had also despaired of the racial climate in Georgia. Tensions had been escalating for some years. Ray had been
active in efforts to encourage the desegregation of higher education in Georgia,
including consultations in 1951 with William M. Boyd, the state's NAACP
chapter president. Boyd was at the time helping Horace Ward in his ground-
breaking, although ultimately unsuccessful, attempt to integrate the University
of Georgia Law School. Then the Mississippi murder of Emmet Till in 1955 set
the whole country on edge.[22] Closer to home, the Montgomery, Alabama, bus
boycott[23] remained in full swing. Still closer to directly affecting the family, the
State Board of Education of Georgia voted to strip Guy H. Wells, the white, former President of the Georgia State College for Women, of his retirement pen-
sion and his President Emeritus title. They did this in retaliation for his public,
pro-integration stance. The trustees of the state retirement system, the system
that represented both Ray and Kay as teachers in the State's employ, opposed
the decision as unconstitutional—and the battle lines were drawn.

Ray felt the tensions threaten to engulf his family; and the children, who had
gotten used to "Northern ways" in Michigan, found it difficult to readjust to the
South's strict rules. Once, Frances was riding with some other teenage friends
in town when they had a minor auto accident with another car that was full of
white teenagers. The youths from both cars got out and were talking together,
inspecting the minor damage and not thinking much about appearances. But,
she recalls, the parents on both sides were greatly alarmed at their casual inter-
action. It just wasn't done!

The 1954 Brown vs. the Board of Education decision had declared "separate
but equal" to be unconstitutional, and mandated the desegregation of schools.
It was clear that Georgia would actively, and perhaps violently, oppose this man-
date—for a long time to come. The Governor insisted that all teachers in the
State's employ must sign contracts agreeing not to teach in integrated schools, if
they wished to continue receiving financial assistance for their own educational
pursuits. Ray decided it was time to permanently remove his family from the
situation:

*Immediately [upon hearing of the Governor's decision to fight desegrega-
tion], I made arrangements for personnel interviews at the University Alumni Office. Five offers were received and I accepted my first California teaching*

22   The incident is noted in Ray's family journal, almost the only journal entry not directly related to the
activities of a family member—an indication of the magnitude of that shock to black people of the South.

23   Sparked on Dec 1, 1955, by the arrest of Rosa Parks.

position, Assistant Professor, Education and Mathematics, at Los Angeles State College. ... After 18 years, I was leaving Fort Valley. My hopes had been to make a real contribution to Georgia, my State, and its People—ALL Georgians, through my chosen career in Higher Education.

He wrote a final, somewhat confrontational letter of resignation to President Troup. "I have voiced my opposition many times and in many places. It appears that my opposition carries little weight within the framework of present developments. I therefore consider it necessary for my own mental health and for my professional security to sever relationships with the college." The Administrative Dean of the college responded at length to the individual points in Ray's resignation letter, and asked Ray to reconsider. However, he foresaw that any attempt to influence Ray's decision would be futile, saying; "You know that is has always been very difficult to explain matters to you because you get your mind set and organize your own interpretations and explanations, and are open to few, if any, others."

Ray did not leave without a final confrontation with Cornelius Troup. A few years earlier, around 1950, the Georgia State College rules had tightened for faculty claiming salary while on sabbatical for graduate study. Ray got caught in the middle of the administrative transition to the new policies. He had previously been promised deferred compensation for one of his early years in Ann Arbor, because at the time he was barred from receiving salary concurrent with the fellowship he'd been awarded. Ray believed he was using this deferred pay during the 1955–56 year in Ann Arbor, but the salary for that year was treated by Troup under the new rules for sabbatical pay. That sabbatical, according to Troup, required his return to the campus for at least one year of additional teaching, subsequent to the leave. Ray argued that the pay was already owed to him, armed with a sheaf of letters documenting every detail of the previous arrangement. But Troup stood his ground. Ray left the college's employ before fulfilling the subsequent teaching requirement, and even in 1959, four years after the Pitts family had moved to California, the two were still battling over whether the funds were owed back to the college as reimbursement.[24]

Ray, Kay, and family were off to California. Only Frances remained back East. She would begin her first year of college at Talladega in the fall.

On To California!

In May of 1956, Kathy Pitts graduated from the Peach County Elementary School in Fort Valley. She expected that summer to be an exciting one. Her

24 Troup eventually threatened to take legal action against Ray, who then appealed to the state Board of Regents. The Board found that Troup was within his rights as President of the college, and said it would uphold whatever decision he made. Troup continued to insist on reimbursement and Ray did eventually (and reluctantly) pay back the amount owed to Fort Valley.

big sister Frances was graduating from high school and would be attending college in the fall. But when the "girls room" became her own, exclusive property, it would not be the same girls room she had always known. The whole family was planning to move to California! During the summer they sold possessions, packed, and the family traveled both north and south along the East Coast, to say goodbye to friends and family. While on the northern leg, they took Frances to her summer job with their Uncle Willis and his wife Fran, at Whispering Willow's camp in Massachusetts. And when they returned from the southern leg, they had added to their number her cousin Ethel.[25] She would be "sister" to Kathy on the trip west.[26] In an interview, Kathy told the story of that cross-country trek:

> On the trip across country we stayed with friends, or at black colleges in dormitories, or wherever the "black network" extended and we knew we could find friends. In those days, such a trip required careful planning and a network of friends and acquaintances. The black community helped one another. I didn't realize it at the time, but reading Wilkerson's book, The Warmth of Other Suns,[27] put it in perspective for me—what my parents experienced during those years of "the black migration."
>
> I remember riding in the car: there were four of us kids (Fran stayed behind, but Ethel came with us) and we each had our own position in the back. Nat curled up in the back window, Ray and Ethel had the seats, and I sprawled on the floor. Mother built up each side of the floor with rugs, to be level with the bump in the middle, and I lay there reading Earl Stanley Gardner for hours on end during the trip. I remember a few other things— eating watermelon in Texas, tying a big bag of water to the hood when crossing the desert to keep the car cool (it didn't work), how long it seemed...
>
> We did a family trip up and down the East Coast to say goodbye to family and friends before we went to California, but we really didn't need to. Once we were established out there, they all came. We had so many visitors that Mother developed a "stock-tour itinerary."
>
> Dad had a naive view of the paradise of California. He thought we would never experience discrimination there. But the first night we arrived in Glendale, he tried to get a motel room and he could not understand why he could not get in. The hotel advertised a vacancy, but when he asked about a room it was suddenly "full up." Mother (who looked white) told him "let me try." She went in with my cousin Ethel (who also looked white), and said they needed a room. They gave her a room right away. Dad's bubble burst that night.

---

25   Also known as "Augie." Daughter of Kathleen's brother James.

26   And would live with the family until the following June, when she flew home.

27   Isabella Wilkerson (2010). *The Warmth of Other Suns: The Epic Story of America's Great Migration*, Random House.

Mother was a realist, but Dad was always a bit of an idealist.

At first we rented, for several months, a two-story house from Mrs. Divine, who lived with us on Hammond Street. Then we had our own house, 489 Atchison Street, where we lived for the next ten years. We went to St. Barnabas Episcopal Church, a small black church, since at that time All Saints in Pasadena was not open to blacks. We kids were "Jack and Jillers."²⁸ Even though it was difficult going to a new school, being in "Jack & Jill" helped. My parents kept both Ray and Nat back a year in school, because we had heard how much more challenging the California schools were, but I did not find them to be so. Pasadena did have many more resources, ones we did not have in Georgia. Mom and Dad were into "experiences," and we took in as many cultural opportunities as possible.

Nat too, recalled the first few months in California:

When we arrived in California, we stayed a short time (maybe five to ten days) in Watts with my mother's brother (Bill Cook). Uncle Bill had stayed in California after the war, when his ship had left him off in Long Beach. He had a son Billy, and a wife. The house was small and we slept on floors, couches, etc. And, since Watts is not where Dad saw himself raising his family, he went directly to researching the best school districts in southern California. He settled on the public school system of Pasadena. So, before school started, we moved into the home of a very religious woman, Ms. Devine. She lived on the black side of town, right down the street from Jackie Robinson's mother. We stayed there for one semester, a very small house for a family of five to move into, but it sufficed until my father could find what he and my mother wanted.

We became "blockbusters" in Pasadena because we were the first black family to move across a certain street line (Los Robles Street) in Pasadena and buy a house in a block that originally was all white. (Today that block is all Mexican, but that's another story.) So, by January of our first year there, we were in our new house, 489 Atchison Street, and we would stay there until my parents moved to Sacramento in 1966. I had to move schools, to basically an all-white school, but my brother and sister remained in their very mixed school. We made friends on the block very quickly and the rest of that Pasadena blending story was great.

My mother, being so fair that she could "pass" in any circumstance, quickly got jobs substitute teaching all over Pasadena. By the time we moved into our own house, she had taken a permanent (fourth grade) position at Altadena Elementary school, a (basically) all-white school near our new house.

Our first or second summer in California, we (the entire family) went

---

28   An intercity organization formed during the Great Depression to bring together black children for social and cultural activities; it focused on instilling values and leadership skills.

camping in Yosemite National Park. We went with another family and had a great time. The other family was Hispanic, of Mexican origin. Dad worked with the father at one of his colleges, either LA State or LA City. From our encounters with them, Mom learned how to make tacos and the Mexican Wedding Cakes that became a house favorite. Yosemite became one of Mom's and Dad's favorite places to go to recharge. They would go to Yosemite even in retirement, and take our friends from the "old country" when possible. Dad would also go there on photo-shoots with senior groups. Visits to Yosemite National Park (camping), in particular, would remain a favorite with Mom and Dad well into their seventies.

Dad was searching for a black middle class in Pasadena, but it was not there. There were very few professional or college educated blacks in Pasadena when we arrived. Those who lived there mostly served the wealthy of Hollywood and aspired to the entertainment industry for advancement. We joined Jack & Jill, which was supposed to be an organization for the children of the black middle class, but Pop was disappointed with this organization because he found out early that the parents did not have the aspiration for their kids that he and my mom had for us. Public education in California was not necessarily excellent education for everyone, and Dad had to watch what was happening to us at every stage. An example was when Ray Jr. went to his first semester of high school. They enrolled him in four shop classes (wood shop, metal shop, auto shop, and photography). Dad had to go up to the school and get his schedule changed for college prep classes. By the time I went through the same school (five years later), Dad already had the reputation as one of those black parents whose children had to be in the college prep courses. But he never quite got used to those Californians, black or white, who had limited ambitions for their children.

Still, Dad felt he had arrived in the land of plenty/opportunity and he wrote back to people in Georgia about the openness of the California experience. He once told us that he took us out of the South, which he sometimes called "the old country" and that if we (his children) went back, we would do it against his wishes or advice.

Ray found the new job at Los Angeles State College exciting, and perfect for his background. With eighteen years of teaching experience in Mathematics and Mathematics Education, and a brand new PhD in the very latest trends and techniques, he landed in California at a time when "the new math" was the watchword, and he was the resident expert:

I was happy and professionally proud to see teachers get converted to using the newer "modern" mathematics materials and methods; and felt prouder yet of the young scientists and engineers who went on to advance our coun-

try's efforts to advance the forefront of productivity in the advancing age of technology. This exposure to broader opportunities in California gave to me greater and broader professional perspectives, which I appreciated. Presenting mathematical papers at professional conferences and giving demonstrations of teaching practices throughout the country and on television literally swelled my head professionally.

Ray added a part-time position at Los Angeles City College and another part-time position at a University of California, LA Extension—for at least one semester teaching at all three schools simultaneously. Even with the additional jobs, the family was struggling to make ends meet. However, Ray and Kathleen deliberately concentrated their greatest energies on rearing, educating, and "spending quality time with" their children.

As parents, our children require more quality time. After all, it was out of concern for our children and development of their self-image that we had left our home state of Georgia. We, as responsible parents, made quality time with our children our highest priority. We have never regretted either leaving the South for a better environment or working seriously with our children at this critical time in their lives. I believe that this is the essence of good and responsible parenting.

And the children were growing up. Providing the type of life they envisioned for their family required as much time and as many resources as both parents could provide. The children were enrolled in music lessons;[29] went to club meetings, summer school, and summer camps; and enjoyed vacations and sightseeing at the many West Coast attractions. Ray Jr. was making a name for himself in tennis. Nat was becoming a budding businessman, running his own pigeon-breeding venture. He was playing baseball, and later he too took up tennis. He was voted Outstanding Tennis Player two years in a row at John Muir High School. Ray, of course, continued to excel in tennis; playing with both sons and often playing doubles with new found friends at LA State. Nat recalls, "While at LA State, as usual, Dad would meet the tennis coaches and spend time playing with them on weekends. He brought one of the coaches (Dr. Joan Johnson) to work with some black youngsters in Pasadena, for a few weekends. This coach of the women's team was also working with Billy Jean King at the time."

Frances completed just one year at Talladega,[30] and then moved to Pasadena to be with the family. Her parents felt that the racial situation was just too tense in the South, and they wanted this last opportunity for the family to all live in their home together. Frances went to Pasadena City College for the 1957–58

---

29 Ray Jr.: saxophone, Kathy: piano, Nat: violin and piano
30 Where she won an award for designing and modeling her débutante ball gown.

school year, and then was able to transfer to nearby Whittier College for her final two years.[31]

Ray loved fatherhood, but did sometimes find it perplexing and a challenge. While he preferred to guide and advise, sometimes he felt compelled to put his foot down. "It is becoming more and more difficult to be a father here. I have to say no to so many things which to me should not even come up. But usually many things are refused for the best interest of all concerned."

Frances was the instigator of one of those times when Ray felt obliged to overrule her decision. She had acquired something in addition to education at Talladega: a fiancé, Paul Smith. They expected to marry soon, before she finished college. Ray felt the circumstances warranted his swift intervention.

Frances invited Paul to visit the family at Christmas, 1957. Paul would graduate the following spring, and the two planned to marry before he left for Hartford, Connecticut, where he intended to train as a minister in the United Church of Christ. The visit went well, and the family fell in love with the intelligent, serious Paul. But Ray had *plans* for this daughter and his other children. He expected those plans to be accomplished, and via the path that he had laid out. His plans included each one finishing college; and, if the eldest child didn't graduate, what might the others expect to get away with?

Ray couldn't bear to ruin Fran's vacation or Paul's visit, but early one morning shortly after Christmas, in his characteristic forthright and self-assured manner, he wrote to Paul:

> *I want to take up the matter of your and Fran's marriage at some length and suggest some changes in plans which I hope will be acceptable to you. ... I have thought at length about this and am suggesting that you and Fran defer any further plans for marriage until she has completed the kind of college education that we had originally planned for her. [An additional] two years of study with the freedom from home responsibilities and with time to develop on her own initiative would make her the kind of person who could be a real asset as a minister's wife. ... The two of you are quite lucky to have gotten together. I want to say this in the light of concern for you. The road to a professional education is not an easy one. I would say that it is the most lonely road that a man can take, if he is serious about really doing something.[32] ... In these two years you could strive to be the top man at the Seminary and get all of the experience and contact that would make you the most desired graduate in your class. The freedom to spend long hours concentrating on the*

---

31   Thanks to the influence of Ray's Talladega friend, Bob O'Brien, now in Whittier's Sociology Department.

32   Paul Smith (later the Rev. Dr. Paul Smith) went on to become prominent in the civil rights movement, and was one of the clergymen who accompanied Martin Luther King Jr., on his famous march in Selma, Alabama. He is Pastor Emeritus of the First Presbyterian Church of Brooklyn Heights, NY

assigned tasks, to take advantage of the unexpected trips for observation and practice, and to make a large number of contacts is yours now, but marriage would make that impossible. ... [A] question raised by Fran was, "What if Paul does not accept the suggestion?" I could hardly answer that, except to say the suggestion is made in the best interest for all concerned. ... If you read this over a couple of times and think through this, you will probably see the wisdom in our suggestion.

Frances was initially disappointed with the delay in her wedding plans, but her years at Whittier would also provide life-changing opportunities. In her senior year she was accepted into the first year of Whittier's new foreign exchange program, for a semester of study at the University of Copenhagen in Denmark. The associated costs of the trip looked prohibitive for the still-struggling family, but Ray immediately contacted potential sources for scholarships and loans. Fran would be the first black student to go on a Whittier sponsored trip of this type. He believed she would be a "goodwill ambassador" in a country where few blacks had traveled, and that the opportunity to travel outside the United States would give her a new sense of herself as a person—one that would be impossible to achieve any other way. Her Uncle Bob provided funds that enabled her to extend the trip, and travel further in Europe over the Christmas vacation. Years later Frances said that, while descending the plane's steps onto European soil, for the first time she was able to say to herself, "I am a free person."

The romance between Frances and Paul survived the additional two years apart. The two were married in Pasadena on the Sunday following Fran's Saturday Whittier graduation ceremony. Despite their rocky start, Ray and Paul became close friends, and remained close and trusted confidants throughout the rest of Ray's life.

That year of 1960, Ray Jr. also got a chance to have a foreign experience. He "summered" in Mexico with his Episcopal Church youth group, before beginning college in the fall at Fisk University in Tennessee. The following summer, he went to Hawaii with the same youth group, to help build a church.

And just when Ray and Kathleen felt that, with one daughter safely married, they could, perhaps, relax for a short while; in July 1961 the seventeen-year-old Kathy went on a fateful blind date with Alfred (Al) Bias. He was quickly "the love of her life," and before long she too wanted to be married. Now it was Kathy's plans that caused a family crisis for Ray. As before, he insisted on the finishing of college before marrying—forbidding the wedding. But Kathy and Al eloped anyway, on Dec 5, 1963. It was extremely difficult for Ray to come around, but he accepted the *fait accompli* and allowed a blessing of that marriage on Christmas Eve, 1963, at the family parish of Saint Barnabas Episcopal Church. He and Kathleen hosted a wedding reception for the young couple later on, in February. Kathy was in her third year at Whittier, and Al was studying pharmacy at the University of Southern California. With their respective colleges so close together, Kathy and Al were able to live together and continue their studies uninterrupted. Despite her father's concerns about the difficulties of getting married while finishing a degree, the two were very happy and Kathy graduated—as planned and on-time—in 1965.

Building the Career

Ray taught a number of traditional mathematics courses while in Pasadena, but he was quickly making a name for himself as a specialist in the training of teachers to use the modern methods of mathematics instruction. He was so much in demand that the family bought a second car because he was driving constantly, all over California. A July 24, 1961 news article in the Los Angeles State College *Summer Times* wrote that:

> *Dr. Pitts ... has earned extensive recognition for his research and experimentation in methods of teaching mathematics in the junior and senior high schools. During recent years he has conducted workshops and in-service training programs for teachers in a number of Southern California school districts. As member of the Summer School faculty at Los Angeles State this summer, he is conducting a laboratory class for teachers in the use of teaching machines for instructing in mathematics.*

Trading on that reputation, and urgently needing a better salary to defray the expenses of a growing family, he decided to seek a job with better long-term promotion potential:

> *With one child in college and three others headed that way, I had to make another choice—how to pay tuition and college fees for four. ... I left my position as Associate Professor at California State University, LA, to develop and direct the Santa Barbara County Mathematics/Science Project, the county's unique joint project with the University of California, Santa Barbara [to comprehensively study mathematics/science teaching in the Santa Barbara County school system]. This move was my introduction to the administrative echelon of California's higher education system. It also gave me the administrative salary, which was a partial answer to my problem of financing our children's college education, and more importantly, it gave me the opportunity to test the feasibility of ideas I had developed about the improvement of the teaching-learning process. I still had to work at two regular jobs, and sometimes three, to meet mortgage payments and pay for college tuition and fees.*

The initial contract with Santa Barbara County was to be for one year (1961–62), but it was extended for a second. When the project was finished, Ray was hired by the University of California, Santa Barbara, to be Assistant Director of the new Center for Coordinated Education. He also began teaching in their Extension Division, on a part-time basis. While Ray worked in Santa Barbara, the family remained living in Pasadena and Ray commuted. He contemplated moving the family, but wanted Nat (the only child still in high school) to be able to remain where he was currently enrolled. Instead, Ray lived during the week in the beach cottage in Goleta[33] that the family had purchased for vacations, and came home on weekends and whenever possible.

Always an advocate for the advancement of race relations, Ray kept abreast of relevant issues in the social and political climate of California. He often consulted about these issues, formally and informally, with his brother Bob, a San Francisco executive in Federal housing. In September 1963, the California Fair Housing Act went into effect, declaring that discrimination because of race, color, religion, national origin or ancestry in housing would be forbidden in the sale, rental, leasing or financing of housing. In November of that year, Ray decided to test the law and put an offer in on a house in an all-white neighborhood.[34] Being informed that the owner refused to sell to a non-Caucasian, he submitted a housing discrimination complaint against the real estate firm and enlisted Bob to write a letters to the California Real Estate Commissioner and the Division of Fair Employment Practices in support of his case. It is not clear whether there was ever any action on the complaint, but the house was not purchased.

In 1964, after the Civil Rights Act forced cities to take actions to deal with *de facto* segregation in schools, Ray took the newly created position of Director, Department of Intergroup Education, in the Pasadena City Schools. Created in optimism, Pasadena was one of only four school districts in the nation to boast such a position. Ray's responsibilities included the administrative and technical challenges of devising a plan to reduce the segregation of the city's schools. They also included the promotion of intergroup understanding and cooperation in the schools, to improve educational opportunities for all Pasadena students. On the first task, Ray was opposed at every step. He generally agreed with the premise that redistricting and busing would be the only way to implement desegregation on a large scale; however, any plans he proposed were shot down by a school board dominated by members who had been elected as a group, in 1965, on a strict anti-busing platform. Because of their opposition, only a small number of the most segregated schools were to participate in student transfers on a limited basis, provided that the students could find their own transportation.[35] Consistently, this school board voted against any other measures that would desegregate the schools.

33   6518 Del Playa Drive.

34   1455 Ontario Ave. in Pasadena.

35   Julie Salley Gray. *"To Fight the Good Fight": The Battle Over Control of the Pasadena City Schools,* 1969-1979. Retrieved April 2, 2015 from http://www.essaysinhistory.com/articles/2012/119

Ray had more success in his efforts to improve other aspects of minority and underprivileged education. He implemented compensatory education programs, supervised teacher training in cultural understanding, and started a program of placing volunteer student aids in needy classrooms. He augmented his own education with a variety of graduate courses in education administration and human relations. In October 1965, to an all-school-district meeting on "The Goals of the Intergroup Relations Thrust," he gave a major address outlining his strategies and successes, and detailing what he had learned. Most significantly, before he left this position he established and endowed the *Raymond J. Pitts Human Relations Award* under the auspices of Pasadena's Human Relations Committee. The award is still given annually for most significant contribution in the field of Human Relations through the Pasadena Unified School District.

Life as an education administrator was not kind to Ray. As his daughter Kathy put it; "He wanted to understand people but he found them difficult. He expected people to behave like math, with logic and consistent results, and people don't work like that!" In November 1965, he suffered a heart attack while driving with Kathleen in Santa Barbara. He took two months off to recuperate, but he was despairing of meaningful progress in Pasadena and began to look elsewhere for employment. He resigned in April 1966 to take a position in Sacramento with Wilson Riles,[36] as Coordinator of Research and Teacher Education for the California Department of Education, Office of Compensatory Education. The family prepared to move.

Sacramento

Nat was about to enter his second year of college[37] and was working at a summer job with the Urban League in St. Louis, Missouri, where Frances and Paul were living at the time. Ray Jr. was in the Navy and on assignment in Istanbul, Turkey. The girls were both married and Frances already had two children: Kathleen Frances (age four) and Heather Marie (age eighteen months). Ray and Kay, with their dog Duchess, were left to pack, sell one house, buy another,[38] and tackle the move by themselves.[39]

Sacramento was, in many ways, a more congenial city for the couple than Pasadena had been. Kathleen found a good job teaching in Sacramento city schools, and commenced making new friends. Always known for her hospitality, it was in this new home that she would most notably indulge in her flair for

36   Then Chief of the Bureau of Compensatory Education with the California Department of Education. Riles later became the first African-American Superintendent of Public Instruction in the state of California.
37   The third Pitts child to attend Whittier.
38   1136 Westlynn Way, Sacramento.
39   With some help from Mary and Mitra (Ray's brother Nathan's wife and daughter), who came for a visit in time to pitch in.

entertaining, becoming renown for her elaborate dinner parties—especially the Valentine's Day parties. Nat writes:

By the time Mom and Dad made it to Sacramento, there was already a reasonably sized black middle class of college graduates, doctors, lawyers, dentists, etc. This was because of the many institutions that had been there for such a long time. It was the state capitol, and was also home to a Federal court house, four colleges (Sacramento State; Sacramento City; MacGeorge Law School; and the University of California, Davis), and the military at Travis Air Force Base. By the time I arrived in Sacramento to attend gradu-ate school, it seemed as though Mom and Dad knew many, if not all, of the middle-class blacks. These educated blacks were members of black fraternities and sororities, as well as other social groups and professional organizations. Mom quickly found her AKA sorority sisters and her Sacramento Chapter of the Links. Pop found his Alpha brothers, but spent more of his social time following his "Kat."

Because this Sacramento group of blacks was well educated, Dad seemed more comfortable in Sacramento than in Pasadena. Even though his own children were mostly out of college by this time, he still enjoyed talking to high school children and their parents about colleges and what they had to offer. These parents had more ambitions for their children than those he encoun-tered in Pasadena. These parents were sending their children to Stanford; University of California, Berkeley; and Ivy League schools. At this stage, few-er were sending their children to the HBCUs of the South, but this continued to be a great debate at parties through the 1980s. Cornell West (of Harvard/ Princeton fame) was in high school during the time my parents were there. His parents and mine were close. As a matter of fact, after my father died and we held a celebration service for him—after the service at our house in Sacramento—Mrs. West was working right next to all of us in the kitchen as we took care of our guests, just like a member of the family.

Sacramento was also a big tennis town and our house was right down the street from a private tennis club (South Hills Racket Club) which was well integrated. Although Dad was never a member there, I played there a lot and taught a number of the children whose parents were friends of my parents. Dad had been kept off the tennis courts for many years because of his heart condition. But he would eventually play tennis in the public park, just a short walk away from the house. Dad enjoyed Sacramento for its multi-racial environment.

While working for the California Department of Education, Ray also kept his finger in other professional pies, continuing to serve in Pasadena as a summer staff member for the NDEA[40] National Institute for Advanced Study in Teaching Disadvantaged Youth, and serving as a consultant for the US Office of Education, for *Operation Follow Through* in Wichita, Kansas.

In 1968, Ray's frustration with his lack of ability to accomplish anything in the Office of Compensatory Education became too much. He resigned with the statement; "My resignation is submitted as a result of a situation created by non-staff personnel to prevent me from carrying out my legal responsibilities (Calif. Educ. Code Sec. 6455). Two alternatives were open: 1) remain and lose my professional integrity or 2) resign. I chose to resign."

Ray's former boss from Pasadena City Schools, Robert Jenkins, had become Superintendent of Schools in San Francisco. Ray left the state Department of Education to join Jenkins as Assistant Superintendent: Instructional Development and Services. Nat recalls; "Jenkins liked Dad and knew what Dad was capable of producing. Dad was a good, deliberate, methodological writer, the type that succeeded in proposal writing. And San Francisco was pushing for Federal funding for some of its system-wide education programs. Dad was the one he wanted on his team, leading that effort." The new job was busy enough that Ray gave up his other part-time positions and rented an apartment in San Francisco, where he would live during the week—commuting to Sacramento as he had previously commuted between Santa Barbara and Pasadena. Nat remembered the apartment with affection:

One of my fond memories when I was in graduate school has to do with when I went to San Francisco my freshman year and stayed in my father's apartment. He worked in SF during the week and came home to Sacramento during the weekends. He had a studio apartment right off Market Street, so he could actually walk to his office. Since I did not need my stereo, I gave it to him for his apartment (and to keep for me—I needed my stereo stored some place). In exchange, he gave me a key to his SF apartment. I would go there on some weekends. At some point, I wanted to see the play "Hair" and informed him. I remember, when I next arrived at the apartment, there were two tickets on the refrigerator, with a note that just said, "Have a good time." I used his apartment a number of times during my graduate student days and got to know SF well, with that apartment as home base.

The work was intense, but the salary was significantly better and the children had, by now, all completed their undergraduate degrees. Frances now had three children, with the addition of Krista Lori in July 1968. The grandparents loved to indulge them, and traveled to St. Louis to visit whenever possible. In 1969, Ray and Kathleen took their first of many foreign trips—to Rome, Venice, Paris and Switzerland; the itinerary arranged by a friend of Ray Jr. (who was, at the

---

40   National Defense Education Act

time, nearing the end of his tour of duty in Turkey). Later that year, Kathleen was presented with a mink stole.[41] In January 1970, Kathy and Al adopted Kelvin Bias, Ray and Kathleen's first grandson. Still living in Whittier, California, the Biases were close enough to the grandparents for regular visits and eager grand-parenting. That June, Ray and Kathleen returned to Europe, purchasing rail passes to see London, Amsterdam, Brussels, Paris, Geneva, Zürich, Madrid and Lisbon. And then in October the two took their first trip back to Georgia together, after a fifteen year absence.

Ray's supervisor, Dr. Jenkins, retired from his position in 1970, and Thomas Shaheen was appointed to the position of Superintendent of Schools. Shaheen's philosophy was quite different than Jenkins', and he led a controversial and ultimately ineffective term, unable to win the confidence of the community or other school administrators. Shaheen had no tolerance for incremental improvement on desegregation, but insisted on full scale busing—implemented immediately. Shaheen decided to reorganize the administration of the San Francisco School District, and in the process demoted eighty-nine white administrators, exempting the city's minority administrators in order to protect the district's affirmative action program. Ray, who clashed with Shaheen on many things, was not officially "demoted," but he was reassigned and his duties were cut. Ray often talked, in later years, of coming back from a trip to find that his office—desk, chair, books, files and all—had been moved to a cramped corner in the dark and clammy basement.[42] The white administrators had gone to court with a reverse-discrimination lawsuit,[43] and Ray threatened to join them if his responsibilities were not reinstated. On June 11, 1971, the San Francisco Examiner reported.[44]

The San Francisco schools' top black administrator threatened today to join demoted whites in their legal fight against district reorganization. Assistant superintendent Raymond J. Pitts, obviously angry, politely but firmly informed the Board of Education that he would not accept a proposed slash in his authority. A curriculum expert, he is the highest-ranking minority group administrator, the only one to hold an assistant superintendency.

The passage of California's Ryan Act in 1970 gave Ray the chance to escape the San Francisco Schools. The Act created an independent body to take over, from the State Board of Education, all teacher preparation and licensing standards and processes. Since he was already a recognized expert in California

41   Costing $1099.35. It was a huge splurge for the frugal couple, who were celebrating thirty-one years of marriage and a family successfully raised.

42   It became his litmus test for how bad someone's job might be: "Have they moved you to the basement?"

43   Which was ultimately successful: Anderson v. San Francisco Unified School District, decided Oct. 1972.

44   Jim Wood (June 11, 1971). *Top Black in Schools Defies Curb on His Job.* San Francisco Examiner, San Francisco, California. (p. 3).

teacher preparation, Ray was able to quit his much-diminished current job, and accepted a position as a consultant in the Program Approval Branch of the new Teacher Preparation and Licensing Commission for the State of California.

But by 1973, Ray felt that he could "no longer contribute anything to the operations of this [Preparation and Licensing Commission] office." He resigned, and next took a position as a specialist in academic affairs in the Office of the Chancellor of the California Community Colleges. He received glowing reports from his supervisor Harlan Stamm,[45] and was promoted to Assistant Dean after only four months in the job. He took over as Dean a few weeks later, when Stamm left to accept a position at another college. As Dean, Ray assumed the responsibility for developing and administering academic policies and programs, coordinating the development of academic master plans, and representing the colleges with other agencies, advisory committees, and various organizations. He remained Dean of Academic Affairs with California Community Colleges until his retirement in 1976.

On the family front, Kathy and Al had adopted a second child, Christopher, in 1973, and had a third child, Brian, in 1975. Ray Jr. had left the Navy, received an MBA from the University of Massachusetts, and spent a year at Washington University Law School. There he met Janice Robinson, who would eventually become his wife. He was now living in New York, with Janice and her daughter Rachel, and working in marketing for IBM. Nat, now married to Carol Shaw, had completed his PhD from the University of California, Davis, in 1975, and was off to a post-doctorate position in Neurophysiology at Rockefeller University in New York. Kathy Smith, their oldest grandchild at age twelve, spent the summer of 1974 with Ray and Kathleen, which started a tradition with the Smith girls. And in 1975, Ray and Kathleen attended the First Talladega College Grand Reunion in Atlanta, visiting the church where they had been wed thirty-seven years before.

As satisfying as life now seemed, the hustle and bustle of family, travel and work were taking its toll on the couple. Ray had suffered a second heart attack in the early 1970s, and Kathleen worried that she might lose him if they did not slow down. Work was now the lowest on her priority scale. She retired at the end of the 1975–76 school year, and set about to convince Ray that his job would also have to go. Nat wrote:

> *My Mom actually forced him to retire, because it was not something he was thinking about. She had him meet with a counselor at our home, and he went over the age/death tables with him. This let him know that a black male who had a heart condition, and was aged 65 ... He was already living past his "scheduled date with death." This woke him up and he went to work the next*

45   "...In all qualifications, if not in outstanding [he is] very close to moving from the standard. Not enough can be said for his ability to assume responsibility in this area."

day and turned in his resignation.

Ray's outstanding contributions to California in the field of education were well-noted when he retired. The State Assembly Rules Committee issued an official resolution recognizing his "dedicated service on behalf of the cause of public education in the State of California." Separately, multiple members from the Assembly's Black Caucus sponsored an Assembly resolution noting his "utmost loyalty and dedication, for which he is deserving of special recognition and the highest commendations." And Yvonne Brathwaite Burke, the first African-American woman elected from the West Coast to the US House of Representatives, read a "Tribute to Raymond J. Pitts" in the House "in commendation for his outstanding record of dedicated and highly effective service to the people of the State of California over the past 20 years." A copy of the tribute was published in the Congressional Record.[46] Following his retirement, Ray received the first *Frank Lanterman*[47] *Award* in 1977 for "outstanding ability, service and achievement in contributing toward the advancement of postsecondary education for and the well-being of disabled people of California."

In Retirement

Concerning the impetus for his retirement, in 2001 Ray wrote:[48]

I retired in the winter of 1976, six months after Kathleen had "called it quits." ... As I retired ..., I made another set of decisions that affected my life. 1) I would get into some of the activities I always dreamed of doing, but had been too busy or too otherwise occupied to try. In other words, I would follow my dreams. 2) I would live a creative and contributing life until my 100th birthday. This would require living a healthful 25 years of senior living with a minimum of stress.

Kathleen and I shared similar thoughts. After a combined 86 years (Kathy 42 and Ray 44) of professional education careers in five states, we shared our hopes and desires to see and to learn more about our world and its many types of inhabitants. Also, by this time, our four children were launched upon their chosen careers as parents and as professionals. Now we were sensing a need to extend our own education.

Both Kathy and Nat recalled how seriously Ray took the pledge for a full retirement and healthful senior living:

---

46   February 9, 1977.

47   Lanterman was a California State Assemblyman who sponsored the Lanterman Developmental Disabilities Act (AB 846), protecting the rights of disabled people.

48   Several quotes in this section are taken from *My Lifetime Contributions and Achievements: A Summary*, which Ray wrote for the Zeta Beta Lambda Chapter of the Alpha Phi Alpha Fraternity, Inc., upon receiving their *Lifetime Achievement Award*. (Dec. 2001).

Kathy: Dad's philosophy on aging was that "your first fifty years are given to you so you can prepare for what's left." He took care of himself and was always exercising. He and Mom were avid mall walkers and swimmers, and he played in his last tennis tournament when he was eighty—they put him in with the sixty-year olds.

Nat: We used to ask Dad to talk about the good old days, but my father would not talk about that. He always preferred to speak about the present or the future. He said, "A man must have goals. It keeps you focused, and productive." He would quote Langston Hughes, "If dreams die, life is a broken-winged bird that cannot fly." So, he always had a project, something he was working towards. He had projects lined up to last him until his 100th birthday, and he expected to complete them all. He made every effort to keep active and healthy. In old age, he would play tennis in the park with Asians he had befriended, and also practiced Tai Chi in the early morning with them.

Regarding Dad's plan of living to be one hundred years old—Pop, as we called him, had placed on a wall in his bed room this goal of being a centurion. I think he got the idea from listening to the Today Show, which he and Mom watched every morning before going to work for many years. The centurions were introduced by Willard Scott on that show on their one hundredth birthday.

Ray believed that being an "international person" was a key to a full and productive life: able to operate in all of society, whether the black community, the larger community, US society, or international society. He believed that all should strive to move freely in whatever environment they found themselves. As a young boy, he remembered once seeing the young girl who would become Madame Chiang Kai-shek on the street, going with her friends from the local Wesleyan College to the Methodist church to worship.[49] He said that seeing her, and wondering about far-away China, "stirred my curiosity to travel and learn." He believed "that people count; knowing their customs and how they think, how they come to do what they do. That is important."

Ray and Kay became serious world-travelers. In addition to the two early trips to Europe, they had traveled with Nat and Carol to Jamaica and Mexico in the early 1970s. But now they wanted to take the opportunity to freely indulge their travel passion, and they had the confidence to take off on their own and go as far afield as they dared. They trained for trips with the dedication of Olympic athletes, and planned itineraries with the meticulous research and organizational prowess that each had employed in their respective careers:

---

49   May-ling Soong only lived in Macon from 1908 to1913, when she transferred to study at Wellesley (leaving Macon when Ray was barely two and unlikely to have remembered seeing her). He may, perhaps, have recalled a time that she traveled there from Wellesley—from which she graduated in 1917—to visit friends.

Armed with a surplus of film, cameras and lenses, tapes and tape re-corders, and notepads filled with suggestions for collectibles, we became the "World Travelers" we had dreamed of becoming during our years of study and teaching. Areas of interest were intertwined with worldwide travel and travel throughout the United States.

After the next dozen years, and in addition to covering much of the US, their foreign trips—at minimum—had encompassed Mexico, Canada, India, Japan, Hong Kong, Thailand, Pakistan, Nepal, the Netherlands, Belgium, England, France, Spain, Portugal, Italy, Switzerland, Germany, Kenya, South Africa, People's Republic of China (twice), Taiwan, Egypt, Greece, Turkey, Russia, Finland, and a Caribbean cruise. Many of the experiences they had during their foreign travels would provide the basis for slide shows and presentations Ray gave for varied educational, civic and social groups back in California.

While not ever in the habit of lavish spending on themselves, Ray and Kathleen decided to each start a collection commemorating their travels. Ray collected letter openers from every country they visited and Kathleen collected dolls. Before Kathleen died, she started sending her doll collection to her grand-daughters. Ray's letter opener collection remains intact.

While the foreign trips nourished Ray's vision of the world's peoples accepting one another, valuing, and celebrating differences; the domestic travel spoke particularly to his sense of family and his search for roots. The year before their retirements, the couple had attended the first Talladega College grand reunion, and also their first Cook family (Kathleen's family) reunion together. Both experiences turned Ray's mind to a variety of history projects that he would complete over the coming years.

The first significant history project was probably his documentation, via a slide show, of the life of his brother Willis for their 1978 family reunion. He called this show *The Squire of Sherborn*, and peppered the show with information about the family's background that he had unearthed during his early research into the history of the Pitts family of Jones County.

A related early project involved documenting the available historical resource material about Ballard Normal School and it's long-term Principal Raymond G. von Tobel. He wrote:[50]

Ballard Normal School served the Central Georgia area in a unique and significant way for three quarters of a century. It seems important to me that an historical documentation of the contributions of Ballard should be made a matter of published record. Secondly, Raymond G. von Tobel served as the principal of Ballard for approximately 22 years. His leadership guided Bal-

---

50   From the *History of the Ballard Normal School Historical Collection* that Ray wrote to accompany the July 1980 Lewis High and Ballard Normal School Grand Reunion events.

174   ROBERTA'S BOYS

lard during the period in which the school was to make its most significant contributions to education. A significant biographical sketch would add to the literature on the work of the American Missionary Association in the State of Georgia. These two projects were being formulated in 1979 as a basis for publications. More importantly, a third idea emerged; that of getting all of the existent materials possible about Ballard Normal School and establishing a collection for use by researchers, writers and exhibitors interested in educational contributions of schools which are no longer in existence.

The Ballard Normal project would result in an elaborate commemorative event and a number of documents, plus the promised collection of historical papers. The summer of 1980 was set as the date of the Grand Reunion of Lewis High and Ballard Normal School. All four Pitts brothers and their wives attended this reunion, the first time the brothers were in Macon together since their school days. For that occasion Ray produced, with Willis, *The Legend of Ballard* historical salute,[51] and wrote the publication *Reflections on a Cherished Past*, incorporating materials collected from more than fifty of the former students and faculty. He also presented his Ballard historical collection to the city of Macon, for their archives.

In conjunction with the Ballard research, Ray also wrote *The Diaries of Raymond Goodwin von Tobel: An Inventory with Notes* for the Georgia Department of Archives and History, which he completed in 1981. And in 1983 he completed an interview project, *Selected Public Secondary Schools Serving Georgia's Black Population Before 1950* sponsored by the Archives Committee of the Fort Valley State College. In the 1990s and 2000s Titus Brown,[52] another chronicler of the American Missionary Association's educational efforts in Central Georgia, heavily cited Ray's works in his own books and articles on the subject.

As Ray's ambition for and engagement in historical projects grew, he and Kathleen built an addition to their house they called "the Pentagon," dedicated to their art and historical collections, and to their genealogical research and family documents. Ray and Kay first sorted out their own papers and collections and "cleaned house." He donated his professional papers to Talladega and to the Armistad Research Center, equipped the new room with an IBM-PC given to him by Ray Jr., and with plenty of table and storage space they now had a place where they could both "do many of things for which we wished time to do while pursuing our careers." The Pentagon, finished in 1982, became Ray's "inner sanctum" and the repository for the many volumes of information and memorabilia he collected, copied, begged, or borrowed from family and friends. As Nat says:

---

51   See chapter on Willis.
52   Of Florida A&M University.

*Pop kept all our records: financial, grades, etc. He once told me that he had
thrown them all away at some point, but he really could not. I found them all
when I was cleaning out the family house after my mom passed away—and
sent all the information collected to the respective sibling. He was a librarian
to the end.*

Another room in the house contained the family "wall of honor," with more
than two dozen family diplomas proudly displayed—from the two Tuskegee
diplomas earned by his parents, Willis Sr. and Roberta, to the latest grandchild's
kindergarten diploma. He collected the diplomas of his children first: high
school diplomas, then college diplomas (which he felt *he* had earned). Next he
added his own and Kathleen's, then his parents'. And then, he started collecting
those of the grandchildren. In the end, he also collected copies of the PhD the-
ses of his two sons and two brothers, and the Master's thesis of his third brother.
It got pretty crowded, but the younger children were always adding something
to the wall and Ray wanted to give them a visible reminder that education is a
worthy goal for which to strive.

Ray had always been an avid photographer, starting early in life with a Brownie and working up to a nice Pentax when the children were little. Although he
suffered from the family's inherited, essential tremor, which made his hands
shake and writing difficult, he loved photography. With Nat's encouragement,
he discovered the techniques of the dark room easy to master. He took some
classes in photography at Sacramento City College, built a home photo-lab,
and became quite proficient.[53] One of the many things Ray passed down to his
children and grandchildren was this love of photography. To pique their interest, he bought cameras for a few of his grandchildren as Christmas presents. He
especially wanted them to get into digital photography, as it was a cheaper and
more versatile option than his usual slides.

One history project combined Kathleen's interest in stamps with Ray's photography. He developed a museum-quality photographic display of "America's
Black Heritage in Stamps," basing it on Kathleen's stamp collection. For another history project, Ray completed a collection of fifteen busts of famous African-Americans, with their histories and contributions. The majority of these,
along with other Civil Rights memorabilia he had collected during his many
years of teaching, had been on exhibit at two Sacramento public libraries. They
were now donated to the Martin Luther King Branch Library in Sacramento, to
stimulate development of a photo-poster contest for the public schools.

When Ray and Kathleen attended the Talladega grand reunion and their
first Cook family reunion in 1975, it started the couple thinking about docu-

---

53   His own or his family's photography, together with his careful reproduction and remastering of aging
and damaged historic photographs from family collections, represent the bulk of the photographs used in
this book.

menting their families' history for posterity. Ray's first large family history project combined his love of photography with this new interest in genealogy. He developed a 125-item family-photo exhibit, which he titled *My Roots Through My Lens*. Many of the items were enlarged and retouched photos that they had collected from Pitts family and from friends and cousins visited on trips home to Georgia. Next, he and Kathleen embarked on a Cook-family project. Cook family reunions had been an ongoing event since 1957, so there was a ready-made network of family who could provide information and an audience. Soon the family had elected Kathleen to the position of Cook-family historian. Over nearly twenty years they collected, analyzed and arranged a huge volume of materials derived from letters, memorabilia, interviews and research trips to Federal, state and local bureaus of records and statistics. They turned this research into a self-published, 300-page volume: *Descendants of George Cook and Calcie Beacham* (1994). Ray wrote a poem for the book preface. This excerpt explains his motivation for the genealogy projects.

> *You, your children and your grandchildren live through your*
> *STAGES OF LIFE knowing well what life means for you.*
> *You, too, must record your life; lest the young who follow,*
> *Like Cedars in the Lane, never know what life was like for you.*

Also at this time, Ray began to contact members of the extended Pitts family to see if there were others interested in reunions and genealogy on that side of the family. Sufficient interest was generated for him to organize, with his cousin, Kathryn Jasper, the First Pitts Family Reunion in 1980. It was well attended and appreciated, and plans were made to do it again. By 1988, the *Pitts Family Association of Central Georgia* had been incorporated in the State of Georgia with Ray as its President and CEO. Ray began seriously researching the Pitts family with the intention of publishing a volume on the Pitts family similar to the one they had done on the George Cook family. He also began pushing his brothers to write their memoirs and collect their important papers, for an additional volume he hoped to publish on their four lives. Ray collected materials for these two projects for the remainder of his life. He wrote once to his brothers, Nathan and Willis, that "In our family collection called *The Pitts Family Archives* there is to be found a treasury of letters, artwork, snapshots, greeting cards and certificates of all kinds ... it will be easy to write a book about the family when time permits." But, he was never able to move the project forward to the point where he would allow himself to stop collecting, and focus on writing.

While he never wrote the full Pitts-family volume, Ray did chronicle, in three separate volumes, his own nuclear family's story. In 1988, he wrote a two-volume set to celebrate his and Kathleen's fiftieth wedding anniversary. *Fifty Golden Years* documented the significant events in their long life together, up to that point. *Letters for a Golden Wedding Anniversary,* produced at the same time, collected the thoughts of their children—with detailed notes about their recollections of growing up in Georgia and California, and stories about their own families and career accomplishments. Then in 2001 Ray wrote a memoir, *My Lifetime Contributions and Achievements: A Summary* for the Alpha Phi Alpha Fraternity, in conjunction with his receipt of their *Lifetime Achievement Award.*

The project that was Ray's ultimate retirement gift to the city of Sacramento was the development of a permanent exhibit for the Sacramento history museum titled *The Dunlap Dining Room.* The Dunlap family were African-Americans having ancestors dating back to Sacramento's Gold Rush days. Dunlap's Dining Room was one of the oldest and most popular restaurants in Sacramento's history, catering to prominent and successful Sacramento businessmen and politicians for over 38 years. Dunlap's oldest daughter donated the family collection to the museum, and their papers to the Sacramento Archival and Museum Collection Center. Ray did the research and photography, and curated the exhibit. He also registered the building itself—a one-story Colonial Revival house with a two-story rear addition, constructed in 1907—with the National Register of Historic Places.

Ray's other, and final, retirement project was the management of his real estate holdings. From early career days in Fort Valley, he had continued to invest in property. The original real estate partnership in Georgia had endured for a number of years, and even after it dissolved he continued to own Georgia property. Later, the family kept the Santa Barbara cottage when they moved to Sacramento, using it or renting it out. He then purchased a condo that Nat rented while he was studying for his PhD at University of California, Davis, and after that purchased several more in the same complex. Other properties were occasionally added. Then, when he was eighty, Ray entered into a real estate partnership with Nat under the name "RJPS." According to Nat:

> *I found myself losing contact with my father and asked my mother if it was OK to get into a business relationship with him. She agreed, and we started RJPS, conceptually, on his eightieth birthday. After age eighty, the banks did not want to loan him money for business purposes, so I became his banker and business partner. I decided our partnership would last ten years. We could purchase a piece of property together, take out a ten-year loan, pay off the loan, and decide what to do with the partnership when he turned ninety. One thing led to another, and I found myself the managing partner of RJPS, with interest in three pieces of property that yielded a decent income. We shared many stories about property management, but those stories were mostly about people and their customs and habits.*
>
> *Dad only wanted enough income to take care of Mom when he died. He had transferred all his property to the Washington, DC, area long before his*

death. I had chosen the property and he had performed property transfers from California. At one time, I was managing seven apartments for him in the DC area, along with the RJPS properties and my own. (Additionally, Ray Jr. managed Dad's apartment in Maryland, and the Fort Valley home that was rented out.) Every time I went to his home in California, I always had to go over the property and income situation with him. I got to know my father as equals after his eightieth birthday.

Ray's Legacy

Ray Pitts was, above all, a family man. In his last decades, the extended family and his legacy to it became his central focus. From reconnecting with and preserving the memory of his brothers, to getting to know and advise his youngest grandchild, family was an all-consuming passion. Together with Kathleen, he continued to read and study, strive to remain healthy and active, and plan for the future. In 2002, he wrote:

> *For me, I believe that the words, "...love for all mankind" translate into the following: Start in each community in which I live, expand my knowledge, improve my skills and use my improved talents to enrich my life and life for my fellow human beings wherever I find them. In Macon, Ann Arbor, Fort Valley, Pasadena, Sacramento and countries on other continents where we have found places of residence, expanding my knowledge, improving my skills and sharing both as a part of life with others has been the focus of my contributions to life so far. I still have nine years and eight months to keep this three-point focus before reaching my century mark. I believe I can keep that focus. It can be done.*

And although he died a few years short of that century mark, he did live this commitment until the end.

In all, Ray and Kathleen had thirteen grandchildren and they were devoted to them all. Fran's three girls, Kathleen, Heather and Krista had each spent a summer with Ray and Kathleen in Sacramento, and the grandparents had frequently visited during summers for camping trips or a holiday. They were now all married, and each had a child of her own.

Ray Jr. and Janice had six children. Their first son, born in 1977, was named Raymond Jackson Pitts III, after his grandfather and his father. Ray III suffered brain damage, and Ray Jr. met the challenge with the same determination that characterized the Pitts men before him, eventually becoming an expert in the needs of developmentally disabled children and a nationally recognized advocate for their well-being. Along with Rachel, Janice's eldest, the couple also had Mitra (named after Nathan's daughter), Jacqueline, and twins Natalie and Robert. The middle girls, Mitra and Jackie, served as occasional tutors for Ray Sr. on the computer. Once Jackie insisted on introducing Ray to her entire class of second-graders, because some of them had never seen a grandfather. Ray described the ceremony she invented as "a tear-jerker for me." He never ceased to marvel at his eldest son's busy, active, and athletic family.

Kathy's boys, Kelvin, Christopher, and Brian, grew up in nearby Whittier, Calif., and were lucky to have their grandparents as a regular presence in their lives. Kelvin, the oldest, remembers numerous conversations about living a good life, and letters that were follow-ups to those discussions. In one sent to Kelvin[54] when he was fifteen, Ray wrote:

> ...*Eating To Win is my recommendation to all young aspiring athletes as well as persons wishing to perform at their peak physically in any field. "You are what you eat" is a truth that everyone should think about more seriously. ... Growing up as the oldest in a family of only boys, you should know how your body works and how it will develop and function. What you learn now and how you treat your body will determine how well you can use it in your path through life. What you do, also, will influence how Kris and Brian use their bodies; so help both yourself and your younger brothers ... I do not know how you are doing with your studies ... I enclose [an attached article] because it might give you an idea of how a good writer uses background in a basic field to produce a good general article. Kelvin, get a good understanding of any area that you might pursue and you improve your chances of becoming a good writer. Think about this.*

Two of the Bias boys, Kelvin and Brian, also used the Pitts family saxophone— retrieved from their Uncle Ray Jr.—that their Great-Uncle Willis first played as a boy back in Macon. But, it was Christopher who was the most frequent visitor to "the Pentagon," and who most shared Ray's love of reading.

Finally, to form a perfect "baker's dozen" of grandchildren, in 1994 Nat and Lisa[55] had a daughter Stephanie. Stephanie (named for tennis great, Steffi Graf) was baptized in a double-baptism with Paula Frances Smith.[56] The two were baptized at Paul's Brooklyn, New York, church. Kathleen made both baptismal dresses. As with all the others, Ray loved to keep track of his youngest grandchild's progress and enjoyed hearing about her interests and accomplishments. He was especially pleased with her continuing the family tennis legacy, with her love for math and science, and with her early proficiency in computers. He called her his "little accountant."

In his last years, Ray turned to his garden as a comfort:

---

54   who later became a writer for Sports Illustrated.

55   His second wife, Lisa Volpe Leonard.

56   Paul and Frances Smith's first grandchild, and Ray and Kathleen's first great-grandchild.

Nat: Dad found peace and serenity in yard work. He focused on planting tomatoes, flowering plants like clematis, roses, and many others. With age, he then studied growing indoor plants, but kept flowering plants both on the outside and inside of the house. He loved the growth and development of plants. And then he would photograph them, of course!

Kathy: Dad was originally a city boy, but he always loved his gardens. He always had both flowers and vegetables, and plants around the house. In Fort Valley we had pecan trees, a peach tree, a pear tree— The last summer he was alive I remember him working with his string beans and tomatoes. His flowers were especially gorgeous that year. I think they were blooming just for him. Frances took some photos of him that summer in the garden, knowing by that time that it would be his last summer. He had always been so robust. It was hard to see him all skin and bones, but he never gave in and his mind was clear to the end.

Ray Jr. came home and lived with Ray and Kay for the final several weeks of Ray's life. At ninety-three, he had outlived his three brothers, and was the patriarch of the entire Pitts clan. Because his was a gradual decline, there were opportunities for family and friends to visit and say their goodbyes before he died on September 9, 2004.

Kathy: When I saw him the last time, we both knew he would not be with us much longer. I went in to tell him the family would all be home for Thanksgiving, assuring him that, even though he wouldn't be there physically, he would still be with us. When I was ready to leave, he said "let me walk you to the door." He was long past getting out of bed at that point, but he had to offer. He was always a gentleman. Whenever we left, he always walked us to the door.

Kathleen survived Ray by several years, well loved and taken care of by her large family. By the time she died in 2011, just a few months shy of her one-hundredth birthday, the family had swelled to include six great grandchildren. After her death, the task of dismantling and selling the house seemed daunting. Nat put boxes of papers, notes, photographs and slides in storage—materials destined to eventually become this book. The house was repainted, furniture donated, and nothing remained to remind anyone that Ray and Kathleen had lived there for forty-six happy and productive years. Ray Jr. wrote:

Both Mother and Dad have died, the family home has been cleaned out, and everything sold—except for The Pitts Family Rifle. As I left the house the final time, the Pitts Family Rifle was packed up and moved to the next generation, just as Dad would have wanted it.

Ray and Kathleen had always felt fortunate that people had helped them through life. In response, they had donated time and talent to various causes, particularly towards helping youth gain education and experiences that would broaden their horizons. But as struggling parents and educators—Kathleen loved retelling how they had put four kids through private college on two school teacher's salaries—they had been little-able to donate money to these favorite causes. During his last six years of employment, when they were in a better position financially, the State of California allowed them to forward all of Ray's salary into a retirement account that they intended to dedicate to this purpose. These funds eventually financed real estate investments in the Washington, DC, area. The timeliness of those investments proved fruitful, and the trust of Raymond J. Pitts and Kathleen C. Pitts eventually became *The Pitts Family Foundation*, directed by their four children. Ray set up the Foundation to do the following, as stated in the trust:

This Family Foundation shall be established for the purpose of supporting creativity in the arts, humanities, and sciences as they relate to cultural diversity in it's broadest sense.

His children are fulfilling this final request.[57]

---

57   Proceeds from this book will also go, in part, to this purpose.

Above Left: Raymond Jackson Pitts, high school
Above Right: Ray, practicing basketball
at Talladega
Left: Ray as a young professional

Below Left: Ray as a young Ballard graduate
Below Right: Ray and Kay at Talladega

Biloxi And Pensacola Teams Divide In Thrillers

The Gators, Pensacola's fast-stepping aggregation of
basket-ball artists, flashed over

Above: Ray (back row, 5th from left), in an article featuring his
Pensacola basketball stars (c1936)

Below: Ray's Fort Valley basketball team

Above: The Fort Valley house that Ray built

Below Left: Kathleen with Frances and baby Ray Jr.
Below Right: Ray with Frances as a toddler

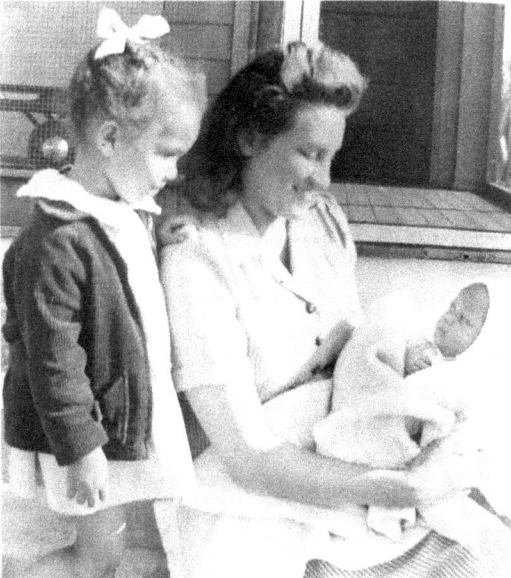

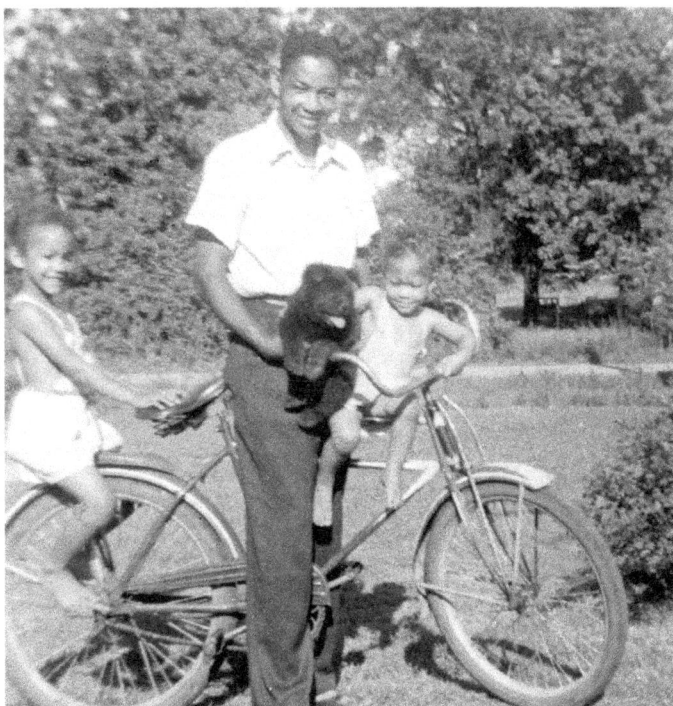

Above: Ray with Frances, Ray Jr., and the first dog, Tang

Below: Frances, Ray Jr., Kathleen, Nathaniel (in wagon) and Kathy

Above: Ray with Kay at University of Michigan

Below: With Catherine Hardy after her Olympic win

C. Hardy & R. Pitts, 1952

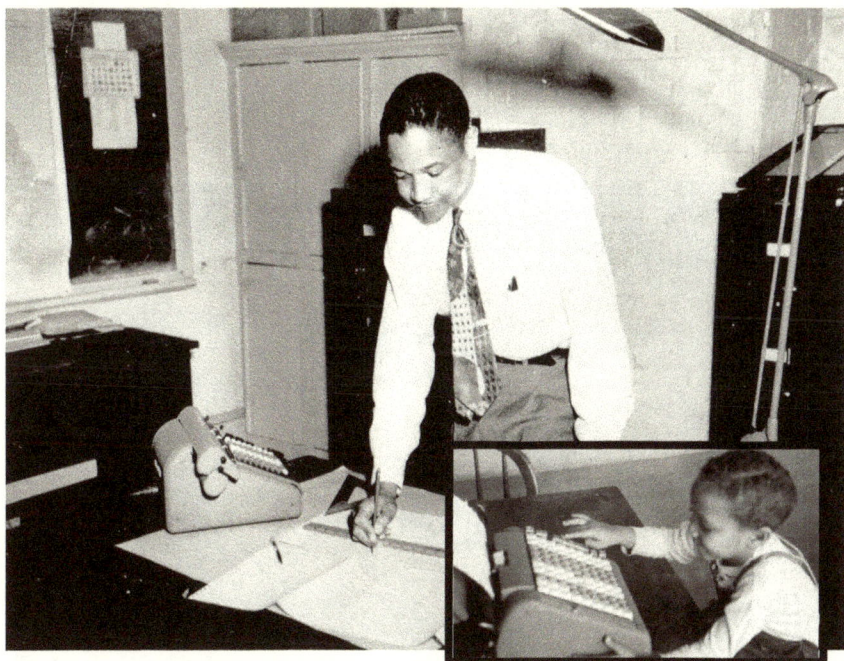

Above: Ray in his lab at Fort Valley State
Inset: Ray's son Nat at one of the lab's calculators

Below: The family, inside the house in Fort Valley (c1953)

A special occasion. (l to r) President Troup (Fort Valley State College), Sara Bailey (Macon school teacher), Ray, Lewis Mounts (Ballard teacher)

Above: Ray teaching Ray Jr. (left) and Nat to play tennis

Photo: Maddox Studio, Fort Valley, GA

Below Left: Written by Ray on the back of the above photo.
Below Right: Prophecy fulfilled.

Ray, Jr., Nat, Ray, Sr.
I started teaching them
tennis this year and in
our first tournament this
summer we were tops.
Ray, Jr. and I won a Doubles
Title and I won men's
singles title here.

MADDOX STUDIO
311 PEAR STREET
DIAL TA 5-5391
FORT VALLEY, GA.

It looks like we will be
in tennis for years to
come.

<u>Above:</u> On the road to California (1956)

<u>Below:</u> Newly arrived. From left, Ray, Nat, Ethel Cook, Kathy, Kathleen, Ray Jr.

Above: Ray in one of his "new math" classes

Below Left: Ray and Kay at the house in Pasadena
Below Right: With Nat at St. Barnabas Church

Above: Frances' Wedding. (l to r) Kathy, Ray, Frances, Paul Smith,
Kathleen, Ray Jr. (back), and Nat

Below: Kathy's college and Nat's high school graduation (1965)
(l to r) Ray, Kathy, Nat, Kathleen, Kathy's husband Al Bias

Above: The Raymond J. Pitts Human Relations trophy

Below: Kathleen and Ray attend Ray Jr.'s graduation
from Fisk University

Above: Frequent weekend trips to the beach in LA

Below: Celebrating their 45th Wedding Anniversary
(l to r) Kathy, Fran, Kathleen, Ray, Ray Jr., Nat

Above: Ray's family diploma "Wall of Honor"

Below: Roberta's Tuskegee diploma

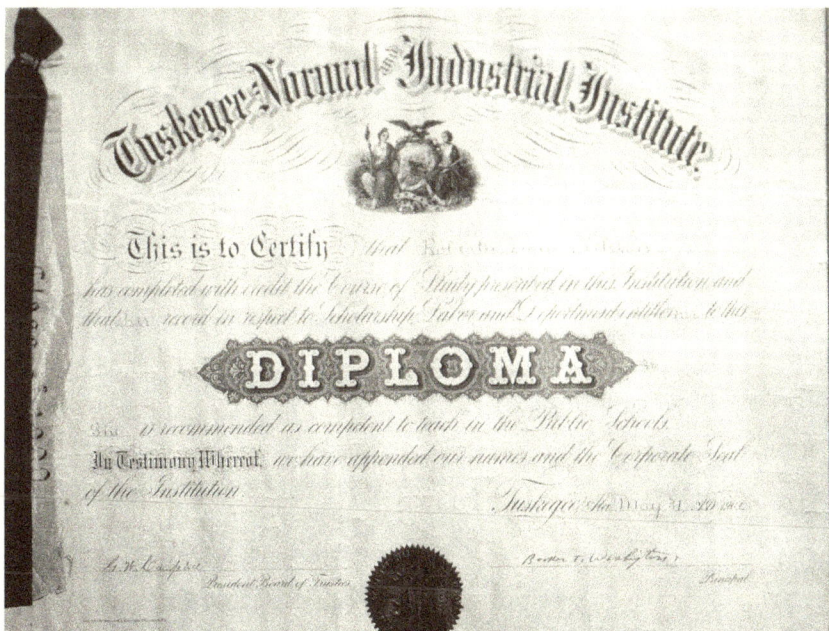

Above: Ray's Ballard Normal School diploma

Below: Ray's PhD diploma

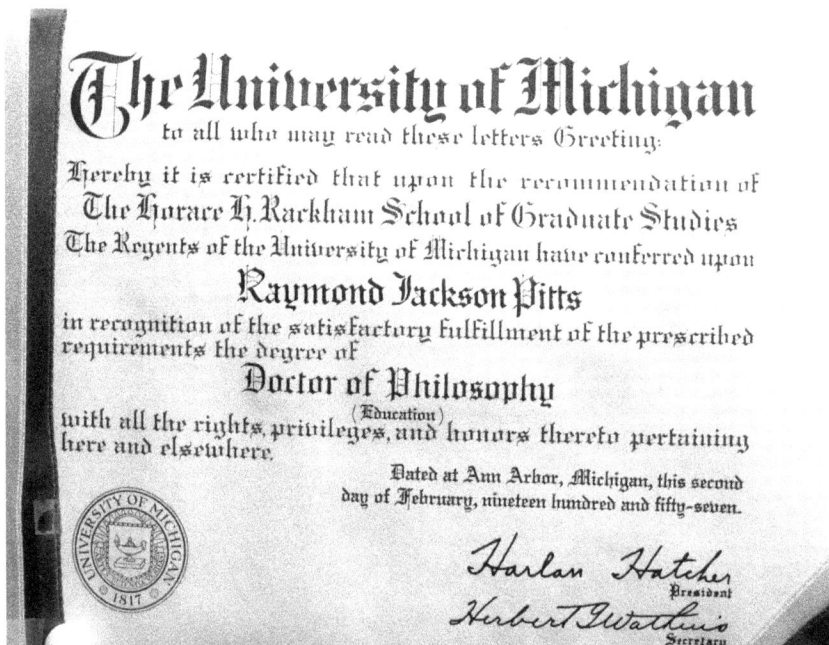

<u>Above:</u> Ray finds his father's grave at Marietta National Cemetery

<u>Below:</u> Visiting Holsey Temple in Macon

Kay and Ray: World Travelers

<u>Below:</u> In front of Kilimanjaro

Left: Great
Wall of China

Below: Venice

One of Ray and Kathleen's many retirement projects

Left: for Ray's
80th Birthday—
A Napa Valley train
excursion, surrounded
by family and friends

Below: Photo
taken at
Nathan Pitts' funeral.
(l to r) Robert Pitts
(Ray Jr.'s son), Ray Sr.,
Ray Jr., Nat

Above: Ray with youngest grandchild Steffie,
at school's Grandparents' Day

Below: With Kathleen, on a trip back to the site of their wedding

Kathleen C. Pitts and Raymond J. Pitts
50th Wedding Anniversary (1988)
(taken at Ray Jr.'s house in Gaithersburg, MD)

Nathan Alvin Pitts

In post-retirement conversation with his brother Ray about their early teen years, Nathan described his life after the family dissolved:

There were two or three years where I had to stop and try to remember even where I lived, because we moved around three or four places. Our father and I were the only two there [in Macon] during that time. My schedule began around four-thirty or five A.M. I would carry papers, go home, go to school, practice some sport after school, go home and study, and then go to bed. On weekends I worked at the bakery shop—Friday nights and Saturdays. So there was not much time spent at home. It was either school or the jobs. When I finished high school there was no talk whatever of college.

Nathan had seen his world turned upside down. His mother was gone for long stretches, to work at schools in North Carolina. His two eldest brothers were working out of state, and Ray was off to Talladega. Going to college had still been a possibility for Ray, and he had been singularly focused on obtaining that dream. He had saved money from his paper route, had obtained work at the college, and Sis had managed to shield some money that had been earmarked for Ray's education. But graduating three years behind Ray from Ballard, there were no funds remaining for Nathan in the aftermath of the family's disaster.

Willis had continued to work in Oklahoma, and helped with the funding for Ray's first two years of college. He returned to Talladega in 1930, Nathan's senior year at Ballard, to finish his own college degree. But, with their father in ill health and only sporadically working, Nathan's own earnings from his various jobs went toward living and school expenses, not college savings. The times were very hard and he found it impossible to save. When he graduated in 1931, he had less than three dollars to his name.

Despite the difficult times, the family did what it could to stay together. Later in life, he occasionally talked to his daughter Mitra about those times. She recounted that:

Sis instilled in them all a sense of respect, and she taught them the value of an education. She told them, "You should always get an education, they can take away a lot of things from you, but they can't take away what's in your mind."

As the youngest son, my dad learned a lot from his brothers about how to survive. He told me that in those days blacks weren't allowed to walk in the center of town. They had to remain in the corners, side streets, and black districts of town. They couldn't be in the affluent downtown area very safely. He once told me about an incident with Aunt Kathleen [she was his high-school friend as well as Ray's high-school sweetheart] that illustrates how difficult things could be. Kathleen was very light skinned and could pass for white. One time he was walking in Macon and out of the corner of his eye he saw this white woman come up behind him, and she put her arms around him and gave him a kiss! He remembered thinking, "Oh no! I'm going to get killed! They're going to lynch me." It turned out to be just Aunt Kathleen. But, even so, if someone had seen them and not realized that she was also black, it could have been very bad.

My father never really talked about his own father. All I knew was that his dad had been arrested; I thought it was probably for something he didn't do. That happened to black people in those days. But, I never knew any details. There was this "code of silence" in those times. If you were an adult people would tell you things, but if you were a child they wouldn't discuss anything in front of you. Everything about their family break-up is a mystery to me today, but I do remember that Dad said Sis always took care of them. She was an independent black woman and that's how she raised them—to be strong and independent. She instilled in them all a sense of respect, tenacity, and the value of an education. They all did very well.

When Willis returned to Macon that summer of 1931, it provided Nathan with an opportunity to get to know his eldest brother as more than just the role model and over-achiever that he always found himself compared to:

I got to know him better when, during the last of my high school days, he had returned to Macon and he and I began to play baseball together on the Bibb Mill Baseball Team. He and I were thrown together on the team with a group where few, if any, of the others had even any high school education. We began to share the type of comradeship that bound us together as friends, in addition to the fact that we were brothers. Since that time, that has been one of the talking points around which he and I share many experiences.

While all the brothers deferred to Willis in terms of innate athletic ability, Nathan was also tremendously talented and had the added advantage of height and weight. He was six-foot-two and powerfully built. A star athlete at Ballard,

Nathan was also smart and popular: he was the Ballard senior class Vice President and won third honor for his academic record. Sis was concerned that their family break-up had affected Nathan the most adversely. She had no financial resources for his college education, but she still had her extensive network of contacts—and her famous determination. She put extra attention into advertising Nathan's athletic potential and academic success. At the end of his senior year, Theodore A. (Ted) Wright,[1] an Alpha man who had taught at Talladega, took notice of the young athlete. Ted had just accepted a position at Florida A&M College in Tallahassee, where he was hired to establish that college's new physical education program. He saw Nathan's potential and his need, and realized that his new job provided an opportunity to give the boy a chance. Ted arranged for Nathan to receive an athletic scholarship at A&M, and the Wright family brought him with them when they moved:

> *It was only when Ted passed through and took me to Florida A&M with him that I had any idea of going to college. Were it not for Ted, I am sure that I could not have stayed in school. Over the four years I was in school, I received a total of fifty dollars from the family. All of my school I was supported by the Wrights, and I considered myself a family member of the Wrights.*

Nathan was the last of the brothers to leave their Macon home, and he didn't look back. He, like his brothers, would make a separate life for himself and would often lose touch with the others. But, while they rarely spoke or wrote to each other, each of them was constantly in touch with Sis. She had little time in her busy schedule to keep them up-to-date on each other's activities, or even whereabouts; but she always knew herself. She helped out when she could—with money, introductions, advice, and encouragement—and kept up a regular correspondence with each one. All the years she worked in North Carolina, through the sheer force of her personality and her mother's love, she remained the dominant influence in their lives. Each son would credit Sis with instilling in them faith and optimism, the determination to excel, and the perseverance to face and overcome whatever hardships life imposed.

College Years

Nathan and Ted remained at Florida A&M for three years, and during that time Nathan won academic letters in four sports: baseball, basketball, football and track. He concentrated on science and mathematics courses, with the dream of eventually becoming a medical doctor. At Tallahassee, he also met Miss Mary Alma Williams, a fellow student who was studying home economics. Originally from Ocala, Florida, Mary came from a strong and close-knit

1 The Wright family had other close Pitts connections. Elzy, one of Ted's sons, later moved to Sacramento. He and his wife Marge were good friends of Ray and Kathleen for many years.

family of four daughters and two sons. According to his nephew Nat, Nathan felt a calmness and security in the large family's stability and affection for each other. He and Mary's deepening romance would be tested when, in 1934, Nathan went to New Orleans with the Wrights. Ted had been selected to develop Xavier University's athletics programs and to coach its football team. But Nathan and Mary kept in close contact. The strength of their affection was proven as their steady, long-distance romance continued to flourish.

Nathan enrolled at Xavier and throve there; academically, athletically, and spiritually. Xavier was a relatively new black institution; founded by Katharine Drexel[2] and the Sisters of the Blessed Sacrament. It was at the time, and remains, the only historically black Catholic university in the US. The college's first degrees were awarded in 1928, and the striking Gothic administration building was finished just the year before the Wrights moved to New Orleans. Nathan continued to do well in pre-medical courses and planned to pursue his dream of becoming a doctor. He starred in the same sports he had played in Florida, but especially excelled in football. He was said to show "uncanny knowledge in selecting the right plays at the right time," and led the Xavier team to many victories. This talent earned Nathan Honorable Mention as an All-American Quarterback in 1935.[3] With his easy nature and innate politeness, Nathan became a favorite pet of the nuns. Under their careful eyes he matured a passion for social justice and for helping the needy that was evident throughout his long life, and before he left Xavier he converted to Roman Catholicism. At his graduation ceremony in 1936, the statement he chose to include in the program was, "I have gained that moral integrity which determines a man's destiny."

Nathan's dream was to go to medical school at Howard University in Washington, DC. Howard was the premier, predominantly-black university in the country, and figured large in all four brothers' college ambitions. Ray had been initially promised a Howard scholarship, Bob would graduate with a Howard degree, and Willis would eventually teach there. Nearly all the prominent black men of his time had some connection with Howard and, despite the formidable obstacle of finances, Nathan was determined to go.

After his Xavier graduation, Ted introduced Nathan to a friend whose father was the headwaiter at a hotel in Atlantic City. He and this friend went to Atlantic City that summer, to work at the hotel, and then Nathan moved to the Washington, DC, area to work towards tuition for Howard University's medical school. During that year, he shared a room with his brother Bob, who was already studying at Howard. With Bob's recommendation, Nathan got a job

---

2   To be canonized, in 2000, as Saint Katharine Drexel.

3   A charming illustration of the talented quarterback, by George Lee, was published in the Chicago Defender, December 15, 1934. Despite repeated attempts, the author was unable to obtain permission to reproduce the illustration for this book. However, it can, for a small fee, be found in their online archives: http://pqasb.pqarchiver.com/chicagodefender/advancedsearch.html

as a waiter at the Southern Club. But, although they lived together, they rarely had time to catch up. Bob went from school directly to his night job at a hotel. When he came home, Nathan was already asleep; and when Nathan left for work, Bob was asleep. They saw each other only on weekends. Still, after their long separation, both felt it was good to have a family member nearby.

Ralph Bunche, the eminent black political scientist, was already teaching at Howard when Nathan set his sites on that university. Another star college athlete, Bunche was the first African-American to receive a PhD in Political Science from a major American university, Harvard, in 1934. He had gone to Harvard after graduating from the University of California, Los Angeles, in 1927—valedictorian of his class and *summa cum laude*. Bunche was already making a name for himself in government and political circles, and ultimately was the first African-American to win the Nobel Peace Prize (1950) for his work on the Arab-Israeli conflict. He chaired the Department of Political Science at Howard from 1928 until 1950. As part of the backdrop of influences on Nathan's future career directions, the fact that Bunche was black and was making significant inroads with his eminent diplomatic career must have been encouraging. He was a role model to all the aspiring and talented young men at the college. Unfortunately for Nathan, the income from his waiter's job was not sufficient to pay the needed tuition, and he could not find better work. However, Bunche's influence may have helped to steer Nathan into a social science career and diplomacy, after the dream of medical school did not work out.

By the fall of 1937, when he had hoped to begin at Howard, Nathan could still not afford the entrance fee. Ted offered Nathan a chance to return to Xavier that fall, where the new gymnasium was just being completed, and he agreed to fill two coaching jobs through football season. Then, in January 1938, Ted alerted Nathan to a job opening at Immaculata high school in Birmingham, Alabama. He was offered, and accepted, a position as faculty member and coach of the basketball and track teams. After just a few short months, Nathan proved his mettle by coaching the basketball team to the regional "best record" of the year, with fifteen victories out of twenty games. His track team also excelled, wining sixteen gold and two silver medals in that year's competitions.

Nathan enjoyed his success and acclaim at Immaculata, but coaching in a high school was not what he wanted to do with his life; nor was the salary sufficient to support a family. His sweetheart Mary wouldn't wait forever, so he continued to search for new opportunities.

First Jobs Together

In the fall of 1938, Ted Wright came through again with a new job lead. Ted had heard, through the religious grapevine at Xavier, of a unique opportunity in Ridge, Maryland. That small coastal community's social-activist priest, Father Horace B. McKenna,[4] had decided to reopen the Cardinal Gibbons Institute, which had closed in 1933 under financial difficulties and amid leadership controversies.[5] McKenna was seeking to hire a school principal and a few good teachers. Both Nathan and Mary applied.

The Cardinal Gibbons Institute, which had initially opened in 1924, was the region's first high school built to educate blacks. It was connected to the mission of St. Peter Claver's Church, the first, and only, all-black parish in St. Mary's County, Maryland, and drew its students from St. Peter Claver's grammar school. Father McKenna, a young white priest who had earlier experience teaching at a Jesuit school in the Philippines, had come to Ridge in 1931 on his first parochial assignment after ordination. He had originally hoped to reopen the Institute in the fall of 1937, even going so far as to gather four graduates of the parish grammar school and begin teaching them himself. However, anticipated funding did not materialize. With his already overtaxed schedule,[6] McKenna only succeeded in putting himself in the hospital. This forced the closing of his makeshift school in November. He did not stop seeking support for the Institute, however, and by late 1938 he had secured eighteen students and enough funding to allow it to reopen. The new teachers would make it a reality.[7]

McKenna hired Nathan to be the Institute's principal and its primary academic teacher, while Mary was hired to teach home economics. They each made plans to move to Ridge and, with the promise of two good jobs, also made plans to marry. Completing the Institute's faculty was Mr. James Wainwright, who taught vocational agriculture. The high school was reopened on annual support of $2000 from the diocese, supplemented with gifts from various patrons. Nathan's and Mary's wedding was held the following June in Baltimore,[8] where most of Mary's family now resided.

The Institute also sponsored a program of adult education and extension work, and McKenna now made it the home of his buyer's-cooperative activism. With the active encouragement of McKenna, Nathan became involved in teaching night classes. He also began to study cooperatives, the credit problems

4 The renowned founder of Washington, DC-based charities: So Others Might Eat (SOME), Martha's Table, and House of Ruth.

5 See David W. Southern (1996). John LaFarge and the Limits of Catholic Interracialism, 1911-1963. Available from http://books.google.com

6 McKenna was also rebuilding St. Peter Claver's Church, which had burned in 1934; had become Superior of the local community of priests; and was actively organizing buyers' cooperatives among the black fishermen in St. Mary's County.

7 Details of the activities at Cardinal Gibbons Institute were gleaned from Francis Michael Walsh (1997). Resurrection: The Story of the Saint Inigoes Mission:1634-1994. (retrieved April 2, 2015 from http://www.reocities.com/RainForest/vines/6480/inigoes1.html)

8 June 14, 1939 at St. Ann Catholic Church. Father McKenna presided. The bride wore pink crepe and carried a corsage of orchids and tiny French rosebuds. (Details from Baltimore Afro American, June 17, 1939)

of rural farmers, and the structure of credit unions. He led work-study groups in three localities of St. Mary's County to investigate the possibilities of organizing a local credit union to benefit the black farm families.

Nathan became convinced of the need for and promise of the cooperative movement in rural black communities. Within a few months he was able to counter initial reluctance of credit associations to extend a charter, and in February 1940 he succeeded in receiving one for their local credit union from the Farm Credit Association. His study group had saved sixty dollars while they worked on the concept. They used this to pay for the charter of the Martin de Porres Federal Credit Union and to purchase necessary supplies, and they still had twenty dollars left over for loans. In this work, Nathan had also discovered the subject for his graduate study. He took a year away from Ridge in 1940–41 and headed to Ann Arbor to begin graduate work at the University of Michigan, where his brothers Ray and Willis were also studying. Although Nathan was away at school, Mary remained teaching at the Institute and he retained his position as principal. He also served as Chairman of the new credit union's Supervisory Committee.

Returning to Ridge in the fall of 1941, Nathan transferred to Catholic University in Washington, DC, to continue his master's degree studies. He received the MA degree in Social Science in 1944, with the thesis topic, "Martin de Porres Federal Credit Union and its influence upon Negro families of St. Mary's County, MD." Planning to continue his education, he immediately enrolled in Catholic University's PhD program.

Life in Ridge must have been both gratifying and frustrating for the young Pitts couple. Nathan achieved considerable success with his credit union activities, and at the school. But other activities that had been intended to benefit the black farmers and fisherman of the county foundered, and a key supporter of the Institute died. The rise of the war effort was changing land use around St. Mary's County drastically, with the building of a Naval air base. Increasing military activities were changing the economy as well, affecting the viability of the Institute-sponsored cooperatives and credit unions. The Institute was also facing financial difficulties. Like Ray, because he was married and employed in teaching, Nathan avoided conscription into the armed services. But the War still changed everyone's lives.

McKenna was rumored to be neither the best parish administrator nor the most financially prudent. With his penchant for activism, he was also something of a lightening rod in a region struggling with increasing economic and racial tensions, as the nation readied itself for war. Those tensions had been exacerbated by the publication of Harry Sylvester's novel, *Dearly Beloved* (1942), based loosely on McKenna's work in the area. McKenna felt the book had over-emphasized racial tensions and injustices in the community, and its positive

review by *The New York Times* had drawn unwanted, and perhaps unwarrant-
ed, attention to their work. Nathan agreed with McKenna that the tone of the
book was exaggerated, and feared that its popularity would only exacerbate the
local problems.

With a view to both to the limitations of his current position and the lure of
better opportunities made possible by his graduate degree, Nathan began applying for positions elsewhere. Several letters of recommendation were written for
him by those who had observed his work at Ridge. One, by Constance Daniel,
who with her husband had run the Cardinal Gibbons Institute in its earlier in-
carnation, hinted that there might have also been conflicts between Nathan and
the Institute's leadership that factored into his decision to leave.[9] This time Ted
Wright, who nevertheless remained a friend of Nathan's and his brother Ray's
for life, was no longer needed to help Nathan find a position. He had achieved
enough stature with his own accomplishments to attract credible offers.

Nathan and Mary left Ridge for good in 1944. He had accepted a one-year
position as an instructor of sociology and economics at North Carolina College for Negroes in Durham, North Carolina. Since the new position was short-
term, and he planned to return to DC to complete his PhD, Nathan moved
alone to North Carolina. Mary moved to the DC-Baltimore area, where she
was able to stay with family.

North Carolina College was the nation's first state-supported liberal arts college for black students. Founded by James E. Shepard in 1910 as a center for
religious training, the school had been through numerous transformations as a
private school before being approved for state funding—all with Shepard as its
head. It had begun offering its first graduate-level courses in arts and sciences
in 1939, had opened the School of Law in 1940, and one of Library Science in
1941. Nathan taught for a salary of $2400 and lived in the dorms.

During his time in Durham, Nathan began studying cooperatives among the
black families of North Carolina, the subject he chose for his PhD dissertation.
He concentrated on these studies during the 1945–46 academic year, while
again looking for a job. He listed his residence as Macon, at his father's place,
but probably divided his time between caring for his father, who was at this
point quite ill, researching North Carolina cooperatives, and studying at Catholic University in DC (visiting Mary while there). In the summer of 1946 Nathan
wrote to Shepard asking for reemployment, but he was turned down. Shepard
did, however, promise assistance; he was perhaps helpful in securing Nathan's
next position. It would be at Shepard's old *alma mater*, Shaw University, the
oldest historically black university in the US.

Mary was able to join Nathan at Shaw in Raleigh, North Carolina. She had

9   Some of the recommendation letters are available from the James E. Shepard archives at North Carolina
Central University: Retrieved April 2, 2015 from http://dc.lib.unc.edu/cdm/search/collection/50001/

continued to further her own education, and soon earned a Masters degree in education from New York University.[10] She too became a faculty member at Shaw, teaching home economics. The two worked together there until the summer of 1950.

While at Shaw, Nathan taught courses in sociology and economics, participated in the community program of teacher training, and became Chair of the Department of Social Science. During this time he also completed the requirements for his PhD, which was awarded by Catholic University in early 1950. His dissertation[11] focused on the leadership activity, organizational procedures, and impact of the cooperative movement on community patterns and behaviors of groups of underprivileged people. The degree was, to the best of his knowledge, the first PhD in Sociology awarded to a black student by Catholic University.

One of Nathan's students at Shaw would have been Angie Brooks, a social science major who graduated in 1949. Later, Miss Brooks became world famous as the Liberian diplomat who, in 1969, was the first (and only) African female elected President of the United Nations General Assembly.[12]

Although Shaw was a Baptist university, Nathan remained an active leader in the Roman Catholic Church, especially working with fellow Catholics on issues of racial and economic justice. In 1947, he was elected to a two-year term as one of eight members of the Board of Directors of the North Carolina Catholic Laymen Association.[13] He was also one of the speakers to address the 1950 *Catholic Conference on Industrial Problems*, in Charlotte, North Carolina. His subject was "economic rights as a basic human right." At that conference, participants were warned that continuing racial problems at home were weakening American influence abroad.[14]

In 1950, Baltimore's Coppin Teachers College became part of the higher education system of Maryland, becoming Coppin State Teachers College. Dr. Miles Connor, the former principal, was named the President of the College. Connor had been a friend of Nathan's since the time he had spent in the DC area after graduating from Xavier.[15] At times, he had written Nathan recommendations for other job applications. Now, he was able to offer Nathan the job of Professor and Chairman of the Social Sciences Department at the new state

10   Awarded in 1947.

11   Nathan Alvin Pitts (1950). *The Cooperative Movement in Negro Communities of North Carolina*. Catholic University of America Press. Washington, DC.

12   She was also only the second woman, from any nation, to head the UN. She served as President of the General Assembly in 1970, while Nathan was on the US delegation to UNESCO in Paris. There is no record of whether they were in contact during that time, however it seems likely that they would have been.

13   Anon. (May 16, 1947). *North Carolina Laymen Select Negro Convert for Board of Directors*. The Guardian. Little Rock, Arkansas. (arc.stparchive.com)

14   Joe Maxwell (March 28, 1950). *Incomplete Democracy at Home Harms America Abroad, Catholic Confab Told*. Washington Afro-American, Washington, DC.

15   Connor and his wife were also listed in the Baltimore paper as attendees at Nathan and Mary's wedding.

college. With so many family and friendship ties already in the Baltimore area, the decision was an easy one. Nathan and Mary happily moved to the city that would become their permanent home.

Settling in Baltimore

Once settled in Baltimore, Nathan and Mary began to both put down roots and to expand their reach. She loved designing and sewing clothes for family members, working in her vegetable garden, and perfecting her cooking skills. She also joined a number of social and service organizations, was involved in her Delta Sigma Theta sorority chapter, and was active in their local church. Mary's three sisters all lived nearby, and they were involved in many of the same groups. They were all regularly featured in the society pages of the *Baltimore Afro American*, both for their charitable activities and for their hosting of elaborate dinner parties and events.

Although they had full, enjoyable lives and an affectionate relationship, one disappointment the couple felt was that they had so far been unable to have children. Settled in Baltimore, they pursued adoption as a possible avenue to having a family together. However, according to daughter Mitra:

> *They went to a Catholic charity to adopt, but the charity didn't have a lot of black kids. One time, they did say they had a child. I remember my father telling me about it when I was young. They brought the child and it stayed with them for the weekend. But, then they came and took the child away and said it wasn't available after all, after my parents had already fallen in love with it. Then they told them they wouldn't have any child for them after all. They couldn't find a black child that would fit with an educated family. I remember being horrified by the whole thing.*

The waiting, excitement and disappointments were taking a toll on the couple. They feared they would never become parents, so tried to find fulfillment in careers, community, and their large, extended families.

Mary returned to full-time teaching in 1955. She taught Home Economics at Morgan State College until 1965, and then taught in Baltimore public schools from 1965 until she retired in 1980.

Nathan, in addition to his teaching and administrative responsibilities at Coppin, assisted in supervising students who were preparing for teaching in the elementary schools of the city, and he represented the college on the State College Curriculum Committee. During the summers of 1951, 52 and 56, he went to Poland, Maine, as the Guidance Director of the Burroughs Newsboys Foundation's Aggasiz Village. At this camp, which served 275–300 boys, he supervised the activities of 25–30 camp counselors, and he prepared the necessary reports for the social service agencies that financed sending boys to the camp. He also used the opportunity to study the adjustment problems of the boys, and published a scholarly article "Educational Implication of Summer Camp Experiences" based upon his observations.

In the summer of 1953, Nathan opted to go to South Carolina State College in Orangeburg, South Carolina, as a visiting professor in sociology. He also, in some years, taught night classes at Morgan State College and the Community College of Baltimore. Committed to continuing his own education, Nathan spent the summer of 1954 at Harvard University, studying administration in higher education and cross-culture contacts. That year he also spent one semester in night classes, studying industrial sociology at Johns Hopkins University in Baltimore. In the summer of 1955, he received a scholarship from the National Conference of Christians and Jews to study at Boston University's Human Relations Center in North Andover, Massachusetts. And in 1957, he was offered a one-year fellowship to return to Harvard to study education administration—but turned it down to explore other, more exciting opportunities.

Nathan and Mary had a friend at Morgan State College, Dr. Regina Goff, who was a professor of social work. She had taken leave from the college to spend time in Isfahan and Tehran, working for the US government on loan to the Iranian Ministry of Education. Her enthusiastic talk about the experience fascinated Nathan, and he applied for the same type of assignment through the State Department's International Cooperation Administration (ICA).[16] He was accepted, and spent two years, 1957 1959, in Tehran and the Azerbaijan Province of Iran, as a teacher-trainer and advisor to the Director General of Education in the province. At that time Iran was considered a "hardship assignment" and he would need to spend much of the time traveling in remote regions, so he went to the country alone and Mary remained teaching in Baltimore. While there, he participated in all the national educational conferences sponsored throughout Iran, served as a consultant to a local university developing a program of teacher education, and studied the sociology of family life in Iran.

Near the end of his stay in Iran, Nathan met some fellow Americans who mentioned knowing a couple who had adopted a child from a local Iranian orphanage. They compared the relative ease of adopting a child in Iran vs. the difficulties in the US. Intrigued, Nathan decided to research the options. On one visit to a recommended orphanage, while being shown around, he picked up a charming little girl who had run out to greet him. When he moved to put her down, she clung to him and would not let go. Always a gentleman, he held on to her as she insisted—carrying her in his arms during the entire tour. By the end of the tour he was as attached to her as she was to him, and he resolved to adopt her. Mary, informed of the possibility of this adoption, quickly flew to

---

16   Which in 1961 became the Agency for International Development (AID).

Iran to assess the situation for herself. She too fell in love with the three-year-old charmer. They soon flew home with their new daughter, Mitra, a "bright-eyed little girl" who seemed as at home in Baltimore as in Iran.[17]

Federal Government and Foreign Service

Back in the States, Nathan returned to Coppin State as Chair of the Department of Social Sciences, and the family adjusted to being a threesome. Daughter Mitra recalls:

> *Growing up with my parents, I thought they were very strict. But, I didn't really have anything to compare it to. It was a great life. I feel like they were great parents. I don't feel like I missed anything or longed for anything—although I would have liked a brother and sister, in order to have an ally when I got in trouble. We did a lot together. We were close knit, although perhaps not like my daughter and I are close knit. She and I tell each other more, and talk about a lot of things that my parents and I would not have talked about. In those days, you didn't talk with children about some things. But we did all the typical family things—eating and talking together at dinner, at breakfast. That's what we did every day. If I could have replicated that life for my daughter, I absolutely would have. But times change. I had to toe the line more than my daughter; my life was very regulated. I grew up in the Catholic Church: we went to church every Sunday. I went to a private school, a religious school. I would get a ride home from a classmate's parents, have a half hour for a snack, practice my piano for a half hour, and then do my homework. Later Dad would come home and we would all sit around the table and have dinner together. Then we'd either watch TV or I would sit with my dad and talk.*
>
> *Now that I'm older, when I look at other people and the way they grew up, I think about how very, very lucky I was to have parents who grew up in an environment where they weren't always given everything. Living in that era in the South, they had lessons they carried with them through life. You work hard, you work together, and you take care of each other. You persevere. Community. Family. That's what helped people to survive back then and that's what they taught me. I had a great life.*

Although always dedicated to education and teaching, the experience of working internationally had left Nathan restless at Coppin State. In July 1961, he left Coppin to take a position in Washington, DC, at the US Office of Education (USOE) International Education Division. He became Chief of International Organizations Recruitment. There he supervised a staff of three

---

17   Carl Schoettler (undated clipping, c1960) *Educator Finds Schools Both Modern, In Tents.* The Baltimore Sun, Baltimore, Maryland.

professionals and three secretaries. He was chiefly responsible for Education's participation in the technical assistance program of the ICA, and for recruiting others to perform similar assignments to the one he had taken in Iran. He was assigned as Education's liaison officer with the Department of State and other US agencies via the United Nations Education, Scientific and Cultural Organization (UNESCO). At first, he had to spend half a day at the Office of Education and half a day at the Department of State. Then in 1964, he was responsible for the transfer of the program entirely to the Office of Education. In addition to US recruitment for ICA, Nathan frequently arranged for and participated in visits from UNESCO personnel to the US to interview potential candidates, and he made periodic trips to UNESCO headquarters in Paris, France, for conferences, training and consultations. While he was in this position, he was responsible for the establishment of a full-time Office of Education position on the US Delegation to UNESCO.

Switching career directions away from teaching did not mean Nathan lost his commitment to students and their educational opportunities. He often accepted speaking engagements, such as delivering the Knoxville College opening convocation in 1965. He challenged the students at this historically black college to be ready to seize the opportunities being opened before them via the Civil Rights Act of 1964, the Economic Opportunity Act, the National Defense Education Act, and other changes in laws or programs that were laying the groundwork for equal opportunity. He told them, "There is no limit to your attainment possibilities if you have the talent." He continued, "There is no excuse for any student today who possesses the ability and talent to study and attain excellence in his academic pursuits to fall by the way-side."[18]

New responsibilities in Washington and frequent travel did not keep Nathan and Mary from investing time with family, either. A nephew, Ray Jr., had a serious girlfriend from Baltimore while he was in college at Fisk University in Tennessee. Since the girl's parents were long-term friends of Nathan and Mary, he eagerly accepted many invitations to enjoy Mary's cooking, and the couple's warm hospitality, while pursuing that relationship. Ray Jr.'s younger brother Nat (who was named after Nathan) also remembered visiting in Baltimore:

Mary was nice, direct, strong, and one hell of a cook. She had her own garden in her back yard and raised some of her favorite greens. She always had a pie of some sort in the kitchen. You never left her house hungry!

And recalling his Uncle Nathan's visits to the West Coast while on government business, his nephew Nat wrote:

He had big, pretty eyes that were stable and focused when he looked at me,

---

18 Anon. (October 9, 1965). *Talented students no longer have any excuses*. Baltimore Afro-American, Baltimore, Maryland. p. 8.

and a smile that would light up the whole room. He was quiet, like my dad, and he spoke with the same directness and focus. He was always well dressed, but of all the brothers he was the one to first get out of the tie and jacket to make and serve up the drinks. We didn't see him often, but my parents kept his vision alive in my head with various stories about his travels through life. He would send me Christmas gifts from various places: Paris, Brussels, or Iran. It made me wonder what my uncle was doing in those places and what were those places like. I was told that he was working for the United Nations in Paris, and that he spoke French! When he came to California, I got to ask him about his life, but he always seemed more eager to know about what I was doing in Pasadena. I think he wanted to understand what California was about for a young black boy.

If Uncle Nathan was out to California on government business, he would come to our home late at night, after he had finished whatever work he was there for. He would be too late for dinner, but Mom would have a plate warming in the oven for him. He would teach them about the latest drink. My folks, never the drinkers, would giggle and humor him by trying his latest concoction. They would loosen up and talk of current and old times, and I would go to sleep to the sounds of their socializing. He would have to leave very late at night to return to his duty station. We were lucky to be close to where he had business, but he had to travel when it would fit in with what the government allowed. When I started working for the government, I did exactly the same thing. My mother, when she was ninety-two, asked me why I had to leave so early to go to the airport. I told her I was just like Uncle Nathan.

In 1968, Nathan left Education's International Education Division to become a program officer in USOE's Bureau of Educational Personnel Development, under Mrs. Iris Garfield, Director of Assessment and Coordination. From 1969 to 1970 he was responsible for coordinating the activities of national advisory groups to the USOE, and for programs serving training directors in over 700 colleges and universities throughout the country. He also served as a liaison officer with training programs in other USOE bureaus, and with other Federal agency training programs, and he assisted in the development of evaluation methodologies for bureau training programs.

Then in 1970, Nathan had the opportunity to himself assume the position he had first established, as the Office of Education liaison to the US UNESCO delegation. His responsibilities included reporting on the education sector of UNESCO; serving as an alternate representative on the Commission dealing with Education, the United Nations University and the International Bureau of Education; and overseeing US concerns in science education in the Education and Natural Science Sectors of UNESCO. He moved to Paris in October of that year; Mary and Mitra joined him there in January 1971. As a black man in the UNESCO office, Nathan found that most people assumed he was from Ethiopia or some other African country. It was thought the US could never send a black man for such a prestigious position. But, he said, "After they were convinced I was from the US, it was very nice."

Because of his many years hosting UNESCO officials in the US, Nathan had contacts in the organization that other Americans didn't have. One of those contacts introduced him to an assistant administrative officer in the embassy, in charge of invitations. Often, if an invitation came and the ambassador or a more senior staffer could not attend, she would call and say, "Does Mary want to go?" The couple loved it, and the family had a great time taking advantage of all the opportunities. Mary was said to have "wined and dined about twenty people at a time, in addition to taking visitors to shows and on sightseeing tours. Those of us [black US ex-pats in France] who live here never refuse an invitation to come out and put away some of her good cooking."[19]

Near the end of his tour, Nathan's position was expanded to include educational activities for the US delegation, and responsibility for the continuing analysis of positions held by Americans in all UNESCO programs. He was the first officer of the USOE to be assigned to an overseas program as an Educational Attaché. In addition to his position as a liaison officer for both Education and for the UNESCOPAS program (assistance to developing states), he had the responsibility of monitoring and evaluating UNESCO education programs in member states, particularly in Africa and the Middle East.

Nathan traveled often, and sometimes the assignments were wearying. He wrote to Ray in 1971; "I spent March 13–31 in Africa. Visited UNESCO projects in Nigeria, Ghana, Ivory Coast, and Liberia. Had a nice, but busy trip. After we do a little traveling in Europe, I will be ready to find a nice quiet spot in the States and settle down." He sometimes felt that the organization had regressed since the days of William Draper Carter, who had run the Department of International Exchange at UNESCO during the years Nathan worked in the International Education Division in DC. "When Carter left, they went back to their old boy network. You couldn't do what you thought was right. You had to carry out the instructions you were given." Still, he said, "In spite of the problems, I was fortunate in being able to travel: France, Afghanistan, Pakistan, India—we saw the Taj Mahal!"

The family returned to Baltimore for a two-month vacation during the summer of 1973, and hit the society pages with a splash. Mary's social club, the Moles, even hosted a "Christmas in July" party for the couple. Then, back in France, Mary continued her tradition of dinner parties and entertaining, hosting two of her sisters, Dorothy and Vera, for nearly a month during the sumer

---

19   Ollie Stewart, Paris correspondent to the Baltimore Afro-American (undated clipping in the archives).

of 1974. Nathan's brother Willis and his wife Frances visited once, as did his second brother Bob and Bob's wife Mattalyn, each taking the opportunity to travel further afield in Europe when they came. Mitra was given all the advantages of a European education, and their family also enjoyed wide and varied travel throughout Europe, utilizing diplomatic recreational facilities. They went all over France, to Berchtesgaden in Bavaria, and to Vienna; they even sent Mitra to ski and skate with old friends in Switzerland.

The family returned home again, briefly, in 1974. But this time Mary, who had been refused another leave of absence from teaching with the school district, stayed in Baltimore while Nathan and Mitra returned to France. It was Mitra's senior year at the American school, and she very much enjoyed the opportunity to play hostess for her dad in the vibrant diplomatic and ex-pat communities.

Dad and I lived in Paris together. That was a great time, because my mom was really strict and Dad was maybe less so. It was the special dynamic of a father-daughter thing. I was definitely "my father's little girl." I used to go to events at the embassies. We would have dinner together all the time, or go out to dinner. If Dad had to go to a party after work, I would get dressed up and go with him and he would introduce me to everyone as "my daughter."

Nathan loved Paris, but he was limited to a five-year leave of absence from his Washington, DC, posting in the USOE. He returned to the states in the fall of 1975 as the Chief of the International Exchange Branch, where he worked until he retired in February 1980. There he directed the teacher exchange program: sending American teachers abroad in direct exchange with teachers from other countries, or directing seminars in selected countries for American teachers. He also directed the International Visitors Program, for foreign visitors' short-term visits to the US; and the Educational Development Program, bringing foreign educators on board for longer-term projects in the US (financed in part by the Fulbright Commission).

In his later years in the USOE, Nathan grew increasingly upset with the inefficiency and cronyism of the government circles to which he belonged. After retiring, he once remarked that the only reason he ever set foot in DC again was to go to his barber. However, colleagues often sought him out for his perspectives and his advice. One such colleague was Frank Pinder, another black diplomat who shared many of Nathan's concerns about the inefficiencies of the government. Frank had been the USAID Ghana Mission Director from 1966–71, and the two had shared many experiences. They would chat over a beer about former colleagues and joint activities, and bemoan changes they saw and could not support in the organization they both had served.[20] Nathan was always generous with his time, and quick to listen or offer counsel.

---

20   There is an audio tape of one such conversation between the two in Ray's archives.

Into Retirement

Mitra went off to college not long after the family returned to the States from Paris. She went first to Spelman College in Georgia, and later to Kent State in Ohio. Without their daughter as a constant companion, Nathan and Mary plunged back into Baltimore society, their social clubs, and service activities.

As he neared retirement age, and particularly after he retired in 1980, Nathan became more and more involved with community education and service activities. In addition to his many professional societies and fraternities, he served on the Baltimore Council for International Affairs, the Baltimore Council for International Visitors, the National Urban League and the Ashburton Area Association. He was also active with the Boulé, the NAACP and the United Negro College Fund. He served, with his sister-in-law Catherine Adams, on the board of the Maryland Committee for Children, and hosted numerous fund-raising events in support of their child-care and day-care programs for disadvantaged families. Most notably, he invested fifteen years in attempts to improve, and ultimately save from closing, the Ashburton public school in his northwest Baltimore neighborhood. He was instrumental in keeping the school open, being a key figure in rousing the community to protest when the city government wanted to close the school and relocate the pupils. He organized the neighborhood in support of the school, lobbied IBM to get donated computers into the classrooms, and ultimately convinced the city to build a new school building that would keep the school within the community. He was constantly searching for grants and other ways to better the school, and besides the computers, also received a grant for the school to purchase books and videos on black history.

In addition, as they transitioned into their later careers and retirement, Nathan and Mary increased their investments in family relationships. Having reconnected with his brothers only after they were all mature and established in their respective careers, Nathan and Mary hosted a large and elaborate Pitts' family reunion in 1978, complete with out-of-town guests and a hosted dinner at a local inn. Then the two attended the great Lewis High and Ballard Normal School Grand Reunion with his other brothers in 1980. He and Mary frequently hosted one or another brother and/or family in Baltimore, or visited them in their respective parts of the country. The door was always open. Nathan and Mary were especially close with Willis and Frances in Stoughton, since the two couples formed "the East Coast Pittses." They tried to spend a minimum of one or two weeks together each summer, had hosted them in Paris and Geneva during Nathan's UNESCO assignment, and Mitra had spent at least one summer at Camp Whispering Willows when she was a girl.

When Mitra finished college she returned to the metro DC area, married, and had a daughter of her own: Mackenzie Mitra Rogers. Nathan and Mary loved having a granddaughter close by, and invested a great deal of time in her early years as well. Mitra mentioned that Nathan loved to tell Mackenzie stories about his many and varied experiences, at home and abroad.

With his history of athletic accomplishment, Nathan was also, naturally, an avid sports fan. He had always focused on his studies, but it was his athletic prowess that had gotten him into college and allowed him to stay there. Given his All-American honorable mention, he must have wondered what it would have been like to have "gone pro"—if only he had been born a decade or two later! A few African-American football players made it to the NFL in the late 40's and 50's, but they played positions other than quarterback. Blacks were not considered capable of being the quarterback.[21] Of course, like many boys-turned-to-men, Nathan would eventually live in a city whose professional team had its own great quarterback. And in this case, the Baltimore Colts had one of the greatest quarterbacks of all times—Johnny Unitas. Nathan was a passionate fan. Under Unitas' leadership, the Colts won the NFL championships in 1958 and 1959, and Super Bowl V[22] in the 1970 season. Until they left Baltimore for Indianapolis in 1983, Nathan faithfully watched, rooted for, and loved his Colts.

Nathan was interested in and supportive of his brother Ray's desire to produce a family history. The two corresponded about the project, and he even allowed himself to be taped for a single, short interview. However, unlike Ray who kept scrapbooks and journals of every trip or project, Nathan and Mary were not avid collectors or diarists. Their daughter Mitra explained:

I don't have old letters or scrapbooks. My mom was not into collecting: she didn't want to keep "junk." Dad would always send cards, but I've never seen the old letters. And Mom wasn't much of a letter writer. I, on the other hand, am a pack rat: I keep everything.

Nathan had intended to write down the details of his life and his career, as Ray frequently prompted him to do. Although he promised to try, he finally wrote to Ray and said that he was making no progress at all at writing anything down. Thus, the details of his and Mary's private lives, especially of their last years, remain sparse.

Nathan and Mary were, however, healthy and active with family and friends, involved in community service and church, and engaged in their several hobbies until both were well into their eighties. Nathan died on June 15, 1998, from complications after hip surgery. Mary continued living, mostly independently, at their northwest Baltimore home until she died of heart failure in 2003.

---

21   Kenny Washington (of UCLA, where he was a teammate of Jackie Robinson), who is considered the first black in the National football league, entered the league in 1946. However the first black to become an NFL quarterback, James Harris, did not enter until 1970 (with Buffalo). Jackie Robinson, considered the first black major league baseball player, entered the league in 1947. Nathan graduated Xavier in 1936; professional athletics was not yet a career path open to him.

22   Although Unitas was himself knocked out with an injury in the second quarter.

On September 29, 2000, a dedication ceremony was held for the new Ashburton school building, which was being christened the *Dr. Nathan A. Pitts–Ashburton Elementary/Middle School.* Sponsors, in addition to several neighborhood associations, included Maryland state legislators, state Senators, the city Mayor, the City Council, and the State Secretary of Public Safety. During the ceremony, Nathan's tireless efforts in securing the new building and his work toward improving the educational resources for the neighborhood were recognized with gratitude. He was eulogized in the program as:

Educator, diplomat, organizer, problem solver: a man of distinction, a man of honor."

Left: Nathan as a
young man

Below: Nathan, high
school and college
football star
(from Ray's scrapbook album)

Nathan (back row, 5th from left), with his fellow Xavier athletes.

Above: Nathan's
championship
Immaculata High
School basketball
team

Right: Nathan's men-
tor, Ted Wright Sr.,
speaking at
Savannah State
University, where he
coached football
and/or basketball
from 1947–62

Photo: Archives of Asa
H. Gordon Library,
Savannah State University

Above: Nathan, probably while at U. of Michigan

Below: 4 Pitts students at U. of Michigan
(l to r) Raymond, Kathleen, Willis, Nathan

Above Left: Mitra as a toddler
Above Right: Mitra as a graduate

Below: In Paris (l to r), Frances, Mitra, a friend, Nathan,
Mary(behind), Willis

Above: Nathan, at an event with Indira Ghandi and colleagues

Below: Nathan at the Taj Mahal

Above: With International Education colleagues, Nathan
was one of the rare black men of the late 60s and early 70s
who served in a senior US diplomatic position

Below: With Kathleen at their Pasadena pool.
"He had a smile that could light up a room."

Nathan (left) in his basement with his brothers (Willis, Bob, Ray): 1978 reunion.

Mary and Nathan at the combined
Lewis High–Ballard Normal School
Grand Reunion in 1980

Epilogue

Roberta "Sis" Pitts lived a difficult life. Trained to optimistically expect that education and hard work would elevate blacks to full participation in the American Dream, she and Willis Sr. ran forcefully into the hard wall of discrimination. They were ultimately unable to navigate socio-economic systems stacked so firmly against them.

Willis Sr. bequeathed to his sons his own love of learning and his pride in their ancestors, but he never recovered from the shock of his arrest and conviction. He died broken and largely alone in June 1948, and was buried at Marietta National Cemetery in Marietta, Georgia.

After their marriage dissolved, Sis—the woman who "never let anyone forget" that she had once been congratulated on her skills by the President of the United States—found it difficult to find work, even work as a domestic servant, in the Jim Crow South. Stress and poor medical care left her with difficult-to-manage high blood pressure and diabetes. In her final years, she endured a stroke and lost one leg to diabetic neuropathy.

But Sis was the strong one, and she had sons who needed her! She never gave up; never allowed herself to become despondent. Thwarted by life on every side, still she continued to hope and to dream—if not for herself; for them. She pinned her aspirations to the fortunes of her sons. She wanted to see them become the good, prominent, and influential men she knew they could be. She knew that sons like hers could change the world: in their hands, they held the promise of a different, brighter, fairer future.

Sis often voiced the concern that her sons, as adults, had lived largely separate lives. She would have been pleased to know that her final illness was the occasion for them to renew the strong family bond. When they heard that her time was near, Bob, Ray and Nathan flew to the home of Willis Jr. in Stoughton, where Sis was in the local hospital. Their joint visit before she died was the first of many regular family reunions that enabled wives and children to also become close, gave nieces and nephews the opportunity to enlarge family connections and expand horizons, and even sparked trips further afield—such as visits to Nathan at his posting in Paris, or trips to Georgia to investigate family history.

That close family bond continued, unabated, until each son, in turn, came to the end of his own life. It continues still, among succeeding generations.

As her life drew to a close that November of 1959, Sis urged each of her sons to cherish their family. She admonished them, "Don't forget who you are. You keep in touch with your brothers." According to Willis, in those final days she constantly repeated, even while semi-conscious; "I want my boys to be good men."

On their last visit, the four men walked into her hospital room together. Sis, prone in bed, observed them standing shoulder-to-shoulder. She slowly and painfully turned to the nurse standing by and, with the proud smack of her lips they all knew so well, she smiled—and said; "Those are *my boys!*"

Roberta's Boys: (l to r) Dr. Nathan Alvin Pitts, Dr. Raymond Jackson Pitts, Robert Bedford Pitts, Dr. Willis Norman Pitts, Jr.

Appendix 1: Family Trees

Emanuel Pitts
Family Tree

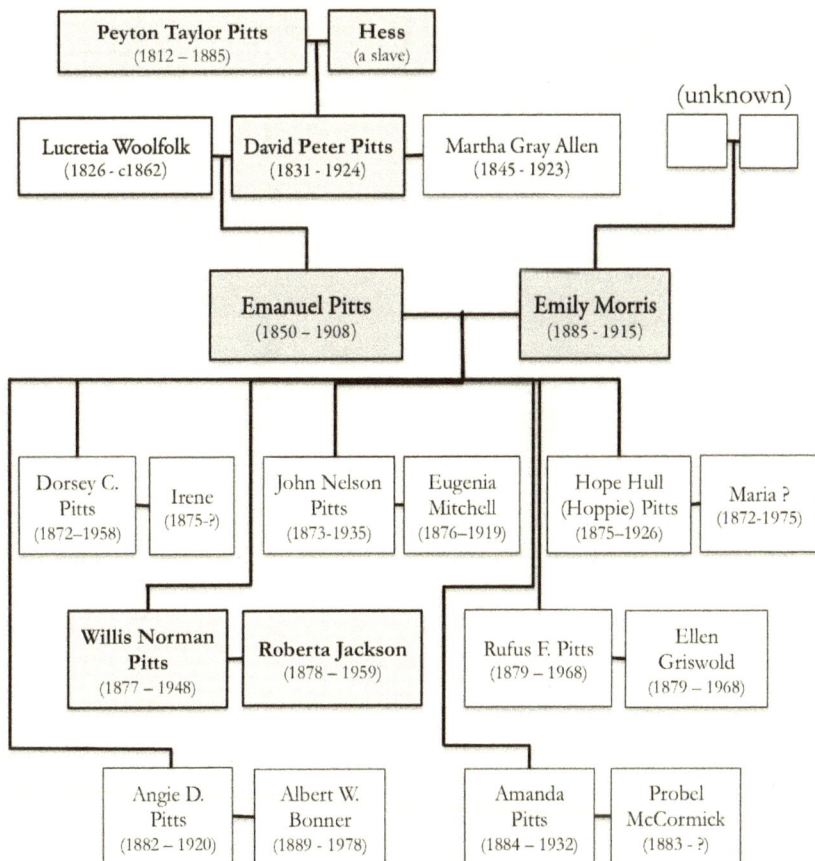

Peyton Taylor Pitts (1812 – 1885)	**Hess** (a slave)

(unknown)

Lucretia Woolfolk (1826 - c1862)	**David Peter Pitts** (1831 - 1924)	Martha Gray Allen (1845 - 1923)

Emanuel Pitts (1850 – 1908)	**Emily Morris** (1885 - 1915)

Dorsey C. Pitts (1872–1958)	Irene (1875-?)	John Nelson Pitts (1873-1935)	Eugenia Mitchell (1876–1919)	Hope Hull (Hoppie) Pitts (1875–1926)	Maria ? (1872-1975)

Willis Norman Pitts (1877 – 1948)	**Roberta Jackson** (1878 – 1959)	Rufus F. Pitts (1879 – 1968)	Ellen Griswold (1879 – 1968)

Angie D. Pitts (1882 – 1920)	Albert W. Bonner (1889 - 1978)	Amanda Pitts (1884 – 1932)	Probel McCormick (1883 - ?)

Willis Norman Pitts Sr.
Family Tree

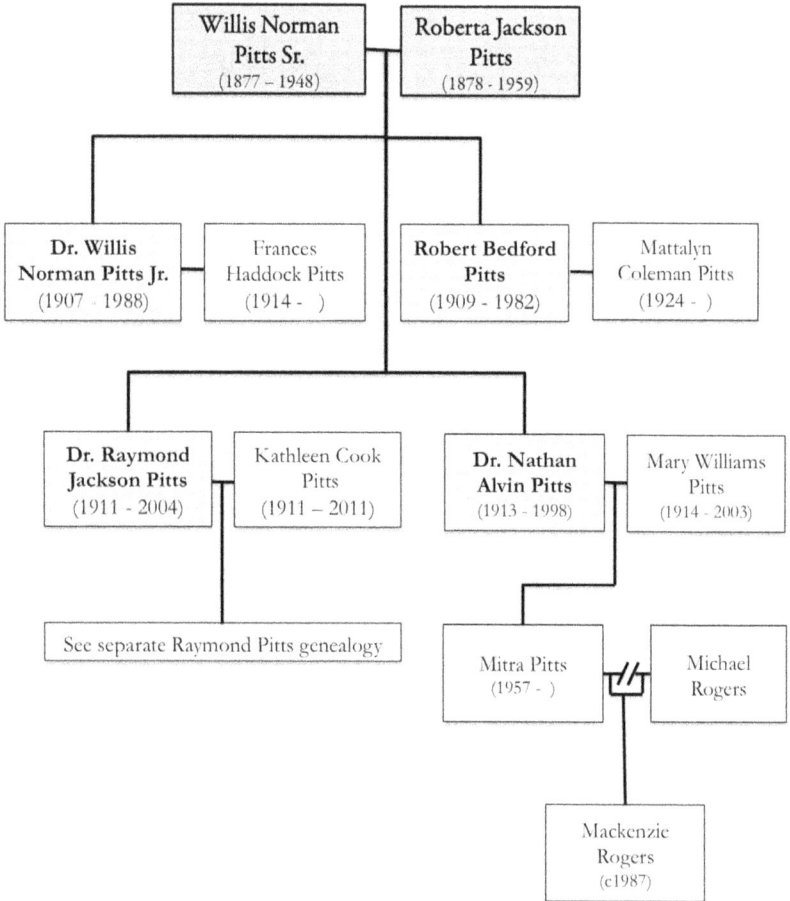

```
┌─────────────────┐   ┌─────────────────┐
│ Willis Norman   │   │ Roberta Jackson │
│ Pitts Sr.       │───│ Pitts           │
│ (1877 – 1948)   │   │ (1878 - 1959)   │
└─────────────────┘   └─────────────────┘

┌─────────────────┐ ┌───────────────┐ ┌─────────────────┐ ┌───────────────┐
│ Dr. Willis      │ │ Frances       │ │ Robert Bedford  │ │ Mattalyn      │
│ Norman Pitts Jr.│ │ Haddock Pitts │ │ Pitts           │─│ Coleman Pitts │
│ (1907 - 1988)   │ │ (1914 - )     │ │ (1909 - 1982)   │ │ (1924 - )     │
└─────────────────┘ └───────────────┘ └─────────────────┘ └───────────────┘

┌─────────────────┐ ┌───────────────┐ ┌─────────────────┐ ┌───────────────┐
│ Dr. Raymond     │ │ Kathleen Cook │ │ Dr. Nathan      │ │ Mary Williams │
│ Jackson Pitts   │─│ Pitts         │ │ Alvin Pitts     │─│ Pitts         │
│ (1911 - 2004)   │ │ (1911 – 2011) │ │ (1913 - 1998)   │ │ (1914 - 2003) │
└─────────────────┘ └───────────────┘ └─────────────────┘ └───────────────┘

┌──────────────────────────────────────┐   ┌───────────────┐ ┌───────────┐
│ See separate Raymond Pitts genealogy  │   │ Mitra Pitts   │ │ Michael   │
└──────────────────────────────────────┘   │ (1957 - )     │ │ Rogers    │
                                            └───────────────┘ └───────────┘

                                                ┌───────────────┐
                                                │ Mackenzie     │
                                                │ Rogers        │
                                                │ (c1987)       │
                                                └───────────────┘
```

Raymond Jackson Pitts
Family Tree

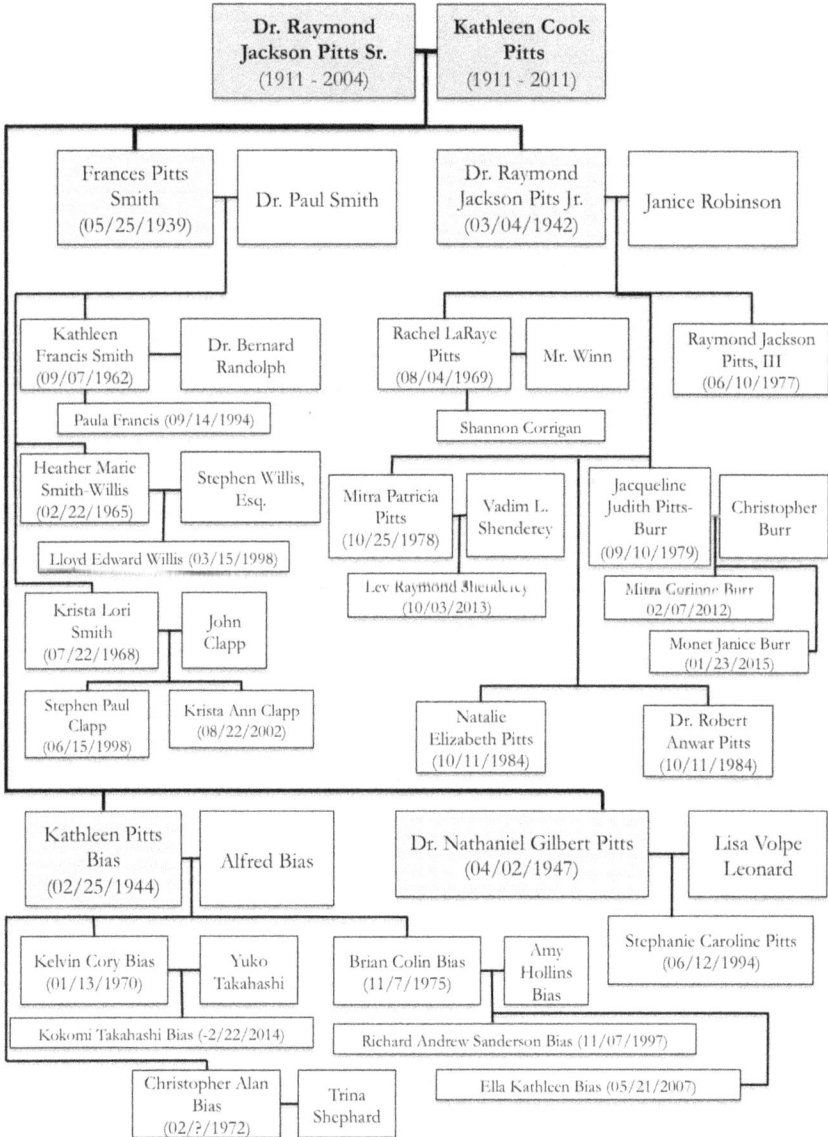

Dr. Raymond Jackson Pitts Sr. (1911 - 2004) — **Kathleen Cook Pitts** (1911 - 2011)

Frances Pitts Smith (05/25/1939) — Dr. Paul Smith

Dr. Raymond Jackson Pits Jr. (03/04/1942) — Janice Robinson

Kathleen Francis Smith (09/07/1962) — Dr. Bernard Randolph

Rachel LaRaye Pitts (08/04/1969) — Mr. Winn

Raymond Jackson Pitts, III (06/10/1977)

Paula Francis (09/14/1994)

Shannon Corrigan

Heather Marie Smith-Willis (02/22/1965) — Stephen Willis, Esq.

Mitra Patricia Pitts (10/25/1978) — Vadim L. Shenderey

Jacqueline Judith Pitts-Burr (09/10/1979) — Christopher Burr

Lloyd Edward Willis (03/15/1998)

Lev Raymond Shenderey (10/03/2013)

Mitra Corinne Burr 02/07/2012

Krista Lori Smith (07/22/1968) — John Clapp

Monet Janice Burr (01/23/2015)

Stephen Paul Clapp (06/15/1998)

Krista Ann Clapp (08/22/2002)

Natalie Elizabeth Pitts (10/11/1984)

Dr. Robert Anwar Pitts (10/11/1984)

Kathleen Pitts Bias (02/25/1944) — Alfred Bias

Dr. Nathaniel Gilbert Pitts (04/02/1947) — Lisa Volpe Leonard

Kelvin Cory Bias (01/13/1970) — Yuko Takahashi

Brian Colin Bias (11/7/1975) — Amy Hollins Bias

Stephanie Caroline Pitts (06/12/1994)

Kokomi Takahashi Bias (-2/22/2014)

Richard Andrew Sanderson Bias (11/07/1997)

Christopher Alan Bias (02/?/1972) — Trina Shephard

Ella Kathleen Bias (05/21/2007)

Appendix 2: Original Documents, Letters and Poems

In the name of God amen. I John Pitts
being in strong minded but weak in body; make this
my last will and testament.
I bequeath to my beloved wife Maria Pitts a
Negro man named Prince a girl named,
Patience a woman named Cate Fib and a
girl named Alsey.
I bequeath unto my beloved son Jack Pitts a
couple of Negro men by the name of Ralph
and Jarrel, a woman named Jenny and her
three children Cintha Joe and Silas.
I bequeath unto my beloved son Noel Pitts two
Negro men named Abner & Jerry a woman named
Winny her son Saul and a girl called little
Milbery.
I bequeath unto my beloved Daughter Mary
Pitts a Negro man Denice a negro woman
named Cloe and three of her children Zach
Letty and Simon and a boy called Warren
I bequeath unto my beloved Daughter Henrietta
Pitts a negro man named Jordan a woman
called Nance and her children Ralph Lewis
Bob Charlotte and Siah.
I bequeath unto my beloved son Ira. W. Pitts
Four Negro boys named Sipp Watson Edmund
and Abram a Negro woman called Beg Mullen
and her Daughter Cinthia Clary.
I bequeath unto my beloved son Peyton Pitts

(Peyton T. Pitts)

Last Will and Testament of John Pitts Sr. (1767–1818):
Lists slaves from the estate bequeathed to Peyton T. Pitts—note both
"Balaam" and "Nelson," which are names repeated in later Pitts generations.

Two negro men called Cato and Balaam also [...]
called Leddy and her children Nelson and Shady
also a boy called Cascott.

I bequeath unto my beloved son William I Pitts
a negro man named Tom a woman called Marge
and her children Moning Edy Beccy and Jacob
also a boy called Jacinth.

I bequeath unto my beloved wife Maria Pitts on
third of my land during her natural life th
other two thirds to be sold and eaqually divid
among my children.

I also give into my wife Maria Pitts three h
a mare called Jin another called Queen and
Dick five cows and calves three ploughs and
Gears Thirty barrels of corn five hundred we
seed cotton one thousand weight of Pork two
feather beds and furniture three Potts and tea
Kettle six chairs tables and crockery ware th
ballance of the crop to be sold and equally
divided among my children after one thousand
weight of clean cotton is taken out for my son P.
If either Payton Iva or William should die &
they have a lawful heir their property shall
to the other two, but if two of them shoul
die before they arrive to the age of twenty, on
years one half of their estate shall be divid
equally
agreeable among the elder children.

I bequeath unto Elijah Boardin Pitts and [...]
[...] Archibald Pitts the negroes which [...]

Preston is to purchase with the twenty five
hundred dollars which he has in his possession
in order to buy Negroes with. if they should
arrive at the age of twenty one or have a lawful heir but if they should die under this age
the property shall be eaqually divided between
my Children.
All my property which is not given away
is to be sold and eqally divided among
my children.
My wish and desire is that my two eldest
sons Jack and Noel shall have the manage=
ment of my four youngest children's property
Henrietta Iva Payton and William Flournoy
until they arrive at the age of fourteen years
they are then at liberty to choose for themselves
I annominate and appoint Jack and Noel
Pitts my sons my Coexecutors.

                                    John + Pitts
                                          his
                                         mark

Richard + Clarke
          his
         mark

William Quinn

Henry + Lord
        his
       mark

Alfred Clarke   Proven in open Court
and the date of the execution of this will
to have been in august 1817. this 1st of Nov.
1819.

                        H. Allen J.P.C.
                        Allen Lockett J.P.C.

December 7th 1815. The property I gave to William
F Pitts knowing that he is dead I expect that
my wife is pregnant I therefore will and bequeath
unto the child which my wife now goes with four
of the Negroes which I gave to the said William
F Pitts namely one negro man named Tom one
Woman named Marget and her two children Cad
and Beck should the child arrive to the age of
twenty one years or be lawfully married but if
not it belongs to Jack and Noel until Iva
and Payton arrives to the age of twenty one, I
will and bequeath unto my Daughter
Mary E Pitts one negro by name Jacinth I
will and bequeath unto Iva and Payton one
negro woman named morning & her increase
but if they die before they arrive to the age
of twenty one years the said negro belongs
to Jack and Noel. but if Iva or Payton sh
die the said Negro morning belongs to
the survivor. I will and bequeath unto m
Son Noel Pitts one Negro boy named Jacob
until he arrives to the age of twenty a
and the remainder part of his life to
my Daughter Henrietta Pitts I wish
peace of writing to be annexed to my

                                        John F Pitt
                                              his mark
m Proven in open Court the 1st   No
H Gillam I.C. Allen & Nicholson I.I.C.
Robt Williams I.C. H Recorded as will Gillam

Woodlawn, Ala.,
Nov. 24th 1898.
Dear Mr. Washington:-
I thought I
would write and let you
know of my whereabout and
what I am doing.
It was my intention
to return to Tuskegee and
finish the course in drawing, but after working home
for awhile I was taken sick
which threw me back in
work and the I saw to
what I wanted would take
until Christmas, so I had
decided to stay out until

Letter from Willis Sr. to Booker T. Washington,
while he was principal of Woodlawn, in Alabama

2

that time when I received
a letter from the Board
of Education of Woodlawn
stating that you had
recommended me as a
capable teacher, and at
that time the colored
school here was without
a principal, and if I
like I might send in
application, which I did
and was notified
shortly afterwards, that
I had be elected principal,
which position I accepted
and began work Sept. 26th,
    I have just closed the
second month of school
with quite a success,
considering the surround-
ing circumstances.
    When I came here the

3

former principal, who for
some reason had been dis-
charged by the board, tried
to make it very unpleasant
for me, although he knew
nothing of me, nor from
what school I came, he
had never heard my name,
nor had I heard his, still
he tried in every way possible to convey the wrong
idea, he even went so far
as to say I voted the
democrat ticket, and
you were also a demverat.
So when I arrived I
was given a cold re-
ception by some of the
citizens of Woodlawn.
After I came he chang-
ed and said I was a
boy and could not man-

age the school, and at
the same time he opened
a private school, there
were at the same time
two other private school
here also all in opposition
to the city school. Yet I am
glad to say after two months
I have succeeded in re-
moving some of my oppositions
and showing the people
they were under the wrong
impression. Two of the private
schools have closed and the
people know I have never
voted any kind of a ticket.
I am very glad to say

now that there is
not so much opposition
against the city school
as when I first came
here.

I hope I shall have no
opposition at the end of
the eighth month when I
close my school.

I hope you will have suc-
cess in all your under-
takings.

Love to Mrs. Washington,
and family.

Yours Gratefully

Willis N. Pitts.

Woodlawn, Ala.,

Macon, Ga, April 29, 1941
209 Middle Street

Dear Nath,

Daddy is doing the best he can do as you ask me. In writing you the history of the family as far as we know.

Grandpa, David Pitts was the son of his master, from that point his history is partly on the other side. His wife Lucretia Pitts, even her children do not seem to remember much about her. But from the records there was born to that union the following children ——

Emanuel Pitts, Hester Pitts Pitts, John Nelson Pitts, Dave Pitts, Henrietta Pitts Gray, Leah Pitts, Carrie Pitts Mabry.

The following children are by the second wife, Martha Gray Pitts ——

Fannie Pitts Gray, Marietta Pitts Benford, Asbury Pitts, Joseph Pitts, Lucretia Pitts, Samuel Pitts, William Pitts, Oliver Pitts, Florence Pitts Adams, Mattie Pitts, Reuben Pitts

Now as to our own immediate family. Here we are Papa Emanuel Pitts, Mamma, Emily Morris Pitts — Papa's record I've just given you. And here is as far as I've been able to obtain concerning her Sisters as follows — Juliet Morris, Catherine Morris Woodall, Sarah Morris Cobb, Melinda Morris, and the following brothers, Louis Morris, Stuart Morris, Bob Patterson (he was sold to a Patterson.)

Letter from Willis Sr. to Nathan on his recollection
of family genealogy

The children of mamma and papa are as follows: Dowey C. Pitts, John Nelson Pitts, Hope Hull Pitts, Willie Norman Pitts, Rufus Pitts, Angie Dequilla Pitts Bonner, Amanda Bell Pitts McCormick.

My family as follows —

Your mother's brothers, Walter J. Jackson, Florence Jackson, Mittie McKenzie,

You four boys as follows:
Willie Norman Pitts, Robert Bedford Pitts, Raymond Jackson Pitts, Nathan Alvin Pitts.

This information at hand except the brothers and <u>sisters of grandpa</u> (Dave) which are as follows:

Names are as follows —

Emmanuel Pitts, Isaac Pitts, Peter Pitts, Balam Pitts, Asburn Pitts a sister Rhonda Pitts Cook. This is the information as far as the family goes.

Hope this will enable you in getting out your Thesis.

Look for a letter from me on or about the 5th.

I have been kind of poorly last few days.

         lovingly, Dad.

Please Make a copy and return to
Raymond J. Pitts
1136 Westlynn Way
Sacramento, CA. 95831

December 30, 1985

Kathy

No apologies —, this is regular Family Stationery!

Roberta Irene Jackson Pitts.

    Born. Tuscaloosa, Alabama   June 30, 1878

    Died. Stoughton, Massachusetts   November 11, 1959 @ 81 years

    Sisters: Millie Corine Jackson Few Cayler.

        B. November 9, 1900. D. June 13, 1970 in Detroit, Mich.

        Florence Jackson   D. March 25, 1947

    Brother, Walter Thomas Jackson D. July 30, 1962.

    Father: A travelling Methodist Minister of 3-4 churches (Methodist in the Alabama area who often took his oldest daughter with him on his numerous church missions.

Mother:

    My father and mother met at Booker T. Washington's Tuskegee Institute, Alabama where both were registered as students in the then highly publicized "School for Negroes" by both blacks and whites.

    As the Mother later expressed to her oldest son: (Your father was the best student in the building trades, and I was selected by Booker T. Washington's wife to be their housekeeper during my last two school years because I was called the best student in Home Economics. So we were sorta attracted to each other. But I almost didn't marry him, because when he graduated ahead of me, he asked me to wait for two years

Letter from Willis Jr. to Kathy Pitts Bias
about family history

2

(Almost her exact words, as I recall)
while he joined the army for that period — and
that was a long time!

At one time in our possession, I remember seeing
a marriage notice, but home fire destructions and
moving, and separations have removed many things
I might have kept — even my Ballard diploma!)

When my father's tragic trouble amid depression years
destroyed a pleasant real home, made so by my
father's construction expertise and my mother's proud
knowledge of Home Economics, I was midway of my
Ballard Normal high school senior year.

I remember my mother's long private talk with
me at that time, first because it was the first time
I had ever seen her really crying while she talked.
She did manage to point out that I was her oldest
son, and she had to talk to someone.

Anyway, I think that was the time I stopped being
an adored, smart little high school student who
had emerged as a sickly little book reading youngster
to become a high school standout.

Since that time, my mother lived with Nath and
Mary at Shaw in North Carolina, and, of course, with
Ray, Kathleen and family in Tabor during your
father's hectic struggle for academic honors.

3

When I returned to Ann Arbor as a war veteron, My
Mother became my partner in residence at Willow Run Village.
She remained with me and frances, in Ann Arbor, Nashville, Stoughton,
until her death.

She is buried in a 4-grave lot in well kept Evergreen
Cemetery, Stoughton, Massachusetts about 25-30 miles
from where frances and I now live in Sherborn.

From my last high school days, often through long
periods of separation, and until her death, the lines of
communication between this Mother and her oldest son
often varied, but was somehow, kept opened.

Passing years and our contacts in moments when
we were "philosophying" with each other gave me
an inner feeling about the woman I dubbed
"Sis" (because there were no girls in our immediate
family) which I shall eternally cherish!

Thus, your request gives me the opportunity
to share a small bit of treasure with my Mother's
favorite little Granddaughter, Kathy:

Pride. My Mother "Sis") had a pride in realistic
achievement, some of which, I feel, was transmitted
into the endeavors of her sons through the so-called
depression years in different ways.) I know I
realized from watching and listening to her as
she went about projects in community and
religion, that one can only make things better by
being persistent in the endeavor.

+

Compassion. I suppose that this is as good a descriptive word as any. That is if you couple a sympathetic consciousness of others distress with a strong desire to eliminate it.

As a small boy, I use to wonder why she wanted to share our "goodies" with neighbors who had little — and always, in some odd dignified way that was difficult for me to understand.

Also, I suppose that somewhere in our genes is an inheritance source of taciturnity (which your father, the family Researcher of the Past would probably credit to our Indian blood inheritance). Anyway, my Mother was an introvert who kept most of her worries, frustrations, hurts, that were physical, mental and deep — to herself.

Warrior. By any other name, I knew my Mother as a fighter. She first passed that on to me in a sick bed of my early youth, and in my athletic efforts. In many forms, I heard her order — "don't quit on your duff" — or, your hopes and dreams.

Few people really knew how she fought when our home life broke down, as did her health. My greatest respect for my Mother, hinges around the deep generous feeling of mine, that "Sis" was a fighter. Much, much more could be told to illustrate from my knowledge gained — let it suffice, I know!

5

We managed to get Bob Ray and Nath to come to Stoughton just before she died.

When the four of us walked into the hospital where she was lying prone in bed. Sis raised her head, turned to the Nurse standing by her bedside, and with that familiar smack of her lips, smiled and said to her, "these are my Boys"! I almost cried!

Soon after one evening late, she whispered to me, "Dont forget who you are! You keep in touch with your brothers."

I left for my hours ride to Stoughton. When I got there, the telephone rang — "Sis, my Mother was gone!"

Kathy

Perhaps distance, personal duties, personal ambitions, personal different goals, different vocations—and even different family individual avocations, akin to the times in which we live — all have kept us from meeting too often as family kin — or even to write!!

Because of my Mother's feeling for you, this sharing which linked her to me, is forwarded.

In all likelihood, I'll never write such a long missive to you again,

Keep Writing,

Willis Norman Pitts

Parents of "Sis":

Rev. Daniel and Mary Few Jackson
— Tuscaloosa, Alabama

I forgot to insert.

Lillis M. P

1/9/86   More detail is somewhere among
my notes ———— dont ask
me where!!

You are the first to ever really
scribble a letter to me from
among yours — Ray Jr., Frances and Nat;
altho I have had less contact with you.
Sis would smile!   WP

Morrison Training School
Hoffman N. C. 11-18-38

Dear Bob,

Your long looked for letter finialy came, glad to hear from you and to know you are well and geting on well. I read your letter three or four times, you are a lucky young man, you have had a tough time, but you toughed it out, and now your luck have changed, the oppotunity is yours to be a great man, use it. I have prayed, and worked hard to see you boys be some body. I hope I'll live to see the finish of this, your letter made me very happy. You can do it, don't doubt you [?] go to it, with a will, do even better than the [?] show them what the Negro [?] in the South can do if given a chance. I payed the $33. — in Oct. Don't worry a bout that. Look out for that cold weather out there Put on

Letter from Roberta to Bob when he first moved to Seattle (1938)

some under clothes, don't
bother Willis he is worried to
death with that baby of his
but Ray + Kathleen can help
you some & understand that
is making $125.00 a month
Ray is geting $100 and board
Kathleene is also geting a nice
salary with board. they are
happy together. I am glad
all you boys need a wife
I want you to hurry &
get married I don't want
to die and leave you alone
your daddy don't care any
thing for you all, as he
he is waiting to see what
you all are going to
do for him.
Take care of your self
put on some wolen
clothes you are near
the North Pole you know
I'll send you a dollar
or two when I get some
write again soon

Yours

Mother

4/5/71

Dear Roy,

Just a note concerning the enclosed. As you see, Bob's lawyer had raised some questions about the fees of the lawyer handling Mittie's estate. Seemingly everything is OK. Willis asked me to send this to you, and you are to return it to him.

I spend March 13-31 in Africa. Visited Unesco projects in Nigeria, Ghana, Ivory Coast and Liberia. Had a nice, but busy trip. After me do a little travelling in Europe, I will be ready to find a nice quiet spot in the States and settle down.

Mary and Mitra are both well and getting settled in life in Paris. Mitra has already had one holiday for 10 days and went on a ski trip with her class to the Alps.

How is Roy, Jr.? Did he get into law school? Mitra asks about him all the time. She is lazy about writing but keeps saying that she is going to write him. Jamie Reddick Graham is a librarian at St. Louis University. Should you write Roy or Frances, you might ask them to look her up.

Tell Kathleen and Nat hello. If you should make another trip this way soon, please spend a little time with us.

Nathan

Letter from Nathan to Ray
while he was stationed in Paris

|2|

I pity thee, girl of slightly darkened hue,
Good fortune's doors seem ever closed to you.
Thy voice that rises in resplendent song,
Falls unheeded through the years — how long!
Thy soul reflected sweetly in thy smile,
Remains unseen, though beaming all the while.
Thy lips that I would gladly beg to kiss —
Seldom are they labeled "perfect bliss".
Curves of body never bring thee praise,
Though Nature fashioned them in perfect ways.
In grace thou art a princess, fair and sweet,
Yet grace in thee with favor never meet.
I pity thee, girl of slightly darkened hue,
Yet how my world has grown because of you.

— Raymond J. Pitts
(May 14, 1933) 2

Poem from Ray's journal

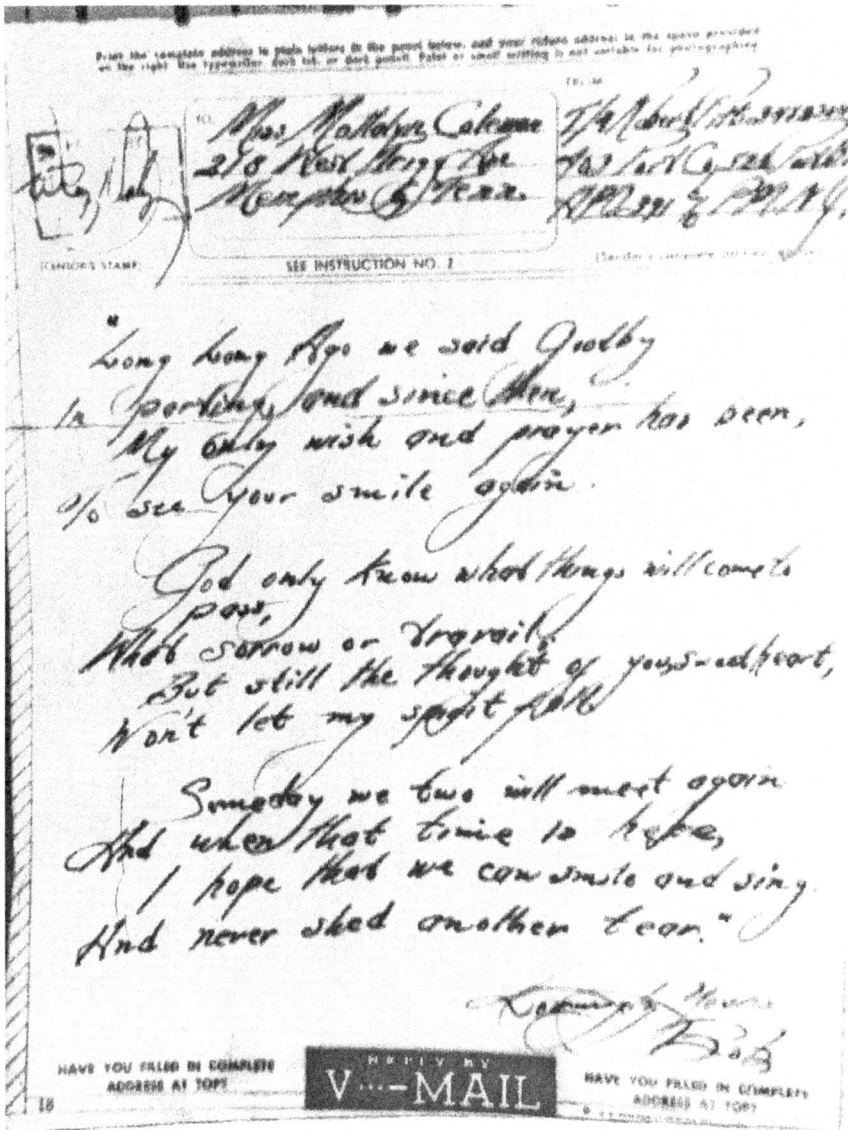

Poem from Bob to Mattalyn
while stationed overseas

<u>To Brother Bob</u>

I am proud of you, Brother
For the job that you have done,
For the Honors that you have won,
For the credit that you have been
To another—
    Our Mother!

While the crowd bestows its laurels
At the dinner hour,
I, too, will walk with you
With pride and good cheer.

Take the bows that you have earned!
Take the lessons that you have learned!
Take the candles of yourself so burned!
And try to travel
    the different way awhile—
To some enjoyment!
    To some rest.
        To some peace—
            My Brother.
Life, too, must take its bow!

    Norman

February 5, 1970
Sherborn, Massachusetts

Poem Willis Jr. sent to Bob
on the occasion of his retirement

Author's Note: Methodology

This book was commissioned by The Pitts Family Trust primarily to serve as an accurate and factual account of the lives of the four Pitts brothers of Macon, Georgia. Ray, who wished to complete this project himself, feared that the lives of successful black professionals in the years immediately before the Civil Rights Era were being "written out of history." He wished to leave a record of his family's struggles, triumphs and successes, for the benefit of Pitts descendants and for future scholars.

In writing this book, I had access to the large collection of personal documents, letters, professional papers, written memoirs, and tape-recorded interviews collected by Ray as background for his own version of this history. I have taken many stories and descriptions verbatim from recordings of, or documents written by, the men who are my subjects, in order to preserve their own voice and tone. In addition, I held extensive interviews with remaining family members. I also spent several days in Macon, Georgia, and environs, conducting my own research. In order to adhere to Ray's wishes for a historical record, I have emphasized factuality and accuracy—at times, perhaps, to the detriment of interest and readability. Thus, although there are data gaps and uncertainties where no records exist, I have avoided the temptation to fill in details with extrapolations, elaborations, or fictionalization.

Despite the plentiful records and my careful reading of them, however, a certain amount of guesswork was involved in reconstructing these life stories. At times, details from events recorded in the men's youths were at odds with their memories of those events in later years. At other times, events recorded in personal letters or memoirs disagree somewhat with newspaper accounts or other historical records from the time. In such cases I have used a hierarchy of sources to minimize errors: trusting first to independently verifiable facts from multiple sources (published histories, newspapers, etc.), relying on writings from closer to the date of the event over events as remembered many years later, accepting personal histories over the memories of family members or friends, etc. The book has also been reviewed for errors by Ray's son, Nat, relying on his extensive knowledge of the family's history. Nevertheless, errors must surely have crept in, and all such errors are solely the responsibility of the author.

About the Author

Ann Carlson is currently a free-lance writer, boutique publisher, and science policy consultant. She lives in northern New York and in southeastern Virginia with her partner, Jan, and their two cats, Amí and Sophia. Formerly employed by the National Science Foundation (NSF), and earlier by the National Aeronautics and Space Administration (NASA), Ann holds a PhD in Aerospace Engineering from North Carolina State University. She has served as both engineer and scientist in several Federal research agency positions and, near the end of her Federal government career, she became a senior agency science policy advisor and specialist in research program advocacy. In that position, she also honed her literary skills through technical writing; science reporting; and drafting speeches, presentations, and correspondence for senior administrators.

Ann and Nat Pitts, youngest son of the Raymond J. Pitts Sr. featured in this book, worked together at the NSF. After they both retired from government service, Nat encouraged Ann to continue to develop and expand her literary endeavors, and also challenged her to learn the ins and outs of the publishing business. He then hired her to produce this Pitts family history.

www.ingramcontent.com/pod-product-compliance
Lightning Source LLC
Chambersburg PA
CBHW021848090426
42811CB00033B/2189/J